International Law in Disaster Scenarios

Flavia Zorzi Giustiniani

International Law in Disaster Scenarios

Applicable Rules and Principles

Springer

Flavia Zorzi Giustiniani
Law
Uninettuno University
Rome, Italy

ISBN 978-3-030-50596-7 ISBN 978-3-030-50597-4 (eBook)
https://doi.org/10.1007/978-3-030-50597-4

This Springer imprint is published by the registered company Springer Nature Switzerland AG.
The registered company address is: Gewerbestrasse 11, 6330 Cham, Switzerland

To my father
Antonio Zorzi Giustiniani

Acknowledgments

Writing a monograph is a solitary activity but not a lonely one. The research for this book and the writing process would not have been possible without the invaluable contribution of many people.

The idea to look at the roots, and beyond, of international disaster response law (IDRL) was conceived at the end of the work on the FIRB research project on IDRL that I directed as the national coordinator. I am thus indebted to all the colleagues who participated in this endeavor, starting with Federico Casolari of University of Bologna for his valuable suggestions and Giulio Bartolini of Roma Tre University. I am particularly indebted to Emanuele Sommario of Scuola Superiore Sant'Anna, for his insightful comments and relaxing coffee breaks at the Institut. I am also grateful to Professors Paolo Benvenuti and Antonietta Di Blase of Roma Tre University for their comments and guidance during the drafting. I am much indebted to Professor Fulco Lanchester of University Roma La Sapienza and Professor Giovanni Serges of Roma Tre University for their constant encouragement and support. Last but not least, I am sincerely grateful to Professor Walter Kälin of University of Bern and David Fisher of IFRC for their time availability and advice.

Special thanks should also be directed to the various academic institutions that hosted me during my research and the drafting process: the Hague Academy of International Law, the University of Geneva, the Institut de hautes études internationales et du développement in Geneva, and the European University Institute in San Domenico (Fiesole).

I would also like to thank the anonymous reviewers at Springer as well as Brigitte Reschke for her precious editorial assistance and help.

More generally, I am grateful to my spouse Christophe and to my mother for their love and support and to little Bianca who always gives me a reason to smile.

I dedicate this book to my father, who passed away prematurely before I began this research but constantly shows me the way like a lighthouse in the dark.

Contents

Abbreviations

AADMER	ASEAN Agreement on Disaster Management and Emergency Response
AP	Additional Protocol
ASEAN	Association of Southeast Asian Nations
CARICOM	Caribbean Community
CESCR	Committee on Economic, Social and Cultural Rights
CPM	Civil Protection Mechanism
CRPD	Convention on the Rights of Persons with Disabilities
CRC	Convention on the Rights of the Child
CtRC	Committee on the Rights of the Child
DAs	Draft articles
DM	Disaster management
DREF	Disaster Relief Emergency Fund
DRR	Disaster risk reduction
ECHR	European Convention on Human Rights
ECJ	European Court of Justice
ECOSOC	Economic and Social Council
EctHR	European Court of Human Rights
EERC	European Emergency Response Capacity
ERCC	Emergency Response Coordination Centre
ESC	Economic, social and cultural
EU	European Union
GA	General Assembly
GC	General comment
GNP	Gross national product
HCT	Humanitarian Country Team
HRC	Human Rights Committee
IAC	International armed conflict
IASC	Inter-Agency Standing Committee
ICCPR	International Covenant on Civil and Political Rights
ICESCR	International Covenant on Economic, Social and Cultural Rights

ICISS	International Commission on Intervention and State Sovereignty
ICJ	International Court of Justice
ICRC	International Committee of the Red Cross
ICTR	International Criminal Tribunal for Rwanda
ICTY	International Criminal Tribunal for the former Yugoslavia
IDI	Institut de Droit International
IDL	International disaster law
IDRL	International disaster response law
IEL	International environmental law
IFRC	International Federation of Red Cross and Red Crescent Societies
IHL	International humanitarian law
IHRL	International human rights law
ILC	International Law Commission
IMF	International Monetary Fund
IRU	International Relief Union
MCDAs	Military and Civil Defence Assets
MS	Member States
NGOs	Non-governmental organisations
NIAC	Non-international armed conflict
OCHA	Office for the Coordination of Humanitarian Affairs
ODA	Official development assistance
OHCHR	Office of the United Nations High Commissioner for Human Rights
OP	Optional Protocol to the ICESCR
PCIJ	Permanent Court of International Justice
R2P	Responsibility to protect
SAARC	South Asian Association for Regional Cooperation
SC	Security Council
SG	Secretary-General
SOFA	Status of forces agreement
TEC	Treaty establishing the European Community
TEU	Treaty on European Union
TFEU	Treaty on the Functioning of the European Union
UCPM	Union Civil Protection Mechanism
UN	United Nations
UNDP	United Nations Development Programme
UNDRO	Office of the United Nations Disaster Relief Co-ordinator
VCLT	Vienna Convention on the Law of Treaties
WSO	World Summit Outcome

Chapter 1
Introduction

Contents

1.1 The Piecemeal Development of the Institutional and Legal Framework of Disaster Response

The first effort to develop an international legal framework specifically devoted to disaster relief dates back to the early 1920s. Indeed, it was only at the beginning of the last century that the international community "became interested with disaster-related issues".[1] The proposal to create an International Federation for Mutual Relief to Peoples Overtaken by Disaster was advanced by Senator Giovanni Ciraolo, acting as the first President of the Italian Red Cross Society.[2] The idea was presented to the 1921 International Conference of the Red Cross and then made its way to the newly established League of Nations, where governments agreed to convene a Conference for the Creation of an International Relief Union (IRU). The Convention and Statute establishing an International Relief Union were finally signed in 1927 and entered into force on 27 December 1932.[3]

[1]Cf. De Guttry (2012), p. 33.

[2]Cf. Macalister-Smith (1986), pp. 364–365.

[3]The Convention establishes the objectives, the structure and the basic principles governing the IRU, while the Statute regulates in greater detail the organisation and the competences of the Union.

F. Zorzi Giustiniani, *International Law in Disaster Scenarios*,
https://doi.org/10.1007/978-3-030-50597-4_1

The IRU's main objective was: "in the event of any disaster due to force majeure, the exceptional gravity of which exceeds the limits of the powers and resources of the stricken people, to furnish to the suffering population first aid and to assemble for this purpose, funds, resources and assistance of all kinds".[4] This was to be made by centralising in the new agency the organisation and coordination of international relief activities.[5] Moreover, in a very farsighted way for the time, the competences of the Union were not limited to disaster response but additionally concerned the promotion of the study of "preventive measures against disasters".[6]

The Red Cross Movement, through representatives of both the International Committee of the Red Cross (ICRC) and the League of Red Cross Societies, was present in the Council and in the Executive Committee of the Organisation. The League and the Red Cross Societies were thus assigned a primary role akin to that attributed to the ICRC by the 1949 Geneva Conventions.[7] Nonetheless, the precise relationship between the two entities was not clarified in the few years of activity of the IRU.[8]

Despite the aura of optimism that surrounded the Union's creation, its mission was doomed to fail. The activities of the organisation, apart from an initial contribution, were to be funded exclusively by voluntary donations from governments and private sources.[9] As a result, the IRU was never provided with sufficient financial means to carry out its activities.[10] Its role in relief operations was limited to a couple of disasters: the earthquakes in Orissa (India) in 1934[11] and in Baluchistan in 1935. In fact, the lack of funding, coupled with the political and economic situation prevailing from the mid-1930s, rendered the Union inoperative in practice. Nevertheless, the IRU's formal demise only took place in 1967, when its assets and

[4]Cf. Art. 2.1, IRU Convention.

[5]Concerning coordination, the intention was "to install a 'command and control' structure over the entire disaster response community" (Fisher 2007, p. 153). According to this author, the failure of such an attempt and the fact that it has not been re-proposed since "has the salutary effect of preserving the independence of actors such as the International Red Cross and Red Crescent Movement and NGOs, which has been acknowledged as a crucial element of their successes in providing rapid and effective humanitarian assistance" (ibid.).

[6]Cf. Art. 2.2, IRU Convention.

[7]Cf. Fidler (2005), p. 6. More generally, Macalister-Smith has remarked that the IRU "gave the Red Cross a potentially important intergovernmental channel by which to further its aims" Macalister-Smith (1986), p. 368.

[8]Cf. Macalister-Smith (1985), p. 21.

[9]Cf. Art. 12. The costs deriving from ordinary administration were instead borne by the international components of the Red Cross Movement, which also undertook the secretariat's functions under the direction of the Executive Committee (cf. Arts. 9–11, IRU Convention).

[10]As noted by Fisher, "an enduring lesson that can be drawn from the IRU experience is the supreme difficulty – even in the waning days of Wilsonian idealism – of persuading the international community to funnel all financial support and coordinating authority for disaster relief into a single agency" Fisher (2007), p. 27.

[11]However, in this case the aid was channelled through the Red Cross because the government refused the assistance offered by the Union (Macalister-Smith 1986, pp. 368–372).

functions were transferred to the United Nations (UN) Economic and Social Council (ECOSOC), while a year later UNESCO assumed its scientific activities.[12]

Despite the outcome, the IRU's experience is relevant in the first place "as evidence of the early recognition by States of the need for collaboration in matters of humanitarian assistance through international organization, on the foundations of international law".[13] Moreover, the IRU Convention still constitutes the sole agreement of universal scope in disaster response. Finally and most importantly, this treaty encapsulates the fundamental tenets of the then nascent international legal framework applicable to disasters: state sovereignty, international cooperation and solidarity as well as non-discrimination in assistance.[14]

Following the IRU's demise, the United Nations decided to establish within its secretariat a permanent office specifically devoted to the coordination of disaster assistance. The body was created in 1971 by a resolution of the General Assembly under the name of Office of the United Nations Disaster Relief Co-ordinator (UNDRO)[15] and was intended to be "the focal point in the United Nations system for disaster relief matters".[16]

Following the UNDRO's establishment, it became evident (in addition as a result of research conducted jointly by the Office and the League of the Red Cross Societies) that various difficulties found in the deployment of relief supplies concerned the unpreparedness of the States' internal orders. The ECOSOC thus decided in 1977 to recommend to States the adoption of a set of non-binding "[m] easures to expedite international relief".[17] A few years later UNDRO prepared a

---

[12]Cf. Agreement on the Transfer to the United Nations Educational, Scientific and Cultural Organization of Certain Responsibilities and of the Assets of the International Relief Union, opened for signature 18 December 1968 and entered into force 24 December 1968. The UN Secretariat's Memorandum on the Protection of Persons in the Event of Disasters remarks, however, that: "While a number of States subsequently withdrew from the Convention, in accordance with article 19, at the time of writing, several States (Albania, Belgium, Bulgaria, China, Ecuador, Finland, Germany, Islamic Republic of Iran, Italy, Monaco, Poland, San Marino, Sudan, Switzerland, Turkey, Venezuela and the former Yugoslavia) had not formally withdrawn from the Convention" (ILC, Memorandum of the UN Secretariat. Protection of Persons in the Event of Disasters, 31 March 2008 (11 December 2007), A/CN.4/590, p. 9, fn. 10).

[13]Cf. Macalister-Smith (1985), p. 21.

[14]Respect for parties' territorial sovereignty and non-discrimination in assistance are codified in Arts. 3–4 of the Convention. Instead, international cooperation and solidarity constitutes the primary reason pushing the States parties to draft the treaty and hence pervades the whole text (see in particular the preambular paras. 1, 3 and 5).

[15]Cf. UN GA Resolution 2816 (XXVI), Assistance in cases of natural disaster and other disaster situations, 14 December 1971. The Resolution authorised the Co-ordinator to carry out, on behalf of the Secretary-General, activities aimed at achieving the two main purposes of the Office: the mobilisation and coordination of international relief; and the promotion of pre-disaster planning, including measures of preparedness and prevention.

[16]Ibid., para. 3.

[17]UN ECOSOC, Res. 2012 (LXIII) (1977), endorsed by the General Assembly with res. 32/56 of 8 December 1977. These measures were also adopted by the International Conference of the Red Cross in the same year.

draft Convention on Expediting the Delivery of Emergency Assistance, which in 1984 was submitted to the ECOSOC for consideration.[18] The text, whose scope addressed natural and human-made disasters with the exclusion of armed conflicts,[19] contained a list of measures to be adopted by States in various sectors (such as customs, transport and communication) in order to facilitate international relief. Despite the support of several States, the Convention was never adopted because of the opposition, on the one side of various non-governmental organisations (NGOs) and both the League of Red Cross Societies and the ICRC, which criticised the emphasis placed on the sovereignty of receiving States,[20] and on the other side of other States, which instead deemed the exercise premature for the time.[21] Even in this case, however, the effort was not without relevance. As was remarked a few years ago, the provisions of the draft Convention, containing as they do both basic general principles and detailed technical rules on various aspects of relief delivery (entry of personnel, communications, customs, costs and liabilities) may still "provide a useful reference point for the kinds of provisions that might eventually be included in a legal instrument were one to be adopted".[22]

Another initiative, also universal in its scope, was undertaken by the UN Secretary-General in 2000 and concerned the deployment and utilisation of urban search and rescue teams.[23] In this case, again, the adoption of a convention was excluded; nonetheless, the General Assembly unanimously endorsed the proposed INSARAG Guidelines in Resolution 57/150 of 16 December 2002.[24]

All in all, the failure of initiatives aimed at providing a binding (institutional as well as legal) framework of comprehensive scope at the universal level explains why it was developed in a piecemeal and fragmented manner.[25] After the creation of the UN, the need to regulate disaster response was satisfied through the drafting of bilateral treaties, whose number has grown exponentially over time.[26] These treaties,

[18]UNDRO Secretary-General, Proposed Draft Convention on Expediting the Delivery of Emergency Assistance, A/39/267/Add.2-E/1984/96/Add.2, 18 June 1984.

[19]The Draft Convention defined "disaster" as "any natural, accidental or deliberate event (not being an ongoing situation of armed conflict) as a result of which assistance is needed from outside the State upon whose territory the event occurred or which has been affected by the consequences of the event" (cf. Art. 1(b)).

[20]UN SG, Report of 24 October 1990, A/45/587, para. 44.

[21]See e.g. Bettati (1991), p. 653.

[22]ILC, Preliminary report on the protection of persons in the event of disasters by Mr. Eduardo Valencia-Ospina, Special Rapporteur, A/CN.4/598, 5 May 2008, para. 40.

[23]Cf. UN GA/ECOSOC, Report of the Secretary-General of 30 May 2000, A/55/82-E/2000/61, para. 135 (m).

[24]These guidelines were prepared by the International Search and Rescue Advisory Group (INSA RAG), an inter-governmental group of search and rescue professionals and the UN Office for the Coordination of Humanitarian Affairs (OCHA).

[25]For a detailed overview of the development of treaties concerning disaster response cf. generally De Guttry (2012), p. 3 ff.

[26]Bilateral treaties, between States as well as between States and international humanitarian organisations, constitute "[t]he bulk of the existing international instruments relevant to disaster response" Fisher (2007), p. 80.

typically but not exclusively concluded between neighbouring States, were initially confined to the regulation of specific aspects of assistance, but from the 1970s they began to cover most disaster response issues related to cross-border operations.[27] However, veritable comprehensive systems of disaster assistance have only been established at a regional or sub-regional level, notably in the contexts of regional organisations like the European Union (EU), the Association of Southeast Asian Nations (ASEAN),[28] the Caribbean Community (CARICOM)[29] and the South Asian Association for Regional Cooperation (SAARC).[30] By contrast, at the universal level, although several treaties regulating different subjects such as customs, human rights and the environment have been provided with ad hoc rules concerning States' duties in cases of disaster, other agreements have been adopted to cover either a specific type of disaster[31] or a sector of assistance.[32]

Another trend that has emerged at the universal level and that partially compensates the paucity of all-encompassing treaties is the adoption of different kinds of soft law instruments, such as resolutions, declarations, codes and guidelines.[33] These

---

[27]The geographical distribution of such treaties is uneven, with Europe and the Americas being the most prolific areas and Africa the least one.

[28]Cf. ASEAN, Agreement on Disaster Management and Emergency Response (AADMER), 26 July 2005.

[29]Cf. Agreement Establishing the Caribbean Disaster Emergency Response Agency (CDERA), 26 February 1991. In 2009 CDERA was renamed by the Caribbean Disaster Management Agency (CDEMA) (cf. Agreement Establishing the Caribbean Disaster Management Agency, 1 September 2009). CDEMA's first and main function is "to make an immediate and coordinated response by means of emergency disaster relief to an affected Participating State" (cf. Art. 4a)) but more broadly the Agency acts "as facilitator, driver, coordinator and motivating force for the promotion and engineering of Comprehensive Disaster Management (CDM) in all Participating States" (cf. CDEMA, About Us, available at https://www.cdema.org/about-us#what-is-cdema-s-mandate>).

[30]Cf. SAARC, Agreement on Rapid Response to Natural Disasters, 11 November 2011. The Agreement, entered into force in September 2016, aims: "to provide effective regional mechanisms for rapid response to disasters to achieve substantial reduction of disaster losses in lives and in the social, economic and environmental assets of the Parties, and to jointly respond to disaster emergencies through concerted national efforts and intensified regional cooperation [...]" (cf. Art. II).

[31]See e.g.: the Convention on the Early Notification of a Nuclear Accident and the Convention on Assistance in the Case of a Nuclear Accident or Radiological Emergency (both of 26 September 1986) and the International Convention Relating to Intervention on the High Seas in Cases of Oil Pollution Casualties of 29 November 1969.

[32]This is the case of the Tampere Convention on the Provision of Telecommunication Resources for Disaster Mitigation and Relief Operations of 18 June 1998. For a thorough survey see Fischer (2003), p. 24 ff; De Guttry (2012), pp. 11–17.

[33]These soft law instruments can be sub-divided into: declarations of principles on cooperation in case of disasters; technical standards for relief activities (e.g. the Sphere Project, Humanitarian Charter and Minimum Standards in Humanitarian Response, Third edition, 2011); codes of conduct for relief personnel (e.g. the Code of Conduct for the International Red Cross and Red Crescent Movement and Non-Governmental Organizations in Disaster Relief, 1994); and guidelines

instruments generally present much more detailed content with respect to treaties, often comprising as they do technical standards, and have the advantage of being more easily updated. It is thus not a coincidence that despite their non-binding character, they constitute the documents most known and utilised by disaster management practitioners, both public and private.

Among the non-binding documents it is important to recall three instruments adopted by the UN General Assembly at the end of the Cold War: Resolutions 43/131 and 45/100 on Humanitarian assistance to the victims of natural disasters and similar emergency situations;[34] and Resolution 46/182 on the Strengthening of the coordination of humanitarian emergency assistance of the United Nations.[35] The latter in particular remains relevant today as it established the international humanitarian system and assigned in this regard to the UN a "central and unique role to play in providing leadership and coordinating the efforts of the international community to support the affected countries".[36] It also provided the creation of bodies that remain at the heart of the UN coordination system of disaster relief,[37] such as the Inter-Agency Standing Committee (IASC), the Consolidated Appeals Process (CAP), the Central Emergency Revolving (now Response) Fund (CERF), the Central Register of Disaster Management Capacities and the position of Emergency Relief Coordinator (ERC). The ERC was created to replace the Disaster Relief Coordinator with a higher status (Under-Secretary General) and was entrusted to manage the coordination of international assistance in both disaster and armed conflict situations.[38]

In summary, by the end of the nineteenth century, international law presented a vast array of instruments of both binding and non-binding character related to disaster response. Within 40–50 years even a veritable field—or regime—of international law had been formed: so-called international disaster response law (IDRL).[39] Unfortunately, the various instruments and frameworks that address disaster response do not constitute a coherent whole and most of those with a binding character are unevenly distributed across different geographical areas. Existing international law on the subject, as highlighted by David Fisher in his Desk Study

---

addressed to States (providing and receiving assistance) to facilitate relief operations (e.g. the IFRC's IDRL Guidelines).

[34]UN GA, Humanitarian assistance to victims of natural disasters and similar emergency situations, Resolution 43/131, 8 December 1988; UN GA, Humanitarian assistance to victims of natural disasters and similar emergency situations, Resolution 45/100, 14 December 1990.

[35]UN GA, Resolution 46/182, 19 December 1991.

[36]Ibid., annex, para. 12.

[37]On the issue see for all De Siervo (2012), pp. 485–515.

[38]At the country level, the ERC is represented by the Humanitarian Coordinator, who coordinates humanitarian assistance on the ground. The resolution also provided for the creation of a secretariat, which was put in place in 1992 under the name of the Department of Humanitarian Affairs (DHA) (currently OCHA).

[39]On the issue see infra, Chap. 2, para. 2.2.3.

for the International Federation of Red Cross and Red Crescent Societies (IFRC),[40] "is poorly organized, leaving gaps in many areas and overlaps in others".[41] This renders the identification and even the development of customary rules on the subject a complex and lengthy process.

In recent decades the ever-growing interest in disaster management, coupled with the dramatic impacts of climate change, has stimulated not just an increase in the instruments amenable to IDRL, but an expansion in the latter's scope. As a result of global awareness of the increasing incidence of natural disasters and of the consequent need to reduce disaster risks, the UN proclaimed the 1990s the International Decade for Natural Disaster Reduction (IDNDR). The IDNDR was followed by a number of important initiatives at the UN level devoted to disaster risk reduction (DRR), such as the so-called Global Platforms.[42] This development and the strengthening of the prevention aspect of disaster management has therefore logically determined in recent times the renaming of IDRL as IDL (i.e. international disaster law).

1.2 The Codification Works of the International Federation of Red Cross and Red Crescent Societies and the International Law Commission

The first effort to bring order among the mass of international rules directly or indirectly addressing disaster response—and ultimately to infer from them some principles of general application—was made by the IFRC. This was achieved through the International Disaster Response Laws, Rules and Principles (IDRL) Programme, initiated in 2001 to both explore the role of the law in disaster response and to strenghten the legal preparedness of governments to disasters.[43] The initial idea was to draft an international treaty framework equivalent to that regulating relief in armed conflicts. However, the majority of governments rejected it and instead

---

[40]The League was renamed the *International Federation of Red Cross and Red Crescent Societies* in November 1991 during the VIIIth Session of its General Assembly (Budapest (Hungary), 25–28 November 1991).

[41]Fisher (2007), p. 85. According to H. Fischer: "[...] there are clearly identifiable areas of disaster response that tend to be regulated by treaties, and within these areas there have emerged some common trends. However in the majority of instances there are no clearly identifiable patterns that lend to the presumption of general principles. Therefore, at least where multilateral and bilateral treaties are concerned, a majority of the law relating to IDRL remains disparate and inconclusive" (Fischer 2003, p. 39). Along similar lines, cf. De Guttry (2012), p. 40.

[42]Cf. UN World Conference on Disaster Reduction, Hyogo Framework for Action 2005–2015: Building the Resilience of Nations and Communities to Disasters (HFA), in UN World Conference on Disaster Risk Reduction, Hyogo Declaration, 22 January 2005, A/CONF.206/6; UN GA, Sendai Framework for Disaster Risk Reduction 2015–2030, 23 June 2015, A/RES/69/283.

[43]Cf. Natoli (2013), p. 139 ff.

agreed to task the Federation and the National Societies with analysing the existing international instruments in order to identify and propose practical solutions in the field.[44]

The first outcome of this effort was the development of the Guidelines for the Domestic Facilitation and Regulation of International Disaster Relief and Initial Recovery Assistance (IDRL Guidelines). The Guidelines contain a set of non-binding recommendations based on various existing international instruments[45] concerning how States should prepare, from a legal point of view, to receive and manage international relief in case of a disaster occurring in their territory.[46] Their content is thus mainly technical and covers several regulatory issues pertaining to the affected State's response, such as the entry of relief personnel, goods and equipment. The Guidelines were unanimously adopted by the States Parties to the Geneva Conventions along with the components of the International Red Cross and Red Crescent Movement in 2007. They are periodically recalled by the General Assembly in its resolutions[47] and have also been taken into account by several regional organisations in their activities.[48] Over time, at least 37 countries have adopted new

---

[44]Cf. XXVIII International Conference of the Red Cross and Red Crescent, Resolution 1, Agenda for Humanitarian Action, Final Goal 3.2, 2–6 December 2003.

[45]Among the several instruments which referred to in the text of the Guidelines or in their Annotations there are e.g.: UN GA Resolutions 46/182 of 1991 and 57/150 of 2002, the draft Convention on Expediting the Delivery of Emergency Assistance of 1977, the Hyogo Framework for Action of 2005, the Food Aid Convention of 1999 and the Tampere Convention. As remarked by Cubie:

> By setting out a series of recommendations to governments on the minimum quality standards and legal facilities that humanitarian actors require to undertake their work effectively, the IDRL Guidelines do not attempt to expand international law or create new rights and obligations for states. The IDRL Guidelines therefore fall squarely into the category of 'technical guidelines' Cubie (2017), p. 280.

[46]The Guidelines expressely aim at "contribut[ing] to national legal preparedness by providing guidance to States interested in improving their domestic, policy and institutional frameworks concerning international disaster relief and initial recovery assistance" (cf. IFRC, Guidelines for the Domestic Facilitation and Regulation of International Disaster Relief and Initial Recovery Assistance (or 'International Disaster Response Laws, Rules and Principles'), adopted by the IFRC on 30 November 2007 (IDRL Guidelines), Introduction, section 1, para. 3). They are divided into the following sections: 1. core responsibilities; 2. early warning and preparedness; 3. initiation and termination of international disaster relief and initial recovery assistance; 4. eligibility for legal facilities; 5. legal facilities for entry and operations.

[47]Already in the year following the Guidelines' adoption, the GA encouraged States to make use of them in three different resolutions (cf. UN GA Res. 63/139, Res. 63/141, and Res. 63/137 of 11 December 2008).

[48]Cf. e.g.: Organisation of American States' General Assembly, Inter-American Plan for Disaster Prevention and Response and the Coordination of Humanitarian Assistance, 2012; EU, The European Consensus on Humanitarian Aid, Joint Statement by the Council and the Representatives of the Governments of the Member States meeting within the Council, the European Parliament and the European Commission, 2008/C 25/01, para. 40.

laws or regulations based on them, while another 10 are planning to do the same.[49] Such an outcome, while undoubtedly important, nonetheless shows the inherent limitations of the bottom-up approach adopted by the Federation,[50] which is very time-consuming and inevitably leads to non uniform results.[51]

To attain its Programme's objectives, the IFRC also elaborated a second, more detailed instrument: the Model Act for the Facilitation and Regulation of International Disaster Relief and Initial Recovery Assistance (Model Act). Developed with the OCHA and the Inter-Parliamentary Union (IPU) as well as with the support of the World Customs Organization (WCO), the Model Act is a practical reference tool intended to assist States in developing appropriate legislation when incorporating the IDRL Guidelines into their own national legal system. It consists of a model domestic statute with commentary and can be used in its entirety or in modules, on the basis of the level of legal preparedness of a given State's internal order and disaster risk profile. A pilot version of the Model Act was presented in November 2011 at the 31st International Conference of the Red Cross and Red Crescent. After an experimental phase, the definitive version of the Act was launched in March 2013 at the IPU's General Assembly.

A different and more traditional top-down approach to the codification of disaster law was adopted by the UN International Law Commission (ILC). The ILC, also building on the research work and the previous findings of the IFRC's Programme, decided to embark on a project concerning the law of disaster relief in 2007, when the topic was added to its agenda under the title "Protection of persons in the event of disasters", with Eduardo Valencia-Ospina appointed as Special Rapporteur.[52]

In the original intentions of the Rapporteur (and as also hinted by the same title of the Project), the primary focus was meant to be on the victims of disasters and their rights. Through a rights-based approach the objective was to identify a certain standard of treatment to which all the individuals affected by a disaster were entitled.[53] However, due to strong resistance both within the ILC and the Sixth Committee of the General Assembly, this initial perspective was sensibly downsized with the result that most of the Draft Articles (DAs) ultimately adopted have a horizontal dimension and concern States' (and other international subjects') rights and obligations in their reciprocal relations. The vertical dimension—related to the relationship between the affected States and the assisting actors with disaster victims—has instead been relegated to three draft articles (4–6), which reaffirm some basic humanitarian tenets that need to be respected and protected in disaster response: human rights, human dignity and humanitarian principles. Being very

---

[49] Cf. https://rcrcconference.org/app/uploads/2019/10/33IC_12.5-Disaster-Law-background-doc-final-EN.pdf, last visited on 25 August 2020.

[50] On bottom-up approaches, see Clement (2014), p. 78.

[51] See generally IFRC, Ready or Not? cit.

[52] See ILC, Report of the International Law Commission, Official Records of the General Assembly, Sixty-Second Session, Supplement No. 10, A/62/10, 2007, para. 375.

[53] Cf. ILC, A/CN.4/598, para. 12.

general in character, these provisions essentially serve as a 'reminder' of the importance of complying with a series of more specific obligations that are posed by international law but are not specified in the text.[54]

An expansion compared to the original objective was realised with respect to the Project's material scope.[55] Indeed, the DAs, while mainly addressing the phase of response, have a broader focus comprising recovery and prevention.[56] Notably, DA 9 poses obligations on States in the field of disaster risk reduction, with a view to prevent disastrous events from occurring again. In this way, the ILC has adopted a progressive stance, not limiting itself to *essentially* codifying the existing rules but manifesting a readiness to capture the recent tendencies of international practice that have yet to be crystallised in customary norms. In fact, even though the ILC in the DAs' commentaries affirms that the Articles "contain elements of both progressive development and codification of international law",[57] as a whole the Project is quite conservative and its only truly innovative provision is constituted by DA 9. Certainly, the latter formulates a clear-cut obligation whose customary character, not being based on particularly solid ground, was questioned by several States.[58]

As a whole, the scope of the Project is extremely broad, covering: ratione temporis, the response to disasters as well as to a certain extent the recovery and the prevention of such events; ratione personae, the affected States, the broad and diverse community of assisting actors as well as the individuals who are victims of disasters; and ratione loci, the territory of affected and assisting States as well as virtually the whole international community as far as the duties of international cooperation and solidarity are concerned. A relevant limitation instead concerns its scope ratione materiae, as a result of the definition of disaster embraced in the text (which only covers events of a certain gravity and having international repercussions) and the primacy attributed to international humanitarian law.

---

[54]As explicitly stated in the commentary to DA 5: "It also serves as a reminder of the duty of States to ensure compliance with all relevant human rights obligations applicable both during the disaster and the predisaster phase" (cf. Draft Articles on the Protection of Persons in the Event of Disasters with commentaries. In Report of the International Law Commission: Sixty-Eighth Session (2 May–10 June and 4 July–12 August 2016), A/71/10, commentary to DA 5, para. 1).

[55]To be fair, Valencia-Ospina had already declared his intention to cover all the disaster phases in his preliminary report (cf. A/CN.4/598, paras. 51, 57), but in practice it was only in 2013 when he proposed two draft articles, respectively related to 'Cooperation for disaster risk reduction' and the 'Duty to reduce disaster risk'. Even though both provisions were adopted on first reading without any change (cf. DAs 10-11, A/CN.4/L.831), in the final text only the second has survived (under the title 'Reduction of the risk of disasters'), while a reference to cooperation in DRR can now be found in the commentary to DA 7 (Duty to cooperate).

[56]However, this expansion is not adequately reflected in all the draft articles, which are primarily focused on disaster response and—to a more minor extent—recovery, as also explicitly highlighted in the ILC Commentary to DA 1, at para. 4).

[57]Cf. ILC, Draft articles on the protection of persons in the event of disasters, with commentaries, preamble, para. 2.

[58]Cf. ILC, Eighth Report on the Protection of Persons in the Event of Disasters, A/CN.4/697, 17 March 2016, para. 193. On the issue allow me to refer to Zorzi Giustiniani (2018), pp. 7–27.

Broadness is accompanied by a certain level of generality. Contrary to the extremely technical and detailed character of the IDRL Guidelines, the DAs lay down general principles, in some cases eventually requiring States to adopt more specific measures at the domestic level.[59] Thus the intent is clearly to establish the basic tenets of international law that should guide the management of disasters with international relevance. This also avoids any risk of duplication with the work conducted by the IFRC; indeed, the Guidelines and the DAs do not overlap but rather are mutually reinforcing and complement each other.[60]

Being drafted in a binding language, the text has the appearance of a treaty—more precisely a framework convention—rather than of a soft law instrument.[61] Nonetheless, the final form of the work has yet to be decided. The ILC completed its project in August 2016, when it adopted on second reading the DAs with their commentaries and, pursuant to Article 23 of its statute, recommended to the General Assembly the elaboration of a convention on the basis of the Articles.[62] In 2018 States were asked to express their opinion on the matter, the results showing a sharp division between those in favour of the prospected solution and those against.[63] As a result of this impasse, the Assembly decided to refer any decision on the topic to its 2020 agenda, in the meantime giving States the possibility to present further comments.[64] In any case, as will be shown in the course of the analysis, regardless of the container into which they will be transferred, the DAs as a whole have binding content as they mainly codify (sometimes even too conservatively) existing law.

Irrespective of the final form they will assume, the DAs have already proved to be an important contribution to the consolidation and the development of international norms applicable to disasters, notably regarding the role of the affected State in disaster response and States' obligations concerning the prevention of disasters. A distinctive and welcome feature of the text concerns its recipients which, contrary to most existing treaties governing disaster response, are not just States but also the different actors making up the broad humanitarian community (i.e. UN agencies, NGOs and the components of the International Red Cross and Red Crescent Movement).

---

[59]This is notably the case of DA 15, concerning the facilitation of external assistance, and DA 16, related to the protection of personnel and equipment and goods. As has been observed, these provisions are typical of a bottom-up approach (Bartolini 2017, p. 1129) even though the ILC does not specify the content of the internal measures to be adopted, instead referring in this regard to the IDRL Guidelines.

[60]The influence of the previous IFRC's work is evident in the discussions held within the Sixth Committee (cf. UN GAOR, 65th Session (1 December 2010) A/C.6/65/SR.25; UN GAOR, 65th Session (1 December 2010) A/C.6/SR.22).

[61]Cf. Bartolini (2017), p. 6, who affirms: "[...] the final result is a sort of framework convention whose content might appear elusive to some extent".

[62]Cf. ILC, Report of the International Law Commission: Sixty-Eighth Session (2 May–10 June and 4 July–12 August 2016), A/71/10, 2016, p. 13, para. 46.

[63]Cf. UN GA Res. 71/141, 13 December 2016, para. 2.

[64]Cf. UN GA Res. 73/209, 20 December 2018.

More deceiving is the place that—contrary to the Special Rapporteur's initial intention and general expectations—has been finally assigned to international cooperation and solidarity. This is all the more so considering the important and peculiar developments which, as will be seen extensively in Part III, international cooperation and solidarity has made, not least in the field of disaster response.

1.3 The Disaster Notion

Before concluding this introductory chapter, a crucial question needs to be clarified: what disasters are we talking about? Is there a generally accepted notion of the term?

In common parlance, *disaster* is a broad term that is utilised (together with catastrophe, emergency and crisis) to depict a situation that is characterized by a certain gravity and urgency. Disasters are generally subdivided into natural and human-made and as such they are identified—or more properly confused—with the *events* or *hazards* from which they originate. This confusion is still extremely common even among jurists and more widely in international practice, with the result that one cannot abstract from the specific context in which the term disaster is utilised. After all, as was noted by Valencia-Ospina in his Preliminary Report: "The term "disaster" [. . .] is not a legal term. There is no generally accepted legal definition of the term in international law".[65]

Various IDL treaties do not contain a definition of disaster but merely refer to particular categories (meant as *events*) such as radiological or nuclear disasters,[66] or more broadly natural disasters.[67] Nonetheless, many others—and indeed most IDL instruments today—contain a definition of disaster. Such definitions are generally characterised by reference to the disaster's origin and its consequences.[68] However, given that treaties on disaster management are based on the willingness of their parties to cooperate, the specific criteria that are generally required in many cases do not hinder a broader application of the treaty if this is in the interest of the parties involved.[69]

---

[65] Cf. A/CN.4/598, para. 46.

[66] Cf. e.g. Convention on Assistance in the Case of a Nuclear Accident or Radiological Emergency, 26 September 1986.

[67] See e.g. the Annex to the Convention on Facilitation of International Maritime Traffic, 9 April 1965, Arts. 5.11 and 5.12; 1990 Istanbul Convention on temporary admission on goods of prime necessity and certain equipment, Art. 1(B), Annex B.9 (referring to "natural disasters and similar catastrophes").

[68] The eventual deliberate character of the act or omission that triggered the emergency is instead of no relevance (cf. De Guttry 2012, p. 7).

[69] Cf. Bartolini (2018), p. 14, who refers to the 1997 Agreement between Argentina and Chile on cooperation in case of disasters, whose Art. 1 after a description of the various features an event should have to be qualified as a disaster for the treaty's purposes, adds that "[d]isaster" shall mean any event so described by the Party requiring assistance".

Although references to the origin and causal elements of disasters are becoming less common given the impossibility of excluding the presence of a human factor from most disasters,[70] the event's consequences are still a crucial feature of the disaster notion. Indeed, it is precisely this element that distinguishes the generic notion of a disaster, which as anticipated considers the historical event per se, from the juridical notion, which instead requires that such an event lead to certain specified effects. In this respect, disaster definitions generally require that a calamitous event be capable of affecting persons, property and/or the environment. The consequences do not need to have a transboundary character; nonetheless, their *international* dimension is given by their scope, which is variously described in treaties by qualifiers such as 'widespread', 'significant' or 'severe'.[71]

A particularly high threshold is set by the DAs, whose disaster definition, as enshrined in DA 3a), demands that "a calamitous event or series of events resulting in widespread loss of life, great human suffering and distress, mass displacement, or large-scale material or environmental damage [has the consequence of] seriously disrupting the functioning of society".[72] This definition is clearly meant to limit the applicability of the Articles to those events that, being characterised by extreme gravity,[73] call for international interest and response. However, it does not provide the necessary tools to unambiguously verify if a certain event satisfies the required elements.[74] To be expressly excluded are only armed conflicts, as is also the case in

[70]This is acknowledged by the same ILC in the DAs' commentaries to justify the choice against limiting the Project's scope to natural events: "[n]o limitation is included concerning the origin of the event, that is whether it is natural or human-made, in recognition of the fact that disasters often arise from complex sets of causes that may include both wholly natural elements and contributions from human activities" (cf. ILC, DAs Commentaries, DA 3a), para. 4).

[71]However, such qualifiers have a relative value as they change from one treaty to another. As remarked by Focarelli: "There is no international agreement on how great a catastrophe has to be in order to be considered a disaster for legal purposes, nor is there any agreement on what criteria should be used to measure its scale" Focarelli (2013) (para. 8).

[72]A reference to the "serious disruption of the functioning of a society" is also present in the disaster notions adopted respectively by the IFRC's IDRL Guidelines and the Tampere Convention (cf. Art. 1, para. 6). Other instruments instead refer to the serious disruption of the functioning of a *community* (cf. e.g., AADMER, Art. 1, para. 3), while still others contain references to both society and community (cf. e.g. SAARC, Agreement on rapid response to natural disasters, Art. 1, para. 3; UN International Strategy for Disaster Reduction (ISDR), UNISDR Terminology on Disaster Risk Reduction, 31 December 2009). The difference is far from being irrelevant, as the term society may be "implied to cover only events having a very significant magnitude toward the entire society of the affected State" Bartolini (2017), p. 1114.

[73]The ILC in this respect affirms that "the reference to a "calamitous" event serves to establish a threshold [...] whereby only extreme events are covered" (ILC, DAs Commentaries, DA 3a), para. 4).

[74]This concerns, in particular, the societal disruption element, which has also been considered as too demanding when the calamitous event has caused an environmental harm (cf. Stephens 2016, p. 155).

many IDL treaties on the assumption that these are largely regulated by rules of international humanitarian law, as well as "serious political or economic crises".[75]

For the purposes of the present work, the term "disaster" will be used to refer to situations of international relevance that result, as stated by the Special Rapporteur, from "the unwillingness or inability of the affected State, region or society to cope with the disaster by using only its own resources".[76] Such a restriction, which is evidently quite flexible as it also considers situations in which the unwillingness/ inability concerns only a part (meant as territory or society) of the affected State, justifies itself in light of the scope ratione materiae of the book, which concerns the *response* to disasters.

1.4 The Scope of the Book

As a whole, this book attempts to conceptualise the main theoretical issues arising in the application of international law to disaster response. This will be achieved by identifying those general rules and principles of international law that have special relevance in disaster contexts and by analysing how they are declined in such contexts in order to guarantee the proper management of one of the major *common concerns* of the contemporary international community.[77]

Throughout the research a privileged point of reference will be the ILC Project on the Protection of Persons in the Event of Disasters, as this touches upon—albeit sometimes tangentially—all of the main theoretical issues that will be addressed in this book. Specific attention will also be devoted, where appropriate, to the regional frameworks developed within the EU and, more lately, the ASEAN. Over time the EU has equipped itself with various instruments specifically addressing disaster management.[78] These instruments, as will be shown, are a manifestation of both internal (among EU Member States) and external solidarity. Meanwhile, ASEAN has approved the most comprehensive regional treaty on disaster management—the AADMER—and has exhibited a willingness to follow the example of the EU to realise a more integrated system in this area.[79]

---

[75] Cf. ILC, DAs Commentaries, DA 3a), para. 10.

[76] Cf. ILC, A/CN.4/598, para. 47.

[77] In its Resolution on Humanitarian Assistance, adopted in 2004 at its Bruges session, the Institute of International Law remarked that great disasters are a "matter of concern for the international community as a whole" (third preambular paragraph). Not coincidentally, the most recent scientific publication on common interests in international law devotes an entire chapter to disaster response (cf. Park 2018, p. 136 ff).

[78] Disaster management, in a broad sense, refers to all the measures undertaken to address disasters, from their prevention, to the response, recovery and reconstruction. As will be seen, in the EU legal order disaster management is more commonly termed civil protection.

[79] Cf. Pennisi di Floristella (2015).

Part I will outline some general and preliminary observations concerning the international legal framework applicable in disaster scenarios. As has already been demonstrated, over time a veritable rule complex concerning disaster response and later disasters tout court was developed, named International Disaster Law (IDL). This is the last of a series of so-called international regimes—intended as rule complexes constituting distinct blocks of international norms ratione materiae—in which international law is generally subdivided by the doctrine. Chapter 2 will thus critically review this doctrinal construct at first in general (as part of the asserted fragmentation of international law) and then with specific reference to disaster contexts. The main features of those regimes that have a particular bearing for disaster response (i.e. international humanitarian law, human rights law and disaster law) will then be scrutinised, alongside their specific relevance in disasters. These reflections will later be taken in Chap. 3 in order to shed some light on the applicable legal framework in mixed situations of disaster and armed conflict. To this end, the two major models of regime selection will be examined, alongside the solution proposed by the ILC. As will be shown, there is no univocal solution and the quick fix proposed by the ILC is problematic. Moreover, it will be argued that the choice must necessarily be made on a case-by-case basis and, most importantly, at the level of single applicable rules and not, once and for all, by choosing one among the various applicable regimes.

Parts II and III will then deal with the role, respectively, of the affected State and the international community in disaster response, in order to apprehend how the fundamental notions of State sovereignty on the one hand and international cooperation and solidarity on the other interact and affect the respective obligations of the State in which the disaster has taken place as well as of the international community at large.

For a long time, the doctrine focused almost exclusively on the obligations of the affected State, notably on the need/duty to accept external assistance. In this respect, relevant rules of international humanitarian law are generally applied by analogy. However, in disaster contexts—as will be shown extensively in Part II—concerns to respect the State's sovereign role are stronger and, apart from situations where the same government is responsible for denying the population's basic needs, generally more legitimate than in a war context. Only in recent times has there been an acknowledgement of the fact that external action in general, even if guided by the noble purpose of relieving the suffering of the affected population, cannot trump the sovereign prerogatives of the territorial State. Indeed, the role of external action needs to be *complementary* to that of the affected State, so as not to undermine national capacities and responsibilities and disempower the affected population. Moreover, international assistance must be conducted in line with human rights principles, even in those cases—best exemplified by the Haiti-post earthquake scenario—where external actors almost completely substitute for State action owing to an institutional breakdown.

Still less investigated has been the actual scope and content of the so-called secondary responsibility of the international community. International cooperation and solidarity are increasingly evoked in international fora as well as in legal literature to address common interests and concerns, with disaster response featuring prominently among the latter.[80] Cooperation and solidarity were also referred to by the ILC Special Rapporteur Valencia-Ospina as some of the "underlying principles" of the Project on the Protection of Persons in the Event of Disasters.[81] Following an overview of the various doctrinal attempts made over time to elaborate on the concept of international solidarity, in Chap. 6 we will outline the main elements that such a principle or value should have. On this basis, at the end of Part III (in Chap. 9) we will assess the extent to which solidarity currently informs disaster response in international law. The research will then proceed, in Chap. 7, by examining the role of international cooperation and assistance within the international human rights law framework. As will be seen, major UN human rights treaties—starting with the International Covenant on Economic, Social and Cultural Rights (ICESCR)—assign an important albeit quite undefined role to international cooperation for the fulfillment of the rights protected. In trying to define the contours of international cooperation, the treaty bodies have convincingly elaborated more specific obligations with which States parties should comply with in order to assist other States, first and foremost in situations of emergency, including disasters. We will also consider the content of the assistance to be provided in disaster settings as well as the actual relevance of the distinction between humanitarian relief and development aid. Chapter 8 will subsequently seek to examine how international solidarity can find and has effectively found realisation in disaster response. This will be achieved first through a re-reading of the R2P doctrine. This doctrine, it is assumed, can be regarded as an institutionalised form of solidarity that is applicable even after a disaster. A specific inquiry will then concern the role of solidarity within the EU legal order, where solidarity is notably at the basis of various instruments of the European disaster management regime. Such specialised analysis will show that solidarity works effectively in an integrated regional framework and that other regional organisations can and indeed are already following suit.

Part IV will subsequently analyse the role of the recourse to foreign military personnel and assets in times of disaster. In particular it will address some of the main legal issues and operational challenges that owe to the involvement of foreign military personnel and assets in disaster response. It will proceed by critically evaluating the solutions proposed in this respect by the existing UN guidelines on the matter, taking as a case study the 2010 Pakistan flood response.

---

[80]In the doctrine cf. inter alia: Wolfrum and Kojima (2010), Hestermeyer et al. (2012), Casini (2013), Carrozza and Crema (2014), O'Donnell and Allan (2016), pp. 453–478. See also the works of the UN independent expert on human rights and international solidarity (notably: UN Commission on Human Rights, Human rights and international solidarity. Note by the United Nations High Commissioner for Human Rights, 1 February 2006, E/CN.4/2006/96; UN Human Rights Council, Draft Declaration on the Right to International Solidarity, annexed to the report of the Independent Expert on human rights and international solidarity of 25 April 2017, A/HRC/35/35), and of the ILC on the Protection of Persons in the event of disasters.

[81]ILC, A/CN.4/615, para. 50.

At the end of the book, some general conclusions will be drawn. As a whole, the analysis of the international legal framework applicable to disaster response will prove that the latter has become a cross-cutting issue in international law that is connoted—but even more connotes—various areas of the discipline.

List of Documents

Agreement on the Transfer to the United Nations Educational, Scientific and Cultural Organization of Certain Responsibilities and of the Assets of the International Relief Union, 18 December 1968

Agreement Establishing the Caribbean Disaster Emergency Response Agency (CDERA), 26 February 1991

Agreement Establishing the Caribbean Disaster Management Agency, 1 September 2009

Annex to the Convention on Facilitation of International Maritime Traffic, 9 April 1965

ASEAN, Agreement on Disaster Management and Emergency Response, 26 July 2005

Code of Conduct for the International Red Cross and Red Crescent Movement and Non-Governmental Organizations (NGOs) in Disaster Relief, 31 December 1994

Convention Establishing an International Relief Union, 12 July 1927

Convention on Assistance in the Case of a Nuclear Accident or Radiological Emergency, 26 September 1986

Convention on the Early Notification of a Nuclear Accident, 26 September 1986

Convention on Temporary Admission (Istanbul Convention), 26 June 1990 (Conventionon the Early Notification of a Nuclear Accident, 26 September 1986)

EU, The European Consensus on Humanitarian Aid, Joint Statement by the Council and the Representatives of the Governments of the Member States meeting within the Council, the European Parliament and the European Commission, 30 January 2008, 2008/C 25/01

Food Aid Convention, 13 April 1999

IFRC, Ready or Not? Third Progress Report on the Implementation of the IDRL Guidelines, Geneva, 2015

ILC, Draft Articles on the Protection of Persons in the Event of Disasters with commentaries. In Report of the International Law Commission: Sixty-Eighth Session (2 May–10 June and 4 July–12 August 2016), A/71/10

ILC, Eighth Report on the Protection of Persons in the Event of Disasters, 17 March 2016, A/CN.4/697

ILC, Preliminary report on the protection of persons in the event of disasters, 5 May 2008, A/CN.4/598

ILC, Second Report on the protection of persons in the event of disasters, 7 May 2009, A/CN.4/615

ILC, Report of the Fifty-ninth session (7 May-5 June and 9 July-10 August 2007), A/62/10

ILC Secretariat, Protection of persons in the event of disasters. Memorandum, 11 December 2007, A/CN.4/590
International Convention Relating to Intervention on the High Seas in Cases of Oil Pollution Casualties, 29 November 1969
Organisation of American States' General Assembly, Inter-American Plan for Disaster Prevention and Response and the Coordination of Humanitarian Assistance, 2012
SAARC, Agreement on Rapid Response to Natural Disasters, 11 November 2011
Sphere Project, Humanitarian Charter and Minimum Standards in Humanitarian Response, Third edition, 2011
Tampere Convention on the Provision of Telecommunication Resources for Disaster Mitigation and Relief Operations, 18 June 1998
UN Commission on Human Rights, Human rights and international solidarity. Note by the United Nations High Commissioner for Human Rights, 1 February 2006, E/CN.4/2006/96
UNDRO Secretary-General, Proposed Draft Convention on Expediting the Delivery of Emergency Assistance, A/39/267/Add.2-E/1984/96/Add.2, 18 June 1984
UN GA, Resolution 2816 (XXVI), 14 December 1971
UN GA, Resolution 32/56, 8 December 1977
UN GA, Resolution 43/131, 8 December 1988
UN GA, Resolution 45/100, 14 December 1990
UN GA, Resolution 46/182, 19 December 1991
UNGA, Resolution 57/150, 16 December 2002
UN GA, Resolution 63/137, 11 December 2008
UN GA, Resolution 63/139, 11 December 2008
UN GA, Resolution 63/141, 11 December 2008
UN GA, Resolution 71/141, 13 December 2016
UN GA, Resolution 73/209, 20 December 2018
UN GA Sixth Committee, Summary record of the 25th meeting, 1 December 2010, A/C.6/65/SR.25
UN GA Sixth Committee, Summary record of the 65th meeting, 1 December 2010, A/C.6/SR.22
UN GA/ECOSOC, Report of the Secretary-General of 30 May 2000, A/55/82-E/2000/61
UN GA, Sendai Framework for Disaster Risk Reduction 2015–2030, 23 June 2015, A/RES/69/283
UN Human Rights Council, Draft Declaration on the Right to International Solidarity, A/HRC/35/35, 22 June 2017
UN International Strategy for Disaster Reduction (ISDR), UNISDR Terminology on Disaster Risk Reduction, 31 December 2009
UN SG, Report of 24 October 1990, A/45/587
UN World Conference on Disaster Reduction, Hyogo Framework for Action 2005–2015: Building the Resilience of Nations and Communities to Disasters (HFA), in UN World Conference on Disaster Risk Reduction, Hyogo Declaration, 22 January 2005, A/CONF.206/6

XXVIII International Conference of the Red Cross and Red Crescent, Resolution 1, Agenda for Humanitarian Action, Final Goal 3.2, 2-6 December 2003

References

Bartolini G (2017) A universal treaty for disasters? Remarks on the international law commission's draft articles on the protection of persons in the event of disasters. Int Rev Red Cross 99 (3):1103–1137

Bartolini G (2018) A taxonomy of disasters in international law. In: Zorzi Giustiniani F, Sommario E, Casolar i F, Bartolini G (eds) Routledge handbook of human rights and disasters. Routledge, New York, pp 10–26

Bettati M (1991) Un Droit d'Ingérence? Revue Générale de Droit International Public 95 (3):639–669

Carrozza P, Crema L (2014) On solidarity in international law. Caritas in Veritate Foundation

Casini L (2013) Solidarity between States in the global legal space. In: Annual Meeting of the European Group of Public Law. Available at https://papers.ssrn.com/sol3/papers.cfm?abstract_id=2368209 (last accessed on 20 August 2020)

Clement C (2014) International disaster response laws, rules and principles: a pragmatic approach to strenghtening international disaster response mechanisms. In: Caron DD, Kelly MJ, Telesetsky A (eds) The international law of disaster relief. Cambridge University Press, Cambridge, pp 67–88

Cubie D (2017) The international legal protection of persons in humanitarian crises. Hart, Oxford

De Guttry A (2012) Surveying the law. In: De Guttry A, Gestri M, Venturini G (eds) International disaster response law. Springer, New York, pp 3–44

De Siervo G (2012) Actors, activities and coordination in emergencies. In: De Guttry A, Gestri M, Venturini G (eds) International disaster response law. Springer, pp 485–515

Fidler DP (2005) Disaster relief and governance after the Indian Ocean Tsunami: what role for international law? Melb J Int Law 6:458–473

Fischer H (2003) International disaster response law treaties. In: Bannon V (ed) International disaster response laws, principles and practice: reflections, prospects and challenges. IFRC, Geneva, pp 24–44

Fisher D (2007) Law and legal issues in international disaster response: a desk study. International Federation of Red Cross and Red Crescent Societies, Geneva

Focarelli C (2013) Duty to protect in cases of natural disasters. In: Max Planck Encyclopedia of Public International Law. Oxford University Press, Oxford

Hestermeyer HP, König D, Matz-Lück N, Röben V, Seibert-Fohr A, Stoll P-T, Vöneky S (eds) (2012) Coexistence, cooperation and solidarity. Liber Amicorum Rüdiger Wolfrum. Martinus Nijhoff Publishers, Boston

Macalister-Smith P (1985) International humanitarian assistance. Disaster relief actions in international law and organization. Martinus Nijhoff Publishers, Dordrecht

Macalister-Smith P (1986) The international relief union: reflections on establishing an international relief Union of July 12, 1927. Legal Hist Rev 54:363–374

Natoli T (2013) L'harmonisation des législations nationales selon des modèles internationaux de réglementation: le programme du droit relatif aux catastrophes de la Fédération Internationale des Sociétés de la Croix-Rouge et du Croissant-Rouge. In: Arcari M, Balmond L (eds) Diversification des acteurs et dynamique normative en droit international. Editoriale Scientifica, Napoli, pp 139–158

O'Donnell T, Allan C (2016) A duty of solidarity? the International Law Commission's Draft Articles and the right to offer assistance in disasters. In: Breau SC, Samuel KLH (eds) Research handbook on disasters and international law. Edward Elgar, Cheltenham, pp 453–478

Park K-G (2018) Law on natural disasters. From cooperation to solidarity? In: Benvenisti E, Nolte G (eds) Community interests across international law. Oxford University Press, Oxford, pp 136–150

Pennisi di Floristella A (2015) Building the ASEAN center for humanitarian assistance and emergency response. Is ASEAN Learning from the Experience of the European Civil Protection Mechanism? *KFG Working Paper, 62*

Stephens T (2016) Disasters, international environmental law and the antrophocene. In: Breau SC, Samuel K (eds) Research handbook on disasters and international law. Edward Elgar, Cheltenham, pp 153–176

Wolfrum R, Kojima C (eds) (2010) Solidarity: a structural principle of international law. Springer, Berlin

Zorzi Giustiniani F (2018) Something old, something new: disaster risk reduction in international law. Quest Int Law (QIL) Zoom-in 49:7–27

Part I
International Law and Disaster Response: The Applicable Legal Framework

Introduction to Part I

As anticipated in the Introduction, the growing interest that the international community has shown over the past century towards disasters and their management led to the development of a set of rules and principles, contained in binding as well as non-binding instruments, which *expressly and directly* apply in disaster contexts. This rule complex or regime was initially termed IDRL and then gradually renamed IDL in order to reflect its broader focus, which today also embraces preventive aspects of disaster management.

Regime is a doctrinal category that—as will be seen throughout Chap. 2—epitomises the increasing specialisation and the accompanying perceived fragmentation of international law.[1] However, like all doctrinal constructions, the regime notion has its limits and its utilisation is not uniform among authors. In particular, when considering the international legal framework applicable in disaster scenarios, we are confronted with a confused picture, which results not just from the lack of a universal flagship treaty, but also from the tendency of many legal theorists as well as practitioners to label as IDRL/IDL *any* instrument whose norms, at least in part, may apply in disaster contexts. This tendency to overstretch the boundaries of a regime is especially evident with respect to IDRL/IDL and it is partly a consequence of the lack of a broadly accepted legal definition of disasters. Be it as it may, the entirety of international rules applicable in times of disasters is much broader and diversified than what could plausibly be considered part of the IDL regime,

[1]On the issue see generally: ILC Study Group on the Fragmentation of International Law, Fragmentation of International Law: Difficulties Arising from the Diversification and Expansion of International Law. Report of the Study Group of the International Law Commission, Finalized by Martti Koskenniemi, A/CN.4/L.682 and Add.1 and Corr. 1 13 April 2006; id., Conclusions, A/CN.4/L.702.

In the doctrine, cf. ex multis: Fischer-Lescano and Teubner (2004), pp. 999–1046; Cogan (2011), pp. 123–125; Young (2012).

comprising as it does rules and principles clearly pertaining to other domains, in primis human rights law, humanitarian law and environmental law.

For the purposes of the present work, particular importance needs to be attributed to the norms and principles of international human rights law (IHRL) and international humanitarian law (IHL). The relevance of IHL notably concerns the various issues pertaining to external actors' access to the territory of the affected State and the disaster's victims. The rules posed in this respect by IHL, even outside the war context, have served as a point of reference for both States and legal scholars in order to devise—originally by analogy—the rules applicable to disaster response. With the growing development of IDRL, the relevance of IHL has diminished, aside from in mixed situations of disaster and armed conflict. As to IHRL, its significance for disaster-related issues has conversely been growing. This is due in primis to the general character and scope of human rights norms as opposed to those characterising norms pertaining to IHL and IDRL/IDL.[2] Secondly, and most importantly, it is in the context of the UN Human Rights Treaty System that the contours and the content of solidarity duties among States in disaster situations have gradually taken form.

Before delving into an analysis of some of the main rules and principles that characterise disaster response at the international level, which will be the object of Parts II–IV of the book, the present Part first seeks to develop some general reflections on the doctrinal category of 'regimes' as distinct sets of rules governing specified subject areas (ratione materiae). This will be done in particular by addressing the debate on the fragmentation of international law and analysing the regime notion. A few considerations will then be made regarding the regimes' descriptive value as well as their impact—if any—on the systemic character of international law. Such reflections will be recalled at a later stage, notably in Chap. 3, when we will address the issue of regime and norm selection in complex emergencies. Certainly, the latter represents a context where typically various regimes, but also simply rules belonging to different regimes, are theoretically applicable.

References

Cogan JK (2011) The idea of fragmentation. Proc Am Soc Int Law 105:123–125

Fischer-Lescano A, Teubner G (2004) Regime-collisions: the vain search for legal unity in the fragmentation of global law. Mich J Int Law 25(4): 999–1046

Young M (ed) (2012) Regime interaction in international law: facing fragmentation. Cambridge University Press, Cambridge

List of Documents

ILC, Fragmentation of International Law: Difficulties Arising from the Diversification and Expansion of International Law. Report of The Study Group of the

[2] Cf. Chap. 2, paras. 2 and 3.

International Law Commission Finalized by Martti Koskenniemi, A/CN.4/L.682 and Add.1 and Corr. 1, 13 April 2006
ILC Study Group on the Fragmentation of International Law, Fragmentation of International Law: Difficulties Arising from the Diversification and Expansion of International Law: Conclusions, A/CN.4/L.702, 18 July 2006.

Chapter 2
The Complex Legal Framework Governing Disaster Response: A General Overview

Contents

2.1 The Growing Specialisation of International Law and the Notion of Regimes

The contemporary international legal system is characterised by a growing densification and specialisation of its norms, accompanied by the multiplication of specialised organisations and judicial bodies. It is generally argued that this phenomenon has led to the development of veritable distinct *regimes* of international norms. There is no universal, legal definition of regime, even though in international law the term has commonly come to refer a specific material field of law—such as international environmental law (IEL) or international human rights law—with its own institutional settings and courts.

While the term regime has become common parlance and it is generally utilised to refer to *any* subfield of international law, international jurisprudence also introduced since a long time a more specific notion, that of "self-contained regime". The latter notion tipically refers to a specific normative sub-set of international norms that exists independently from any other international law and as such does not tolerate any fall-back on common principles of customary international law. The term 'self-contained regime' was first utilised by the Permanent Court of International Justice (PCIJ) in *S.S. Wimbledon* (1923). In this case the Court, confronted with an issue of treaty interpretation concerning the determination of the status of the Kiel Canal,

F. Zorzi Giustiniani, *International Law in Disaster Scenarios*,
https://doi.org/10.1007/978-3-030-50597-4_2

asserted that the special rules on the Canal as laid down in the Treaty of Versailles were "self-contained; if they had to be supplemented and interpreted by the aid of those referring to the navigable waterways of Germany in the previous Section of Part II, they would lose their "raison d'etre"".[1] The term was subsequently used by the International Court of Justice (ICJ) to refer to diplomatic law. The Court in particular argued that the regime of specific legal consequences contained in the 1961 Vienna Convention on Diplomatic Relations was self-contained because no resort may be had to any remedy provided for by customary international law.[2] This second meaning of the term was later adopted by the majority of scholars. For instance, Bruno Simma defines self-contained regimes as a limited sub-category of subsystems of international law that embraces "a full set of secondary rules".[3]

Against this background, scholars raised the alarm against the asserted risks of a *fragmentation* of international law.[4] In the ensuing debate, the same unity and systemic nature of international law was called into question.[5] However, such risks are more apparent than real. In the first place, calls for unity overlook the fact that international law was never fully integrated. To the contrary, as lucidly remarked by P.-M. Dupuy, "one of the characteristics of international law is precisely its decentralization".[6] The growing expansion and diversification of international law is just a sign of the latter's "vitality"[7] and ultimately of its "maturisation", a process already experienced by national legal orders.[8] Secondly, such a process has not ultimately jeopardized international law *as a system*. Indeed, none of the many existing branches of international law that are generally considered as veritable

[1]Cf. PCIJ, Case of the S.S. Wimbledon, Judgement of 17 August 1923, in P.I.C.J. Series A., No. 1 (1923).

[2]Cf. ICJ, Case concerning the United States Diplomatic and Consular Staff in Tehran (United States of America vs. Iran), judgement of 24 May 1980, in I.C.J. Reports, 1980, 40, para. 86.

[3]Cf. Simma (1985), pp. 111, 115 and 117. On self-contained regimes see generally ILC, Fragmentation of International Law: Difficulties Arising from the Diversification and Expansion of International Law. Report of The Study Group of the International Law Commission Finalized by Martti Koskenniemi, A/CN.4/L.682 and Add.1 and Corr. 1, 13 April 2006, paras. 123 ff., where three distinct notions of the term are identified.

[4]Fragmentation is here meant strictly as *substantive* fragmentation, not covering its institutional dimension (also referred to as the *proliferation* of international courts).

[5]See e.g. Koskenniemi and Leino (2002), p. 533.

[6]Dupuy (2014), p. vi.

[7]"Nous pensons [...] que le phénomène [...] est un signe evident de la vitalité du droit international; un droit qui a toujours trouvé dans les règles conventionnelles, et dans les institutions crées par celles-ci, une possibilité d'expansion" (cf. Conforti 2007, p. 18).

[8]"It is because international law is in fact evolving and because institutions are being created to ensure its implementation and, occasionally, its enforcement that there now exists this growing concern for its unity. The irony, then, lies in the fact that international lawyers, having long fought for the recognition of 'their' law as 'real' law, are now concerned that there may be an excess of international law. In other words, the achievements of international law may institute its own downfall" (Prost and Kingsley Clark 2006, p. 343).

regimes, with the notable exception of EU law, can be deemed truly self-contained.[9] Last but not least, excessive emphasis on fragmentation is often placed by those legal scholars who, specialising in a single branch of international law, treat the latter *as if it were* fragmented.[10] More generally, the asserted fragmentation of international law is nothing more than a subjective and negative perception of the discipline's expanding specialisation in multiple subject areas.

As to regimes, a distinction must be drawn between regimes tout court and self-contained regimes. The latter notion was for a long time the object of academic debate but in the end it was rightly dismissed.[11] Admitting the existence of completely independent international regimes would in fact amount to denying the same viability of international law as a legal order. By contrast, the use of the term 'regime' as a subject area with its own internal logics and, most importantly, its own objectives has established itself among scholars and courts alike. However, the fact that any international regime has "neither clear boundaries nor a strictly determined normative force",[12] together with the general horizontal character of the international legal order,[13] render interaction and coordination among various regimes (at least

---

[9]As Simma and Pulkowski affirm in this regard: "Social systems cannot exist in splendid isolation from their environment. This point is conceded even by ardent proponents of regime specialization. According to Niklas Luhann's System theory, for example, all systems are to some extent interlinked by structural coupling. Similarly, legal subsystems coexisting in isolation from the remaining bulk of international law are inconceivable" (Simma and Pulkowski 2003, p. 491). "[O] ne may argue that special regimes are not so different from specific material regimes in national law. [. . .] [T]hey are not autonomous legal orders - with the exception of EU law which is not only a special regime, but arguably also a self-contained and independent legal order - but merely groups of specific legal norms with territorial or material specificity in application" (Besson 2010, p. 169). "[T]he chimera of 'self-contained regime' remains a phantom with no legal basis in international law, a notion which, despite its persistent appearance in jurisprudential debate, is best confined to the lively world of myth and fable" (Lindroos and Mehling 2006, p. 877). The opinion that totally self-contained regimes do not exist in international law has already been affirmed by the former ILC Rapporteur on International Responsibility Gaetano Arangio-Ruiz (cf. ILC, Fourth report on State responsibility, by Mr. Gaetano Arangio-Ruiz, Special Rapporteur, 12 and 25 May and 1 and 17 June 1992, A/CN.4/444 and Add.1-3, paras. 112, 124) and later by the ILC Study Group on the Fragmentation of International Law in its final report ("[. . .] the term "self-contained regime" is a misnomer. No legal regime is isolated from general international law", A/CN.4/L. 682, para. 193).

[10]"[A] vrai dire, s'il existe une 'fragmentation', elle se trouve davantage dans l'esprit des juristes, qu'ils soient enseignants, chercheurs ou praticiens, qui, à cause de cette complexification et de cette extension du droit international, se spécialisent à l'excès dans un domaine particulier [. . .] Le droit international n'est pas fragmenté – ou plutôt, s'il se fragmente, c'est surtout parce que les universitaires et les praticiens en traitent de manière fragmentée" (Pellet 2014, p. 758).

[11]Marti Koskenniemi, as Chairman of the ILC's Study Group on Fragmentation, considered the notion of self-contained regimes as "simply misleading" arguing that "there is no support for the view that anywhere general law would be fully excluded" and in its place proposed the expression "special regimes" (see Koskenniemi, M. Study on the Function and Scope of the Lex Specialis Rule and the Question of 'Self-Contained Regimes', Preliminary Report to the International Law Commission, ILC(LVI)/SG/FIL/CRD.1/Add.1 (2004), para. 134).

[12]ILC, A/CN.4/L.682, para. 173.

[13]As was famously held by the ICTY, "fragmentation is the product of a system of laws that, by and large, lacks a sense of vertical integration, of hierarchy" (ICTY, *The Prosecutor v. Dusko Tadic (Jurisdiction)*, Decision on the Defence Motion on Jurisdiction, Case No. IT-94-1, 10 August 1995,

those that are commonly recognised as such) and their norms quite difficult. Particular problems arise in the case of overlap, whenever rules pertaining to different regimes in principle are applicable to the same subject of regulation, that is, to the same facts. This issue will be explored further in Chap. 3 with respect to the scenarios of complex emergencies, i.e. situations where a disaster breaks out during an armed conflict.

Additional problems also arise as a result of inconsistencies in the application of the regime notion as well as of the utilitaristic recourse to a given regime (so-called regime-shifting) and/or its related court (forum shopping) "based on the strategic consideration which forum and regime will respond best to [law-appliers'] claims based on their parochial interest".[14] Furthermore, the proliferation of regimes, as evidence of the fragmentation of the international legal order, is considered a threat to legal certainty and ultimately to the coherence of international law *as a whole*.

The contrast between the growing specialisation of the discipline and its overall coherence should not be dramatised. Absolute coherence cannot be realised in a complex and pluralistic system like international law.[15] While conscious of this, an answer to the problems and challenges posed by the fragmentation *rectius* specialisation of international law[16] can and indeed (we argue) needs to be found within the normative ambit of general international law.[17] From the perspective adopted in this book, regimes thus have some—albeit limited—value. Three regimes in particular have a special importance for our purposes: IHL, IHRL and IDL. Their relevance is

---

(1995) 105 ILR 458). The only exception to the asserted lack of verticalisation is given by the—admittedly few—international norms having a peremptory and/or *erga omnes* character.

[14]Cf. Peters (2017), p. 675.

[15]"We, as theoreticians, need to think about international law's complex unity without complexes, in a dispassionate way, by seeking to achieve greater coherence where possible, but also by being prepared to welcome legal advances in their spontaneous and disorderly irruption, in the play of their differences and immediacy, even if contradictory or conflictual. Kant himself, who was anything but an advocate of fragmentation, conceded that good can come out of friction, opposition or conflict" (Prost 2012, p. 210).

[16]A. Peters argues that fragmentation, which she re-conceptualises as "refinement", should also be seen as an opportunity: "Accepting that '[t]here is no God's Eye Point of view that we can know or usefully imagine,' then the plurality of the view-points of actors involved in global governance need not only be seen as inevitable, but may even be appreciated as beneficial. Espousing such a perspectival pluralism in turn suggests qualifying the plurality of institutions and of their legal acts, the policy results, frictions, and conflicts created by the multiplicity of sites, actors, and acts, no longer as 'fragmentation' but as a refinement of international law" (Peters 2017, p. 703).

[17]Indeed, as recalled by Caflisch, all specialised regimes "are founded on, and connected with, general international law, and many disputes arising in their context can be settled only by reverting to rules of that law" (cf. Caflisch 2008, p. 297). Along similar lines, see inter alia Brownlie (1987), p. 160; Simma and Pulkowski (2003), pp. 507–12; Weil (1972), p. 34. However, central relevance in the more limited sense of general international law has also been underlined by A. Peters: "General international law always constitutes the normative environment, and is applicable to fill gaps or when the rules of a given regime cannot in themselves fulfill the regime's stated objectives" Peters (2017), p. 675.

especially due to the fact that the main principles and rules that inform disaster response arose from such subject areas'—necessarily restricted—context. Against this background, the overall objective of the present work is to establish the (potentially) universal—ultra regimes—relevance of some of these rules and principles, that is the existence either of norms belonging to general international law or of values which, being supported by a growing practice and opinio juris, could become part of general international law in the near future.[18]

2.2 International Regimes Applicable to Disaster Response

The international legal framework applicable to disaster response, as anticipated, is extremely diverse. Importantly, it does not end with instruments exclusively dedicated to the subject. A vast array of rules pertaining to different regimes are in principle applicable. Three such rule complexes are particularly relevant as a whole: IHL, IHRL and obviously IDL. In the analysis that follows we will thus outline the main features peculiar to each of these three rule complexes.

2.2.1 IHL

IHL applies precisely and exclusively[19] in situations of armed conflict (of an international as well as a non-international character) and belligerent occupation. The core discipline is contained in a set of multilateral treaties, mainly the four 1949 Geneva Conventions and their two 1977 Additional Protocols. These treaties, which for a significant part have attained customary status,[20] provide a distinct discipline for each of the three contexts.

Previously known as the law of armed conflicts, after the signing of the Geneva Conventions the regime was progressively renamed IHL in order to emphasise its essentially humanitarian objectives, consisting of limiting the effects of war and

[18]By general international law we mean customary international law and general principles as sources giving rise to norms that bind generally. On this and the other possible meaning of general international law, cf. Besson (2017), p. 839. On the difficulties inherent in defining general international law, see for all Wolfrum (2010).

[19]Aside from some limited exceptions, such as obligations to prosecute war criminals and to disseminate IHL norms.

[20]Cf. in this regard the study on customary humanitarian law conducted by the ICRC (Henckaerts and Doswald-Beck 2005), which claims that over time, differences between international and internal conflicts have in many cases disappeared. Indeed, according to the ICRC Study, out of 161 rules of customary humanitarian law applicable as treaty law to international armed conflicts, 136 would also apply to internal conflicts. Nevertheless, this reading is overly optimistic and simplicistic: on the various difficulties of detecting customary humanitarian norms, see e.g. Sassòli (2019), para. 4.40 ff.

protecting those who are not, or are no longer participating in hostilities. Indeed, IHL norms and their application are the expression of a careful balance between military necessity and humanitarian exigencies, in which the latter in principle should be prioritised.[21]

IHL is a special regime *par excellence*, as it applies only to the very specific contexts of war and occupation. However, this is not the only constraint circumscribing its applicability. Ratione temporis, the majority of IHL rules apply from the beginning to the cessation of hostilities or of the occupation.[22] As to personal limitations, it is necessary to distinguish between IHL's beneficiaries and addressees. The Geneva Conventions limited the former, identified under the category of "protected persons", to specified groups of civilians as well as to combatants who were *hors de combat*. These persons had to be protected by the adverse party whenever they came under its control. With the adoption of the Additional Protocols and thanks to the growing influence of the human rights movement, the scope of personal limitations has been sharply reduced. In particular, all civilians[23]—in a non-international armed conflict (NIAC) as long as they do not take direct part in hostilities[24]—are IHL's beneficiaries. Irrespective of nationality, these persons have to be protected by all parties to the conflict.[25] Moreover, to the extent that they have attained customary status, IHL norms need to be respected not only by the belligerents but by any other international subject acting in a conflict scenario, such as third States and international organisations.

Last but not least, the reach of IHL is limited geographically. In the absence of treaty provisions clarifying the regime's spatial scope, some interpretative doubts persist. In any case, it is generally accepted that, with the exception of the law of

[21]Cf. Sassòli (2019), p. 435 ("the object and purpose of IHL is not only to offer the best possible protection to individuals but also to find a balance between the principles of humanity and military necessity").

[22]Cf. common Article 2, paras. 1 and 2 of the Geneva Conventions.

[23]Cf. e.g. Art. 70.1 of the First Additional Protocol to the Geneva Conventions, which refers to "the civilian population of any territory under the control of a Party to the conflict".

[24]Cf. Art. 13, Additional Protocol II.

[25]In Art. 70, Protocol I provides that "[i]f the civilian population of any territory under the control of a Party to the conflict, other than occupied territory, is not adequately provided with [relief supplies], relief actions which are humanitarian and impartial in character and conducted without any adverse distinction shall be undertaken". The civilian population comprises "all persons who are civilians", i.e. all those who are not members of the armed forces, irrespective of nationality (cf. Art. 50.2, Protocol I). It follows that, according to Art. 70, it is primarily up to each party to the conflict to satisfy the essential needs of its nationals. However, in contrast to that applying in occupied territories, this obligation can be derived only implicitly, because the Contracting Parties at the time took for granted that each State would protect its own population. Giacca also remarks:

"[While IHL] has not been designed to regulate human relief in response to [...] non-conflict related-disasters [...], none of the above-discussed IHL provisions governing humanitarian relief in times of armed conflict appears to be restricted to humanitarian needs arising only from armed conflicts. Rather, it is the need of the civilian population that is decisive, irrespective of where those needs come from" Rodenhäuser and Giacca (2016), p. 147. A restrictive and indeed outdated interpretation of "protected persons" is instead adopted by Gavshon (cf. Gavshon 2009, p. 256).

occupation, which applies only to the areas over which the occupying power exercises effective control, in international armed conflicts (IACs) IHL is applicable to the whole territory of the belligerents. In other words, on the basis of the principle of unity of territory, IHL's spatial scope is not limited to those areas where active hostilities are ongoing.[26]

In the case of NIACs, the territorial scope of IHL's application is more contentious. The international jurisprudence of both the ICTY and the ICTR indicates that IHL norms apply to "the whole territory under the control of a party to the conflict, whether or not actual combat takes place there".[27] However, the situation becomes increasingly complicated further away from the battlefield. Beyond the territory of the State party to a NIAC or in which the NIAC originated, it is debatable whether IHL should apply and, in the affirmative, within which limits. In this respect it is necessary to distinguish between cases of spillover to the territories of neighbouring countries and other cases in which the conflict spreads to multiple States. In the latter scenario, acceptance of IHL's applicability could have the effect, as remarked by the ICRC, of transforming the world into a global battlefield.[28] It has thus been convincingly argued that a case-by-case approach should be adopted, in which a decisive role is played not by geography but rather by the *nexus* of a given conduct to the armed conflict.[29] This nexus must be stronger "the further away from the NIAC [the conduct] occurs".[30] However, the uncertainties surrounding the *abstract* applicability of IHL in such trans-national armed conflicts prompt authors supporting the nexus criterion to add that IHRL—if applicable—*in concreto* in

---

[26]"Although the Geneva Conventions are silent as to the geographical scope of international 'armed conflict', the provisions suggest that at least some of the provisions of the Conventions apply to the entire territory of the Parties to conflict, not just to the actual vicinity of the hostilities. Certainly, some of the provisions are clearly bound up with the hostilities and the geographical scope of those provisions should be so limited. Others, particularly those relating to the prisoners of war and civilians, are not so limited" (ICTY, *The Prosecutor v. Dusko Tadic (Jurisdiction)*, Decision on the Defence Motion for Interlocutory Appeal for Jurisdiction, Appeals Chamber, Case No. IT-94-1, 2 October 1995, para. 68). On the principle of unity of territory cf. Kolb and Hyde (2008), p. 95.

[27]ICTY, *The Prosecutor* v. *Dragoljub Kunarac, Radomir Kovač and Zoran Vuković*, Appeals Chamber, Judgment, Case No. IT-96-23 & IT-96-23/1-A, 12 June 2002, para. 57. See also ICTR, *The Prosecutor* v. *Laurent Semanza*, Judgment, Case No. ICTR-97-20-T, 15 May 2003, para. 367.

[28]ICRC, International humanitarian law and the challenges of contemporary conflicts, Report prepared for the 31st International Conference of the Red Cross and Red Crescent, 31IC/11/5.1.2, 9–11, October 2011, 22.

The ICRC *nonetheless* acknowledges the possibility that a NIAC spills over the territory of a neighbouring country. Cf. also Dinstein, who argues that "the idea that a NIAC can be global in nature is oxymoronic: an armed conflict can be a NIAC and it can be global, but it cannot be both" Dinstein (2012), p. 400.

[29]Cf. Sassòli (2019), 187, para. 6.3; Giacca (2014).

Giacca (2014), p. 313. Sivakumaran instead holds that it is the "persons, objects, and the like that are affected by the armed conflict and the conduct at issue rather than any geographic location [that] would provide a more appropriate solution to the question of the geographic scope of application of the law" Sivakumaran (2012), p. 252.

[30]Cf. Sassòli (2019), p. 190; Lubell and Dereijko (2013), p. 65 ff.

most cases would dominate over IHL.[31] Such a caveat is in fact fully understandable considering the low level of protection offered by the law of NIACs.

2.2.2 *IHRL*

While IHL is intended to impose limits to the horrors of war, notably by protecting civilians and soldiers *hors combat*, IHRL's guarantees apply in principle without limits, being of universal application.[32]

This means that even in situations of disasters or broader complex emergencies, IHRL constitutes one of—if not the main—major set(s) of applicable rules. The crucial role of IHRL in disasters has also been recognised in the ILC DAs, whose Art. 5 (Human rights) provides that: "Persons affected by disasters are entitled to the respect for and protection of their human rights in accordance with international law". Additionally, it is worth noting that human rights have had a decisive impact on disasters at the operational level, as they have helped shape disaster management policies and inform a rights-based approach to disaster response, as exemplified by the IASC Operational Guidelines on the Protection of Persons in Situations of Natural Disasters.[33]

The fact that, ratione temporis, human rights in principle continue to apply even in times of disasters probably explains why only a few human rights treaties contain references to such emergencies.[34] Nevertheless, this does not mean that States in dire straits should respect and protect human rights to the same extent as in peaceful times. As remarked by Venturini:

> As a matter of fact, when a catastrophic event strikes a country, the ability of a government to ensure full respect of a number of CPRs [civil and political rights] and ESCRs [economic, social and cultural rights] may be seriously impaired. To cite an example, the liberty of movement or the right of assembly may sometimes prove incompatible with the

---

[31] Cf. Sassòli (2019), ibid.

[32] See for all Kolb (2013), para. 33. However, the duty-bearer changes depending on where the individual beneficiary is located. While international human rights were traditionally territorially based, today it is generally recognised that States are bound by them within their jurisdiction and wherever they exercise "effective control".

[33] "The Guidelines are addressed to intergovernmental and non-governmental humanitarian actors. They focus on what humanitarian actors should do in order to implement a human rights-based approach to humanitarian action in the context of natural disasters" (Brookings-Bern Project on Internal Displacement, Human Rights and Natural Disasters. Operational Guidelines and Field Manual on Human Rights Protection in Situations of Natural Disaster, Pilot version (March 2008), 2).

[34] Express references to disasters can be found in the following human rights treaties: 1990 African Charter on the rights and welfare of the child (Art. 23); 2006 International Convention on the rights of persons with disabilities (Art. 11); 2006 Great Lakes Protocol on the Protection and Assistance to internally displaced persons (Art. 1); 2009 African Union Convention for the protection and assistance of internally displaced persons in Africa (Art. 1).

management of assistance and relief. In extreme cases, floods of persons forced to abandon a disaster area could even threaten the life of a weak State.[35]

Apart from ordinary limitations, which are envisaged by the same content of a specific right, human rights can be derogated in a time of public emergency threatening the life of the nation.[36] Derogations are permitted by treaties on civil and political rights, which establish procedural requirements and also demand that derogation measures be temporary, non-discriminatory and proportional. Only a few rights are considered non-derogable under such treaties and these generally correspond to those having a peremptory character, like the right to life and prohibitions of torture and slavery. Although war is the quintessential public emergency, some doubts were raised in the past over the possibility of invoking derogation clauses in the case of disaster. Practice, though quite scarce, nonetheless seems to confirm such a possibility.[37] Contrary to war, however, disasters in most cases affect a narrow geographical area and hence the territorial scope of derogation measures generally is—and indeed should be—limited accordingly.

As to economic, social and cultural (ESC) rights, human rights treaties do not admit the possibility of derogations.[38] Only limitations are permissible, on the condition that they are established by law, but "only in so far as this may be compatible with the nature of these rights and solely for the purpose of promoting the general welfare in a democratic society".[39] This differential treatment finds its origin in the asserted particular nature of ESC rights, whose realisation States have to ensure only progressively. Nonetheless, as will be seen in depth in Chap. 7, the ESC Committee has clarified that some of the obligations deriving from the ICESCR are of immediate effect and must be complied with in all situations, even notably in the case of disaster.

2.2.3 IDL

IDL comprises a plethora of instruments, both of a binding and a non-binding character, which have been developed over time to regulate natural and human-made disasters. The vast majority of these instruments lack a universal reach, having

---

[35]Venturini (2012), p. 50.

[36]For a broad overview of limitations and derogations in human rights treaties, see UN Commission on Human Rights, The Siracusa Principles on the Limitation and Derogation Provisions in the International Covenant on Civil and Political Rights, 28 September 1984, E/CN.4/1984/4, Annex, 28 September 1984.

[37]In this sense, cf. Sommario (2018), p. 111, who also remarks that "Article 4 ICCPR has been invoked by at least five States in cases of natural disasters". Furthermore, Schultz and Castan affirm that "a severe natural disaster, such as a major flood or earthquake" could qualify as a serious public emergency (Schultz and Castan 2000), p. 624.

[38]This is the case, e.g., of the ICESCR and the African Charter on Human and Peoples Rights.

[39]Cfr. Art. 4 ICESCR.

been concluded either at the regional or the bilateral level. Their content is also very specific, typically addressing a certain type of disaster and/or a disaster-related issue.[40] As was noted in the Introduction, the ILC DAs were meant to fill this gap, but the objective was fulfilled only in part. The consequence is that in IDL there is no global instrument of a general character equivalent to the 1949 Geneva Conventions for IHL or the 1966 International Covenants for IHRL. Moreover, existing instruments do not form a coherent framework as they often regulate the same issue in different and contrasting ways.[41]

As one of the latest special regimes of international law, IDL has benefited from developments occurring in older regimes, notably IHL, IHRL and IEL. As regards IHL, its principles and rules concerning humanitarian access were initially applied by analogy to disaster relief and then ultimately contributed to the formation of similar rules that specifically address disaster contexts.[42] IEL has also been—and continues to be as far as disaster prevention is concerned—an essential source of inspiration for IDL. Indeed, the latter has borrowed extensively from IEL in laying down substantive as well as procedural obligations and standards for disaster risk reduction. Despite the differences that still exist between the two branches, the growing preventative focus that now features IDL has rendered the dividing line with IEL more blurred. Finally, as far as IHRL is concerned, it is evident that IDL shares with it its protective focus vis-à-vis the victims of disasters. Nevertheless, IDL has an equally strong focus on the protection of the affected State's sovereignty (and integrity), which is in fact constantly recalled in treaties regulating disaster response. More specifically, by emphasising the primary role of the affected State in disaster response, IDL aims to reinforce national capacity and build resilience in order to avoid the recurrence of disasters in the future.

List of Documents

African Charter of Human and People's Rights, 27 June 1981

African Charter on the Rights and Welfare of the Child, 11 July 1990

Brookings-Bern Project on Internal Displacement, Human Rights and Natural Disasters. Operational Guidelines and Field Manual on Human Rights Protection in Situations of Natural Disaster, Pilot version (March 2008)

Convention for the Protection and Assistance of Internally Displaced Persons (IDPs) in Africa (Kampala Convention), 22 October 2009

[40]With specific reference to IDRL, Sivakumaran remarks that "disaster relief law has been described as being composed of a 'pot pourri' of, or 'strewn with', instruments, all of which tend to regulate the same sorts of issues" Sivakumaran (2017), p. 1099.

[41]As claimed by De Guttry, "[t]his anarchic accumulation of treaties and rules is due to the fact that most international regulations have been agreed upon and enacted without reference to each other, and sometimes as a reaction to new kinds of disasters" De Guttry (2012), p. 4.

[42]Cf. Chap. 3 of this book.

Convention on the Rights of Persons with Disabilities, 13 December 2006
Geneva Conventions for the protection of war victims of 12 August 1949
ICJ, Case concerning the United States Diplomatic and Consular Staff in Tehran (United States of America vs. Iran), Judgement of 24 May 1980, in I.C.J. Reports, 1980
ICRC, International humanitarian law and the challenges of contemporary conflicts, Report prepared for the 31st International Conference of the Red Cross and Red Crescent, October 2011, 31IC/11/5.1.2
ICTR, *The Prosecutor* v. *Laurent Semanza*, Judgment, Case No. ICTR-97-20-T, 15 May 2003
ICTY, *The Prosecutor* v. *Dragoljub Kunarac, Radomir Kovač and Zoran Vuković*, Appeals Chamber, Judgment, Case No. IT-96-23 & IT-96-23/1-A, 12 June 2002
ICTY, *The Prosecutor v. Dusko Tadic (Jurisdiction)*, Decision on the Defence Motion on Jurisdiction, Case No. IT-94-1, 10 August 1995
ICTY, *The Prosecutor v. Dusko Tadic (Jurisdiction)*, Decision on the Defence Motion for Interlocutory Appeal for Jurisdiction, Appeals Chamber, Case No. IT-94-1, 2 October 1995
ILC, Fragmentation of International Law: Difficulties Arising from the Diversification and Expansion of International Law. Report of The Study Group of the International Law Commission Finalized by Martti Koskenniemi, A/CN.4/L.682 and Add.1 and Corr. 1, 13 April 2006
ILC, Fourth report on State responsibility, by Mr. Gaetano Arangio-Ruiz, Special Rapporteur, 12 and 25 May and 1 and 17 June 1992, A/CN.4/444 and Add.1-3
Koskenniemi, M. Study on the Function and Scope of the Lex Specialis Rule and the Question of 'Self-Contained Regimes', Preliminary Report to the International Law Commission, ILC(LVI)/SG/FIL/CRD.1/Add.1 (2004)
International Covenant on Civil and Political Rights, 16 December 1966
PCIJ, Case of the S.S. Wimbledon, Judgement of 17 August 1923, in P.I.C.J. Series A., No. 1 (1923)
Protocol Additional to the Geneva Conventions of 12 August 1949, and relating to the Protection of Victims of International Armed Conflicts (Protocol I), 8 June 1977
Protocol Additional to the Geneva Conventions of 12 August 1949, and relating to the Protection of Victims of Non-International Armed Conflicts (Protocol II), 8 June 1977
Protocol on the Protection and Assistance to Internally Displaced Persons to the Pact on Security, Stability and Development in the Great Lakes region (Great Lakes Protocol), 30 November 2006
UN Commission on Human Rights, The Siracusa Principles on the Limitation and Derogation Provisions in the International Covenant on Civil and Political Rights, E/CN.4/1984/4, Annex, 28 September 1984

References

Besson S (2010) Theorizing the sources of international law. In: Besson S, Tasioulas J (eds) The philosophy of international law. Oxford University Press, Oxford, pp 164–185

Besson S (2017) Sources of international human rights law. How general is general international law? In Besson S, d'Aspremont J (eds) The Oxford handbook on the sources of international law. Oxford University Press, Oxford, pp 837–870

Brownlie I (1987) Problems concerning the unity of international law. In: International law in the time of its codification: essays in Honor of Roberto Ago, Giuffrè, 1987, pp 153–162

Caflisch L (2008) International courts and tribunals – the challenges ahead: the law – substantive and procedural questions. Law Pract Int Courts Tribunals 7(3):289–299

Conforti B (2007) Unité et fragmentarion du droit international: "glissez, mortels, n'appuyez pas!". Revue Générale de Droit International Public 111(1):5–18

De Guttry A (2012) Surveying the law. In: De Guttry A, Gestri M, Venturini G (eds) International disaster response law. Springer, New York, pp 3–44

Dinstein Y (2012) Concluding remarks on non-international armed conflicts. In: Watkin K, Norris AJ (eds) Non-international armed conflict in the twenty-first century. Naval War College, Newport, Rhode Island, pp 399–421

Dupuy P-M (2014) Foreword. In: Pulkowski D (ed) The law and politics of international regime conflict. Oxford University Press, Oxford, pp v–viii

Gavshon D (2009) The applicability of IHL in mixed situations of disaster and conflict. J Conflict Secur Law 14(2):243–263

Giacca G (2014) The relationship between economic, social and cultural rights and international humanitarian law. In: Riedel E, Giacca G, Golay C (eds) Economic, social and cultural rights in international law. Contemporary issues and challenges. Oxford University Press, Oxford, pp 308–342

Henckaerts J-M, Doswald-Beck L (2005) Customary international humanitarian law. Cambridge University Press, Cambridge

Kolb R (2013) Human rights and humanitarian law. In: MPEIL. Oxford University Press, Oxford

Kolb R, Hyde R (2008) An introduction to the international law of armed conflicts. Hart, Oxford

Koskenniemi M, Leino P (2002) Fragmentation of international law? Postmodern anxieties. Leiden J Int Law 15(3):553–579

Lindroos A, Mehling M (2006) Dispelling the Chimera of "Self-contained regimes". International law and the WTO. Eur J Int Law 16(5):857–877

Lubell N, Dereijko N (2013) A global battlefield?: Drones and the geographical scope of armed conflict. J Int Crim Just 11(1):65–88

Pellet A (2014) Notes sur la "fragmentation" du droit international: droit des investissements internationaux et droits de l'homme. In: Alland D, Chetail V, de Frouville O, Viñuales JE (eds) Unité et diversité du droit international/Unity and Diversity of International Law - Ecrits en l'honneur du Professeur Pierre-Marie Dupuy/Essays in Honour of Professor Pierre-Marie Dupuy. Martinus Nijhoff, Leiden & Boston, pp 757–784

Peters A (2017) The refinement of international law: from fragmentation to regime interaction and politicization. Int J Const Law 15(3):671–704

Prost M (2012) The concept of unity in public international law. Hart Publishing, Oxford & Portland

Prost M, Kingsley Clark P (2006) Unity, diversity and the fragmentation of international law: how much does the multiplication of international organizations really matter? Chinese J Int Law 5 (2):341–370

Rodenhäuser T, Giacca G (2016) The international humanitarian law framework for humanitarian relief during armed conflicts and complex emergencies. In: Breau SC, Samuel KLH (eds) Research handbook on disasters and international law. Edward Elgar, Cheltenham, pp 132–152

Sassòli M (2019) International humanitarian law – rules, solutions to problems arising in warfare and controversies. Edward Elgar, Cheltenham

Schultz J, Castan M (2000) The international covenant on civil and political rights. Oxford University Press, Oxford

Simma B (1985) Self-contained regimes. Neth Yearb Int Law 16:111, 115, 117

Simma B, Pulkowski D (2003) Of planets and the universe: self-contained regimes in international law. Eur J Int Law 17(3):483–529

Sivakumaran S (2012) The law of non-international armed conflict. Oxford University Press, Oxford

Sivakumaran S (2017) Techniques in international law-making: extrapolation, analogy, form and the emergence of an international law of disaster relief. Eur J Int Law 28(4):1097–1132

Sommario E (2018) Limitation and derogation provisions in international human rights law treaties and their use in disaster settings. In: Zorzi Giustiniani F, Sommario E, Casolari F, Bartolini G (eds) Routledge handbook of human rights and disasters. Routledge, London, pp 98–118

Venturini G (2012) International disaster response law in relation to other branches of international law. In: De Guttry A, Gestri M, Venturini G (eds) International Disaster Response Law. Springer, The Hague, pp 45–64

Weil P (1972) Le droit international économique, mythe ou réalité? In: Aspects du droit international économique. Elaboration, contrôle, sanction. Colloque d'Orléans pour la SFDI, pp 1–34

Wolfrum R (2010) General international law (principles, rules, and standards). In: Max Planck Encyclopedia of international law. Oxford University Press, Oxford

Chapter 3
The International Legal Framework Applicable in Mixed Situations of Disaster and Armed Conflict

Contents

3.1 Preliminary Remarks

'Disaster' is a broad notion that, as was shown in the Introduction, encompasses both natural and human-made events. Among the latter, the most destructive is undoubtedly war. International law has long recognised this sad record by devising a specific legal framework—international humanitarian law (IHL)—which aims to limit the effects of armed conflicts and in particular to manage their humanitarian consequences. IDL instruments, which are mostly newer than IHL treaties, generally take account of such a specialised protective regime by adopting a definition of disaster that excludes war events.[1] A similar reasoning explains the decision of the Special Rapporteur Valencia-Ospina—later to be confirmed in the DAs as approved on

[1] An explicit exclusion of armed conflicts from the definition of disaster is contained in soft law instruments as well as in treaties, including the DAs and the Report of the UN Open-ended intergovernmental expert working group on indicators and terminology relating to disaster risk reduction (cf. UN GA, Report of the Open-ended intergovernmental expert working group on indicators and terminology relating to disaster risk reduction, 1 December 2016, A/71/644) in recent years.

F. Zorzi Giustiniani, *International Law in Disaster Scenarios*,
https://doi.org/10.1007/978-3-030-50597-4_3

second reading—to exclude armed conflicts “per se” from the disaster notion enshrined in DA 3(a).[2]

Nonetheless, reality often confronts us with a more complicated picture, with disasters breaking out in the territories of countries involved in an armed conflict. This scenario falls under the more general notion of so-called complex emergencies: those “humanitarian cris[es] in a country, region or society where there is total or considerable breakdown of authority resulting from internal or external conflict and which requires an international response that goes beyond the mandate or capacity of any single and/or ongoing UN country programme”.[3] In these mixed situations of disaster and armed conflict, the problem arises of determining which rules or sets of rules to apply, additionally considering the difficulty of “separately addressing the situations of a population in need as a result of an armed conflict and a disaster situation”.[4]

Although the applicable legal framework in disaster settings is extremely varied and changeable depending on the actors involved, the main branches of international norms that are typically deemed applicable to mixed situations, as well as to disaster contexts at large, are IHL, IHRL and obviously IDL. These branches, as was shown in Chap. 2, are generally described as veritable ‘regimes’ of international law. Such a qualification, it is worth remembering, has a mere classification purpose. Therefore, it will be utilised in this chapter in order to assess the relevance of the two major doctrinal models devised sofar to select the set of rules to be applied in complex emergencies. The approach envisaged in this regard by the DAs will then be addressed. The inquiry will show the limits of reasoning in terms of regimes—which are generally evident in any disaster context but even more so in complex emergencies—and the consequent need to search instead for the most suitable *rule* to apply on a case-by-case basis. The said limits are particularly evident in complex emergencies.

3.2 Identification of the Applicable Legal Framework

With the growing frequency of disasters, it is increasingly likely that these will occur in a war-torn country, especially when considering the large number of ongoing conflicts around the world.[5] In such mixed situations, the problem arises of determining which international rules apply to regulate the various legal issues that may

[2]The first version of DA 3 directly envisaged such exclusion in the text of the provision. In the DAs as approved on second reading, a clarification in this respect was instead relegated to the commentary.

[3]IASC, Working Group XVIth Meeting, Definition of Complex Emergencies, 30 November 1994.

[4]Cf. Bartolini (2017), p. 1113.

[5]A list of ongoing conflicts worldwide is available at the following link: https://www.warsintheworld.com/?page=static1258254223(last accessed on 25 August 2020).

emerge in disaster response. It would seem logical that the rules governing armed conflicts as well as those protecting internationally recognised human rights (if not derogated) continue to apply. However, it is probable that many disaster-related issues do not fall within the geographical or material scope of these norms, or that the latter contrast among each other or with IDL rules, or even that no international rule specifically addresses the needs of disaster victims or other disaster-related issues.

In order to determine which international rules are applicable in a given situation, a two-step process is usually utilised. First, the various sets of norms (generally qualified as regimes) that are potentially applicable are identified. Next, recourse is made to a model of regime selection in order to decide, once and for all or on a case-by-case basis, which regime or rule(s) of a certain regime should be applied.

3.2.1 *Applicable Regimes and Models of Regime Selection in Complex Emergencies*

In a complex emergency characterised by a disaster and an armed conflict, a vast array of rules pertaining to different regimes are in principle applicable, rendering overlap between rules pertaining to different regimes a common situation. Three such rule complexes are, as anticipated, particularly relevant in general: IHL, IHRL and IDL. In order to determine which regime's rules should be applied to regulate a certain factual situation, two main models of regime selection are normally used: lex specialis and complementarity.

3.2.1.1 Lex specialis

The lex specialis model is rooted in the principle of lex specialis derogat generali.[6] This finds its origins in Roman law and has become a general principle common to many municipal orders. Generally utilised as a tool for resolving conflicts between legal norms, it suggests that the law governing more specifically a subject matter (the *lex specialis*) prevails over the more general rule (the *lex generalis*).

Despite some authoritative exceptions in scholarly writings,[7] the principle was first used quite recently in international law, notably to describe the relationship between IHL and IHRL. It was only after—and indeed as a result—of the International Court of Justice's (ICJ) recourse to the principle that it began to receive

[6]On the lex specialis principle, see e.g.: Pauwelyn (2003), pp. 385–439; Koskenniemi, M. Study on the Function and Scope of the Lex Specialis Rule and the Question of 'Self-Contained Regimes', Preliminary Report to the International Law Commission, ILC(LVI)/SG/FIL/CRD.1/Add.1 (2004); Lindroos (2005), p. 27; Prud'homme (2007), pp. 356–395.

[7]Already Hugo Grotius referred to the lex specialis principle with respect to agreements to be regarded as equal. Cf. Prud'homme (2007), p. 367 ff., who also refers to Vattel.

substantial attention in academic circles. In the Advisory Opinion rendered in the *Nuclear Weapons* case the Court, when examining the interplay between human rights and humanitarian law in armed conflicts, affirmed that:

> In principle the right not arbitrarily to be deprived of one's life applies also in hostilities. The test of what is an arbitrary deprivation of life, however, then falls to be determined by the applicable lex specialis, namely, the law applicable in armed conflict which is designed to regulate the conduct of hostilities.[8]

This opinion has sometimes been (incorrectly) interpreted as IHL completely displacing IHRL during armed conflicts, or at least having primacy *as a regime*.[9] A little more clarity was brought by the Court in the later Opinion on the *Legal Consequences of the Construction of a Wall in Occupied Palestinian Territory*. Here the ICJ expressed itself in a slightly different way, stating that the parallel application of the two regimes of IHL and IHRL can result in three possible scenarios:

> some rights may be exclusively matters of international humanitarian law; others may be exclusively matters of human rights law; yet others may be matters of both these branches of international law. In order to answer the question put to it, the Court will have to take into consideration both these branches of international law, namely human rights law and, as lex specialis, international humanitarian law.[10]

However, the Court failed to specify which rights belong to each regime or establish on the basis of which criteria IHL or IHRL norms should be applied in practice. The co-application of the two branches was subsequently affirmed by the ICJ in a contentious case, *Democratic Republic of the Congo v. Uganda*. With no reference made to lex specialis, such silence was interpreted as "a possible abandonment" of the principle,[11] even as a possible "tacit acknowledgement of the bankruptcy of that approach to the matter".[12]

Lex specialis was then thematised in the context of doctrinal debates on the fragmentation of international law. According to the first position, the lex specialis maxim must be seen in terms of legal regimes. This clearly advantages IHL as it was specifically developed for the context of armed conflict. Such an approach, also

---

[8]Cf. ICJ, The Legality of the Threat or Use of Nuclear Weapons, Advisory Opinion, 8 July 1996, para. 25.

[9]Rather, as remarked by Koskenniemi in commenting on the cited passage: "[e]ven as [the lex specialis test] works so as to justify recourse to an exception, what is being set aside does not vanish altogether. The Court was careful to point out that human rights law continued to apply within armed conflict. The exception – humanitarian law – only affected one (albeit important) aspect of it, namely the relative assessment of 'arbitrariness'. The use of the lex specialis test did not intend to suggest that human rights were abolished in war. It did not function in a formal or absolute way but as an aspect of the pragmatics of the Court's reasoning" (cf. ILC(LVI)/SG/FIL/CRD.1/Add.1 (2004), para. 76).

[10]ICJ, Legal Consequences of the Construction of a Wall in the Occupied Palestinian Territory, Advisory Opinion, 9 July 2004, para. 106.

[11]Sic Márquez Carrasco et al. (2015), p. 55.

[12]Cf. Eden and Happold (2009), p. 442.

termed the displacement approach, has found the support of only a few States[13] and is generally rejected by the doctrine.[14] In fact, its major consequence is that IHRL—as well as any other regimes or norms pertaining to a regime *different from IHL*—cannot be applied in armed conflicts.[15] Much more acceptable is the second position, which contends that lex specialis operates at the level of individual norms and not of regimes. This position has the advantage that no regime is a priori and as a whole singled out in times of war. Nonetheless, the absence of hierarchy that typically features international rules and the fact that all specialised regimes generally have their own conflict rules render particularly challenging the application of the lex specialis principle. Moreover, it has been rightly observed that "the vagueness of lex specialis allows the principle to be interpreted in all directions, to the benefit of diametrically opposed stances".[16] Not coincidentally, various versions of the latter position have been proposed.

According to some authors, in the case of genuine conflict (i.e. a conflict that cannot be avoided through interpretation) between specific norms of IHL and IHRL, IHL as lex specialis "would displace or qualify the conflicting rule of IHRL *to the extent strictly required* to resolve the conflict".[17] This interpretation evidently assumes that IHL is always the lex specialis. An alternative reading proposed by Sassòli instead suggests that "one must determine which conflicting rule constitutes the lex specialis in every specific situation, taking into account as well the overall systemic purposes of international law".[18] The factors to be considered in this case-by-case evaluation of specialty, he claims, are several:

> Specialty, in the logical sense, implies that the norm that applies to a certain set of facts must give way to the norm that applies to that same set of facts as well as to an additional fact that

[13]In particular, this is the opinion expressed by Colombia (cf. Inter-American Commission on Human Rights, Report No. 112/10: Inter-State petition IP-02: Admissibility: Franklin Guillermo Aisalla Molina, Ecuador – Colombia, OEA/Ser.L/V/II.140, 21 October 2011, para. 114); Russia (cf. European Court of Human Rights (former Fifth Section), Georgia v. Russia (II), Decision on Admissibility of 12 December 2011, para. 69) and Israel (see UN Human Rights Committee (HRC), Second Periodic Report: Israel (2001), CCPR/C/ISR/2001/2, para. 8)). It was also the approach of the United States of America under the Bush Administration (cf. United States of America, Response of the United States to Request for Precautionary Measures – Detainees in Guantanamo Bay, Cuba (15 April 2002) (2002). *International Legal Materials*, *41*, 1020–1021 ff.; UN HRC, Comments by the Government of the United States of America on the Concluding Observations of the Human Rights Committee (2008), CCPR/C/USA/CO/3/Rev.1/Add.1, para. 12). Previously, the ICRC additionally supported the absolute primacy of IHL as lex specialis in times of war (cf. Kolb 2013, paras. 10 and 21).

[14]The displacement approach is supported e.g. by: Dennis (2006), pp. 472–480; McCarthy (2008), p. 107.

[15]The lack of acceptability of such an outcome has been confirmed, inter alia, by the works of the ILC on the effects of war on treaties.

[16]Cf. Prud'homme (2007), p. 394.

[17]Cf. Milanovic (2017), p. 104, emphasis in the original. See also Krieger (2006), p. 272; Droege (2008), p. 524.

[18]Cf. Sassòli (2019), p. 433.

> is present in a given situation. Between two potentially applicable rules, the one that has the larger 'common contact surface area' with the situation applies. A norm that is either more precise or that has a narrower material or personal scope of application constitutes the lex specialis. The norm addressing a problem explicitly prevails over the one that treats it implicitly. A norm that provides more details prevails over another's generality, while one that is more restrictive prevails over one that covers a problem fully but in a less exacting manner.
>
> A less formal (and less objective) factor that permits determination of the applicable lex specialis is the extent to which the solution conforms to the systemic objectives of the law.[19]

As acknowledged by the same author, the last factor does not formally fit the lex specialis model, but nevertheless needs to be considered in "hard cases" without a clear solution. It should be noted that this factor, taken alone, is the distinguishing feature of the second model, to which we now turn.

3.2.1.2 Complementarity

Contrary to lex specialis, complementarity is based on the assumption that the regimes whose application is at issue are on an equal footing and can thus mutually support one another. In this case, again, reference is generally made to the relation between IHL and IHRL. As both regimes, it is asserted, have a common objective—the protection of humanity—their norms, which frequently overlap, have to be interpreted in a coherent way and inform the interpretation of each other. Indeed, they are in a relation of interpretation.[20] This implies that whereas in peacetime only IHRL is applicable and should hence be applied, in armed conflict IHL has to be applied in conjunction or better in coordination with IHRL.

This model clearly relies on the principle of systemic interpretation ex Art. 31.3 (c) of the Vienna Convention on the Law of Treaties, according to which in interpreting a treaty rule account must be taken of "[a]ny relevant rules of international law applicable in the relations between the parties". Advocates of such model also call in their support the ICJ's advisory opinion on *Nuclear Weapons*, notably the passage where the Court holds that the meaning of an "arbitrary deprivation of life" ex Art. 6 ICCPR in armed conflicts has to be established in light of IHL.[21] Reference is then routinely made to General Comment 31 of the UN Human Rights Committee, which affirms: "[w]hile, in respect of certain Covenant rights, more specific rules of international humanitarian law may be specially relevant for the purposes of the

[19]Ibid., 439.

[20]Hathaway et al. (2012), p. 1886.

[21]Cf. ICJ, Nuclear Weapons cit., para. 25. According to V. Gowlland-Debbas, this paragraph "serves to reinforce the consistent trend in human rights case law that the individual is entitled to both human rights and humanitarian law protection in complementarity fashion in time of armed conflict" (cf. Gowlland-Debbas 2004, p. 359).

interpretation of Covenant rights, both spheres of law are complementary, not mutually exclusive".[22]

However, as was remarked with respect to lex specialis, the same term or language can be used to mean different things, especially in the absence of a clear explanation. The ambiguities surrounding the *Nuclear Weapons*'s opinion are a case in point. More pertinent and straightforward seems the reference to the ICRC's Customary Study on IHL, which describes IHRL's role as being to "support, strengthen and clarify analogous principles of international humanitarian law".[23] Finally, support for the complementarity model is found in the doctrine, notably by those authors who underscore the limits of lex specialis.[24]

The objective as well as the attractiveness of this model is found in its harmonious interpretation and application of international law "understood as a coherent system".[25] However, the means to attain such an objective (i.e. interpretation) is not always adequate, especially when we are confronted with a genuine conflict of norms.[26] Moreover, even when the norm conflict is apparent and could thus be solved through interpretation, the risk is that in the most complex cases, the solution, or stated better the compromise, "might require a dilution of both norms [which are in tension] to force them into a relationship of interpretation".[27]

3.3 The ILC's Approach

The interplay between IDL and other applicable regimes or rules during complex emergencies was also addressed by the ILC in its works on the Protection of Persons in the Event of Disasters. In this respect the Commission proceeded in two stages. Initially the issue was addressed indirectly in the context of the discussion on the disaster notion. The Special Rapporteur, also on the basis of the opinions of States'

[22]UN HRC, General Comment 31 - Nature of the General Legal Obligation on States Parties to the Covenant, CCPR/C/21/Rev.1/Add.13 (2004), 10 December 2005, para. 11.

[23]Cf. Henckaerts and Doswald-Beck (2005), p. xxxvii.

[24]We refer in particular to Robert Kolb, Richard Hyde and Gilles Giacca. The first two authors, who term their approach "renvoi", suggest indeed "using both sources of law [IHL and IHRL] in a complementary manner in order to obtain a proper interpretation" (cf. Kolb and Hyde 2008, p. 271). Giacca, instead, argues that there is "a general presumption of complementarity of the two sets of norms" and that "the question of complementarity between IHL and human rights, as discussed, can reflect the principle of systemic integration" (Giacca 2014, p. 316).

[25]Cf. Droege (2008), p. 521. See also Giacca, who argues: "[t]he main rationale is to contribute to greater coherence in international law and to the avoidance of further fragmentation, making the application of human rights practicable and realistic, having in mind that states have not created two legal regimes which complement each other perfectly" (Giacca 2014, p. 317).

[26]On the difference between a genuine and an apparent conflict of norms, see Pauwelyn (2003), p. 178.

[27]Cf. Hathaway et al. (2012), p. 1902.

delegations,[28] proposed to expressly exclude armed conflicts from the definition of disaster "with the understanding that a well-developed body of law exists to cover such situations".[29] However, as a result of the subsequent discussions within the Sixth Committee and the ILC, the decision was made not to exclude situations of complex emergencies from the scope of the DAs. While the majority opinion both within the ILC and among States was that armed conflicts per se should not be qualified as disasters,[30] it was recognised that "[t]o simply exclude the applicability of the draft articles because of the co-existence of an armed conflict would be detrimental to the protection of the victims of the disaster, especially when the onset of the disaster pre-dated the armed conflict".[31] The Drafting Committee thus suggested including in the DAs a new provision devoted to clarifying the relationship between the Articles and humanitarian law.[32]

As approved on first reading, the Article (DA 21) provided that "[t]he present draft articles do not apply to situations to which the rules of international humanitarian law are applicable".[33] The provision was intended to give precedence (i.e. primacy) to IHL whenever applicable in complex emergencies. This objective, while resulting from the drafting history and the commentary, was not however clearly detectable from the text of the article. Consequently, the provision was finally redrafted as follows:

> [t]he present draft articles do not apply to the extent that the response to a disaster is governed by the rules of international humanitarian law[34]

This last version of the provision, which was approved on second reading as DA 18.2, accords undisputable primacy to IHL as lex specialis without wholly displacing the IDL rules contained in the DAs. Indeed, the latter can still apply in complex emergencies, although residually, "'to the extent' that legal issues raised by a disaster are not covered by the rules of international humanitarian law".[35] As clarified by the same ILC commentary, the role of IDL rules as spelled out in the

[28]ILC, Second Report cit., para. 6.

[29]Ibid., para. 48.

[30]Cf. ILC, Report. Sixty-first session, 4 May–5 June and 6 July–7 August 2009, A/64/10, para. 62; ILC, Eighth report of the Special Rapporteur on the protection of persons in the event of disasters, 17 March 2016, A/CN.4/697, para. 365 ff.

[31]Cf. ILC, Statement of the Chairman of the Drafting Committee Mr. Marcelo Vásquez-Bermúdez, 31 July 2009, available at https://legal.un.org/ilc/sessions/61/pdfs/english/2009_dc_chairman_protection_31july2009.pdf (last accessed on 25 August 2020).

[32]Ibid.

[33]Cf. ILC, Report of the International Law Commission: Sixty-Sixth Session (5 May–6 June and 7 July–8 August 2014), UN Doc. A/69/10, 2014, para. 55.

[34]Cf. Art. 18.2 of the DAs.

[35]ILC, Draft Articles on the Protection of Persons in the Event of Disasters with commentaries. In Report of the International Law Commission: Sixty-Eighth Session (2 May–10 June and 4 July–12 August 2016), A/71/10, p. 46, para. 9.

DAs consists in "contribut[ing] to filling legal gaps in the protection of persons affected by disasters during an armed conflict while international humanitarian law shall prevail in situations regulated by both the draft articles and international humanitarian law".[36] In other words, in the case of overlap and regardless of whether it results in a genuine or apparent norm conflict, IHL rules will always prevail as lex specialis. Considering the strong influence exerted by IHL on the Articles and the quite limited regulation provided by the latter, the entity of such overlap conflict would appear minimal.[37] At the same time, however, it concerns some basic rules and principles revolving around the role of the State affected by the disaster, thereby revealing the different approaches and the partially non-coinciding objectives of the two regimes. This clearly renders the application of the lex specialis principle problematic, all the more so in the absence of any guidance by the Commission.[38] As a matter of fact, the Commentary makes reference to just one case in which IHL should trump: where at issue is "the ability of humanitarian organizations to conduct, in times of armed conflict (be it international or non-international) even when occurring concomitantly with disasters, their humanitarian activities in accordance with the mandate assigned to them by international humanitarian law".[39]

The special position assigned to IHL by the DAs is also illustrated by the fact that this regime has been singled out in a dedicated provision. The "other applicable rules of international law" are considered in Art. 18.1, which was formulated as a no-prejudice clause. Such wording intends to cover *any* international rule "that

[36]Ibid.

[37]According to Perez, "[i]n sum, the concurrent application of the Draft Articles and IHL during armed conflicts and complex emergencies does not present the grave danger of conflict that has been suggested" (cf. Perez 2018, p. 273).

[38]In this regard, OCHA "expressed the concern that the draft article [. . .] did not provide a clear understanding of the relationship between the draft articles and international humanitarian law" (cf. A/CN.4/697, para. 379). Along the same lines are the considerations expressed by Williams and Simm: "[t]he relationship clause does little to address the complexities of this area of humanitarian assistance and the overlap and potential interaction between IHL and IDL. In fact, while aiming to produce text that was simple and elegant, the ILC gave fairly superficial consideration to this relationship. In this sense, it was a lost opportunity to collect State practice and to explore the issues fully in an attempt to provide more clarity, consistency and uniformity in this area. [. . .] As it presently stands, the ILC Draft Articles leave responders to consider the applicability of each area of law on a case-by-case basis" (Williams and Simm 2018, p. 56). *Contra*, Rodenhäuser and Giacca deem that "there are good reasons for the ILC not to question IHL as the *lex specialis* during complex emergencies" (cf. Rodenhäuser and Giacca 2016, p. 150).

[39]ILC, A/71/10, p. 73, para. 9. Such reference seems an answer to the concern, expressed by the ICRC, that DA 10.2 "is potentially very intrusive for impartial humanitarian organizations such as the ICRC [. . .] IHL only authorizes the concerned parties to the armed conflict and States to verify the humanitarian nature of the assistance through a so-called right of control" (ICRC comments on The ILC Draft Articles on The Protection of Persons in the Events of Disasters, January 2016.

might interact" with the DAs,[40] including more detailed rules contained either in IDL treaties or addressing disaster situations.[41]

The IDL rules enshrined in the DAs have thus been conceived by their same authors as a totally *residual* discipline, to be applied only in the absence of more detailed IDL treaty rules and, in a complex emergency, to the extent that a certain disaster-related issue is not governed by IHL rules.[42]

3.4 Summing Up: Disaster Norms as *normae speciales*?

As the preceding analysis has tried to show, determining which rule complexes—or better rules—to apply in a mixed scenario of disaster and armed conflict is not an easy task. The doctrine, having in mind in particular the interplay between IHL and IHRL, has devised two major models of regime selection that should facilitate this exercise. Nonetheless, as is true of all categorisations, the partition of international law in different regimes ratione materiae runs with it the risk of arbitrariness.[43] This is also true of the attribution of a certain rule or group of rules—typically a treaty—to a regime as opposed to another. The growing densification of international law has increasingly blurred the boundaries between the different regimes, increasing these risks. This is especially pertinent for the last addition to the regimes' list: IDL. Such complexities also explain why, irrespective of the model utilised in a given scenario, the selection is now generally made at the level of single rules and not of regimes.

Of the two models examined, both have been supported by the doctrine for being used in a situation of complex emergency. Complementarity is generally praised as the best model to manage the interplay of the three regimes at hand—IDL, IHL and IHRL—based on the latter's assumed common objective, i.e. the protection of

[40]Ibid., p. 73, para. 6.

[41]Ibid., p. 72, para. 3.

[42]For instance, Bartolini remarks that "[i]n some cases [...] the DAs might additionally detail some aspects not exhaustively addressed by IHL, such as the procedural obligations to consult and notify on the termination of external assistance (Article 17)" (Bartolini 2017, p. 1113). The opinion that "the Draft Articles could represent an added value to protect victims of disasters" was shared by various participants to the Expert Meeting on the ILC's Draft Articles on the protection of persons in the event of disasters, held at the Roma Tre University in June 2015 (Bartolini, G., Natoli, T., & Riccardi, A. (2015). Report of the expert meeting on the ILC's Draft Articles on the Protection of Persons in the Event of Disasters. Roma Tre University Department of Law - 8 and 9 June 2015. *International Law and Disasters Working Papers Series*, *3*, 87).

[43]Indeed, as notoriously argued by Koskenniemi: "'fragmentation' and 'coherence' are not aspects of the world but lie in the eye of the beholder" (ILC, Fragmentation of International Law: Difficulties Arising from the Diversification and Expansion of International Law. Report of The Study Group of the International Law Commission Finalized by Martti Koskenniemi, A/CN.4/L.682 and Add.1 and Corr. 1, 13 April 2006, para. 20).

humanity.[44] However, such an assumption, although possible to call into question with respect to IHL, remains somewhat inadequate vis-à-vis IDL.[45] In the chaos that typically follows a disaster, care for victims is not the only objective of the stricken State, which is equally and legitimately concerned with protecting its sovereignty in the classical sense against internal and external threats. Such concern, which even and excessively permeates the DAs, is routinely expressed in IDL treaties on disaster response. Consequently, the *only partial* coincidence of the three regimes' aims accentuates the evoked risks of dilution of the applicable norms.

As to lex specialis, apart from the lack of agreement regarding its implications, its application is particularly challenging in a complex emergency. Indeed, as a preliminary it is necessary to clarify which is the lex specialis—i.e. the most specialised regime—between IHL and IDL. The ILC in the DAs has recognised this privilege once and for all to IHL. This decision, which as has been shown can already be criticised with respect to the DAs, would be even more objectionable if it concerned *all* IDL instruments. In fact, while the rules contained in the DAs are quite limited in scope and to a great extent are inspired by analogous IHL principles,[46] the same cannot be said of IDL as a whole. IDL instruments on disaster *response* in particular address various technical and regulatory issues related to the provision of humanitarian assistance lato sensu (i.e. facilitation, coordination in delivery, content of relief items, status of relief personnel, quality and accountability etc.). The level of detail of such instruments is thus generally much higher than that of IHL or IHRL treaties.[47] Moreover, as is true of the interplay between IHL and IHRL as well as between IHL and IHRL on the one side and IDL on the other, genuine norm conflicts are the exception.

---

[44]Cf. Venturini (2012), p. 251 ff.; Gavshon (2009), p. 260; (and partially) Williams and Simm (2018), pp. 45, 56.

[45]This point is also emphasised by Williams and Simm, who warn of the risk that "IHL prioritises international rather than national responses inconsistently with the emphasis on building resilience through the development and implementation of national plans in IDL" (Williams and Simm 2018, p. 55).

[46]With the notable exceptions already mentioned in para. 2.4.

[47]Gavshon deduces from this that "IDL may be *lex specialis* in that it expands on an existing general rule of IHL" (Gavshon 2009, p. 261). By contrast, according to Rodenhäuser and Giacca: "Important reasons suggest [. . .] that IHL should nonetheless be considered the governing framework during complex emergencies.

At present, IDL is still not a unified body of international law but an assembly of rules drawn from different sources, including legally non-binding instruments. It has been repeatedly emphasized that one obstacle for effective humanitarian relief is a lack of clarity of the applicable legal framework. Thus, the need for rapid humanitarian action in times of complex emergencies would benefit from a coherent legal framework. Despite existing deficiencies in the IHL framework, it is doubtful whether the current piecework of provisions that constitutes IDL should take precedence over the well-established IHL framework" (Rodenhäuser and Giacca 2016, pp. 149–150).

This being the framework, the choice of the lex, or better of the norma specialis should be made on a case-by-case basis, taking into account different factors.[48] To the list proposed by Sassòli, who notably mentions the level of detail of norms and the more or less precise scope of application, should be added the following priority factors: the nexus of the situation with the armed conflict or the disaster; the geographical proximity of the disaster with the areas of active hostilities;[49] and eventually the presence of exigencies of military necessity. While such a case-by-case approach does not allow one to anticipate which norms should be applied in a given situation, it is possible to predict that whenever a disaster occurs outside of the area of active hostilities, the normae speciales will probably belong either to IDL or to IHRL.[50] This assumption is corroborated by two pieces of evidence. First of all, statistically complex emergencies concern internal conflicts, whose IHL regulation, despite growing convergence with the discipline of international armed conflicts (IACs), is essential. Additionally, practice shows that IHL is not relied upon in complex emergencies, not even in areas directly affected by conflict.[51] However, this practice is limited and in numerous cases predates many IDL instruments, which are generally quite recent. Moreover, as far as non-State belligerents are concerned, because IDL customary rules remains scant, it is more likely that IHRL will apply to such actors. The same holds for third States, whose obligations in disaster settings and more broadly in humanitarian crises have largely been developed in the realm of IHRL.[52]

We are aware that the proposed approach would require a quite elaborate reasoning, which might prove excessively demanding in a war context. It is therefore desirable that the practice in this regard develops rapidly, so as to provide adequate guidelines ready to be used by the belligerents in the near future.

In conclusion, in complex emergencies IHL norms cannot be and indeed are not the only rules to apply. Given the multiplicity of subjects acting in such contexts—mainly States, armed groups and humanitarian organisations of both intergovernmental and non-governmental character—and the scarcity of customary norms specifically addressing disasters, the applicable framework is *necessarily* variegated

---

[48]A case-by-case approach has been recommended, inter alia, by Gavshon (2009, p. 263), while Williams and Simm warn of the risks associated with such an approach without any clear direction indicated by the ILC (Williams and Simm 2018, p. 56).

[49]More broadly, Williams and Simm suggest that "where the disaster affects an area that is geographically removed from and does not impact, or is not impacted by, the armed conflict, IHL should not regulate the provision of humanitarian assistance" (ibid., 53).

[50]As anticipated, we have focused on the three most relevant regimes which are applicable in complex emergencies. However, in practice norms pertaining to other regimes may also be applicable and consequently applied.

[51]Cf. Gavshon (2009), p. 251. See also Venturini (2012), p. 259 ff., who in the five cases of complex emergencies examined (occurring in Ethiopia/Eritrea, Colombia, the Democratic Republic of the Congo, Indonesia and Sri Lanka) found that IHL was either not applied or played a limited role.

[52]See extensively Part III, in particular Chap. 7.

and case-specific. Nonetheless, greater attention should be devoted by scholars as well as by States and the broader international community to identifying the criteria and standard situations that could facilitate the norms' selection in the field.

List of Documents

Bartolini, G., Natoli, T., & Riccardi, A. (2015). Report of the expert meeting on the ILC's Draft Articles on the Protection of Persons in the Event of Disasters. Roma Tre University Department of Law - 8 and 9 June 2015. *International Law and Disasters Working Papers Series, 3*

European Court of Human Rights (former Fifth Section), Georgia v. Russia (II), Decision on Admissibility of 12 December 2011

IASC, Working Group XVIth Meeting, Definition of Complex Emergencies, 30 November 1994

ICJ, The Legality of the Threat or Use of Nuclear Weapons, Advisory Opinion, 8 July 1996

ICJ, Legal Consequences of the Construction of a Wall in the Occupied Palestinian Territory, Advisory Opinion, 9 July 2004

ICRC comments on The ILC Draft Articles on The Protection of Persons in the Events of Disasters, January 2016, available at https://www.icrc.org/en/document/report-international-law-commission-icrc-statement-united-nations-2016, last accessed on 25 August 2020

ILC, Draft Articles on the Protection of Persons in the Event of Disasters with commentaries. In Report of the International Law Commission: Sixty-Eighth Session, A/71/10, 2 May–10 June and 4 July–12 August 2016

ILC, Fragmentation of International Law: Difficulties Arising from the Diversification and Expansion of International Law. Report of The Study Group of the International Law Commission Finalized by Martti Koskenniemi, A/CN.4/L.682 and Add.1 and Corr. 1, 13 April 2006

ILC, Report. Sixty-first session, A/64/10, 4 May-5 June and 6 July-7 August 2009

ILC, Second report of the Special Rapporteur on the protection of persons in the event of disasters, A/C.4/615, 7 May 2009

ILC, Eighth report of the Special Rapporteur on the protection of persons in the event of disasters, A/CN.4/697, 17 March 2016

ILC, Report of the International Law Commission: Sixty-Sixth Session (5 May–6 June and 7 July–8 August 2014), UN Doc. A/69/10, 2014

ILC, Statement of the Chairman of the Drafting Committee Mr. Marcelo Vásquez-Bermúdez, 31 July 2009, available at https://legal.un.org/ilc/sessions/61/pdfs/english/2009_dc_chairman_protection_31july2009.pdf (last accessed on 25 August 2020)

Inter-American Commission on Human Rights, Report No. 112/10: Inter-State petition IP-02: Admissibility: Franklin Guillermo Aisalla Molina, Ecuador – Colombia, OEA/Ser.L/V/II.140, 21 October 2011

Koskenniemi, M. Study on the Function and Scope of the Lex Specialis Rule and the Question of 'Self-Contained Regimes', Preliminary Report to the International Law Commission, ILC(LVI)/SG/FIL/CRD.1/Add.1, 7 May 2004

UN GA, Report of the Open-ended intergovernmental expert working group on indicators and terminology relating to disaster risk reduction, A/71/644, 1 December 2016

UN HRC, Second Periodic Report: Israel (2001), CCPR/C/ISR/2001/2, 4 December 2001

UN HRC, General Comment 31 - Nature of the General Legal Obligation on States Parties to the Covenant, CCPR/C/21/Rev.1/Add.13 (2004), 10 December 2005

UN HRC, Comments by the Government of the United States of America on the Concluding Observations of the Human Rights Committee, CCPR/C/USA/CO/3/Rev.1/Add.1, 12 February 2008

United States of America, Response of the United States to Request for Precautionary Measures – Detainees in Guantanamo Bay, Cuba (15 April 2002) (2002). *International Legal Materials*, *41*, 1015 ff.

References

Bartolini G (2017) A universal treaty for disasters? Remarks on the International Law Commission's Draft Articles on the protection of persons in the event of disasters. Int Rev Red Cross 99 (3):1103–1137

Dennis MJ (2006) Application of human rights treaties extraterritorially to detention of combatants and security internees: fuzzy thinking all around? ILSA J Int Comp Law 12(2):459–480

Droege C (2008) Elective affinities? Human rights and humanitarian law. Int Rev Red Cross 90 (871):501–548

Eden P, Happold M (2009) Symposium. The relationship between international humanitarian law and international human rights law. J Confl Secur Law 14(3):441–447

Gavshon D (2009) The applicability of IHL in mixed situations of disaster and conflict. J Confl Secur Law 14(2):243–263

Giacca G (2014) The relationship between economic, social and cultural rights and international humanitarian law. In: Riedel E, Giacca G, Golay C (eds) Economic, social and cultural rights in international law. Cambridge University Press, Cambridge, p 316

Gowlland-Debbas V (2004) The relevance of Paragraph 25 of the ICJ's advisory opinion on nuclear weapons. Am Soc Int Law Proc 98:358–365

Hathaway OA, Crootof R, Levitz P, Nix H, Perdue W, Purvis C, Spiegel J (2012) Which law governs during armed conflict? The relationship between international humanitarian law and human rights law. Minnesota Law Rev:1886

Henckaerts J-M, Doswald-Beck L (2005) Customary international humanitarian law. Cambridge University Press, Cambridge

Kolb R (2013) Human rights and humanitarian law. Max Planck Encyclopedia of Public International Law. Oxford University Press, Oxford

Kolb R, Hyde R (2008) An introduction to the international law of armed conflicts. Hart, Oxford

Krieger H (2006) A conflict of norms: the relationship between humanitarian law and human rights law in the ICRC customary law study. J Confl Secur Law 11:265–291

Lindroos A (2005) Addressing norm conflicts in a fragmented legal system: the doctrine of lex specialis. Nordic J Int Law 74(1):27–66

Márquez Carrasco C, Abrisketa J, Salmón E, Nagore M, Marinelli C, Zafra R, Alamillos Sánchez R, García Martín L, Íñigo Álvarez L (2015) Applicable regulatory frameworks regarding human rights violations in conflicts. Work Package No. 10 – Deliverable No. 2, Large-Scale FP7 Collaborative Project GA No. 320000

McCarthy C (2008) Legal conclusion of interpretative process? Lex specialis and the applicability of international human rights standards. In: Arnold R, Quénivet N (eds) International humanitarian law and human rights law: towards a new merger in international law. Brill, Leiden/Boston, pp 101–132

Milanovic M (2017) The lost origins of lex specialis: rethinking the relationship between human rights and international humanitarian law. In: Ohlin JD (ed) Theoretical boundaries of armed conflict and human rights. Cambridge University Press, Cambridge, pp 78–117

Pauwelyn J (2003) Conflict of norms in public international law: how WTO law relates to other rules of international law. Cambridge University Press, Cambridge

Perez A (2018) In defense of concurrent application: the ILC Draft Articles on the protection of persons in the event of disasters and international humanitarian law. Denver J Int Law Policy 46:273

Prud'homme N (2007) Lex specialis: oversimplifying a more complex and multifaceted relationship? Israel Law Rev 40(2):356–395

Rodenhäuser T, Giacca G (2016) The international humanitarian law framework for humanitarian relief during armed conflicts and complex emergencies. In: Breau SC, Samuel KLH (eds) Research handbook on disasters and international law. Edward Elgar, Cheltenham, pp 132–152

Sassòli M (2019) International humanitarian law. Rules, solutions to problems arising in warfare and controversies. Edward Elgar, Cheltenham

Venturini G (2012) Disasters and armed conflict. In: De Guttry A, Gestri M, Venturini G (eds) International disaster response law. Springer, New York, pp 251–266

Williams S, Simm G (2018) Assistance to disaster victims in an armed conflict: the role of international humanitarian law. In: Zorzi Giustiniani F, Sommario E, Casolari F, Bartolini G (eds) Routledge handbook of human rights and disasters. Routledge, London, pp 43–62

Part II
The Role of the State Hit by the Disaster

Introduction to Part II

As long as the affected State's apparatus is still functioning after a disaster, disaster response and assistance to victims will be undertaken first and foremost through it, even when the necessary (material, logistical and human) resources have an external origin. Disasters, like other national emergencies, fall within the sovereign competences of a State, which is entitled to address them as it deems appropriate while respecting the constraints imposed by international law.

The concept of sovereignty has undergone an evolution over time and hence must now be interpreted in terms no longer—or not only—of State rights, but in terms of the sovereign's responsibility towards its own population. According to this reinterpretation, it is primarily up to the State to guarantee the safety, life and well-being of its citizens. As will be seen throughout this Part, from an international law point of view the primary role of the State hit by the disaster in managing disaster response has various implications. Such implications essentially concern and affect the (eventual) role of external relief actors, be them third States, international organisations or NGOs.

Indeed the affected State's primacy has two facets, which are amenable respectively to a more traditional vision of sovereignty and to a people-centred one. The first understanding of sovereignty is expressed by the control of relief activities in all its phases, i.e. initiation, organisation, co-ordination and implementation. This primary control by the affected State, while routinely recognised by all relevant international documents, is often disavowed in practice, notably in mediatised crises. Nonetheless and also as a result of the disaster risk reduction (DRR) agenda, the inevitable centrality of the State in managing disasters is the object of renewed recognition. The second facet is instead expressed internally by the sovereign's primary duty to protect and assist its population and externally by the increasing limits set by international law to an outright refusal of any external help.

Drawing from the categorisation proposed by Arnold Pronto, Senior Legal Advisor to the Secretariat of the ILC, the specific legal issues addressed in this

Part are amenable to the following categories: “a) the legal aspects of the initiation of disaster assistance (consent, notification, requests and offers); [and] b) the conditionality of assistance (e.g. retention of national control, compliance with international and nationals rules and standards)”.[1]

Part II is organised as follows. Chap. 4 “State sovereignty in disasters” examines the role of State sovereignty in disaster response. To this end, some general reflections are made about the changes that the notion of sovereignty has undergone over time up to its contemporary understanding. The analysis proceeds by illustrating the crucial and diverse role played by the State hit by the disaster in addressing the consequences. This part shows how after decades of preponderance—sometimes to the level of arrogance—of external (humanitarian) actors, recent practice has seen a renewed recognition of the affected State’s primary and essential role in disaster response. Finally, a re-reading of the Nargis case is undertaken, with a view to identifying a list of lessons learned potentially applicable to other disasters for which an international response is needed. Chap. 5 “The legal framework” next investigates the international rules and principles revolving around the role of the State affected by the disaster, notably in its relations with external assisting actors. In particular, the following issues are examined: offers and requests of assistance; the consent requirement and its exceptions; and other corollaries of the affected State’s primary role in disaster response. For each of the topics scrutinised, the solutions proposed by the ILC in the Draft Articles on the Protection of Persons in the Event of Disasters are critically reviewed in light of on the one hand the broader existing legal framework and on the other hand recent international practice.

References

Pronto A (2009) Consideration of the protection of persons in the event of disasters by the International Law Commission. ILSA J Int Comp Law 15(2):449–457

[1]Cf. Pronto (2009), p. 451.

Chapter 4
State Sovereignty in Disasters

Contents

4.1 State Sovereignty as an Ever-Changing Notion and Its Reshaping by International Human Rights Law

Respect for State sovereignty remains one of the major pillars of disaster response. The present research, devoted as it is to investigating the role of international law in disaster scenarios, could not thus help but analyse the significance—in its double sense of meaning and importance—and the actual scope of sovereignty in such contexts.

Sovereignty is indisputably the salient notion of international law. It can be said to coincide with the birth of the discipline in its modern sense. Nonetheless, it has been the object of endless debates and a variety of meanings have been attributed to it overtime. Even today, there is no single internationally recognised definition of sovereignty.[1]

According to its more traditional understanding, which dates back to the birth of the Westphalian system in 1648, sovereignty consists of a government's exclusive

[1]The bibliography on sovereignty is immense. Cf. ex pluris the following works: Anghie (2004); Arand (1986); Bartelson (1995); Carrillo Salcedo (1996), p. 39 ff.; Cohen (2010), p. 261 ff.; Falk (1981, 1995); Hart (1961); Henkin (1994), p. 351 ff.; Kelsen (1944), p. 207 ff.; Krasner (1999); Kreijen (2002); MacCormick (1999); Roth (2004), p. 1017 ff.; Schrijver (1999), p. 65 ff.; Shue (2004), p. 11 ff.; Warbrick and Tierney (2006).

F. Zorzi Giustiniani, *International Law in Disaster Scenarios*,
https://doi.org/10.1007/978-3-030-50597-4_4

power and control over a given territory and a given population. Such control is frequently characterised as absolute, as opposed to the one featuring the contemporary view of sovereignty. However, despite the undeniable evolution that it has undergone over time, sovereignty in its modern sense was never conceived as completely absolute.[2] Donnelly reminds us that the same "Treaty of Westphalia, while mandating religious non-interference, [. . .] imposed substantive restrictions on sovereigns. For example, Article 28 guarantees adherents of the Confession of Augsburg 'the free Exercise of their Religion, as well in publick Churches at the appointed Hours, as in private in their own Houses'".[3] What has changed during the course of time and exhibiting a cleavage between the traditional and the contemporary understandings of sovereignty—the latter imposing itself after World War II with the establishment of the UN—is the role played in this respect by international law. Indeed, "modern international law binds sovereign States in their internal and external dimensions, often without their consent".[4]

The external dimension of sovereignty entails independence and signifies that a State within its own territory is not legally subordinated to the will of any foreign power.[5] While being the primordial aspect of sovereignty, since 1945 it has been expressed by the principle of sovereign equality as enshrined in Art. 2.1 of the UN Charter.[6] Internally, sovereignty instead involves the supreme authority of the State to rule over those who find themselves within its own jurisdiction.

Sovereignty's internal dimension corresponds to the domain réservé ex Art. 2.7 of the Charter, according to which "[n]othing contained in the present Charter shall authorize the United Nations to intervene in matters which are essentially within the domestic jurisdiction of any state". The scope of domestic jurisdiction has been progressively shrinking as international law regulates more and more aspects of what were typically a State's internal competences. This growing invasion of the pitch is particularly evident in the field of human rights protection, to the point that some authors have argued that State sovereignty has become *people*'s sovereignty.[7] Even without embracing such a radical position, it must be admitted that the international

[2]Indeed, sovereignty has never been completely absolute, except as conceived by authors like Jean Bodin and Thomas Hobbes in their respective theories.

[3]Cf. Donnelly (2004), p. 8. According to Samantha Besson sovereignty "is inherently limited since public international law and external sovereignty imply each other" (Besson 2011, para. 75).

[4]Besson (2011), para. 75. The main constraints to States' sovereign liberty are in fact amenable to new concepts such as jus cogens and erga omnes norms.

[5]"Sovereignty in the relations between States signifies independence" and "[i]ndependence in regard to a portion of the globe is the right to exercise therein, to the exclusion of any other State, the functions of a State" (Island of Palmas Case [Netherlands v United States of America] 838).

[6]Art. 2.1 UN Charter states: "The Organisation is based on the principle of the sovereign equality of all its Members".

[7]Cf. Reisman (1990), pp. 866, 869; Besson (2011), paras. 83, 153.

human rights legal framework has reshaped sovereignty as never before.[8] As a result of this process, at the beginning of the 1990s sovereignty was notoriously (re)defined in terms of *responsibility*.

Such a reconceptualisation was first proposed by Francis Deng, who argued that sovereignty should be understood not only as protecting against external interferences but also as entailing responsibilities towards the population.[9] The notion of responsible sovereignty was then enshrined in the 1998 Guiding Principles on Internal Displacement[10] and additionally endorsed by former UN Secretary-General Kofi Annan[11] and the International Commission on Intervention and State Sovereignty (ICISS) in its study on the Responsibility to Protect (R2P).[12] The ICISS' report in particular is centred on the idea that sovereignty is no longer characterised *as control* but rather *as responsibility* "in both internal functions and external duties".[13] Nonetheless, the opposition between the two concepts "is neither clear, nor does it appear coherent within the report. In fact, it could be objected that it is precisely thanks to control that states can be responsible. Furthermore, the report underscores in various points that sovereignty (as control) is still necessary inter alia to respect and ensure respect for human rights".[14] Indeed, the same report recognises that "sovereignty does still matter" and that "a cohesive and peaceful international system is far more likely to be achieved through the cooperation of effective states, confident of their place in the world, than in an environment of fragile, collapsed, fragmenting or generally chaotic state entities".[15]

In any case, despite recurrent claims that the multiple and relevant changes affecting the international legal order via globalisation—such as the expansion of international substantive regulation, the emergence of new actors and the establishment of various innovative accountability mechanisms—will lead to the unavoidable decline of States, State sovereignty is not withering away.[16] Faute de mieux, the

---

[8]According to Theodor Meron, in the second post-world war we have assisted to a humanization of international law as human rights have shifted the focus of the latter from the State to the individual (Meron 2003, p. 26).

[9]Cf. Deng et al. (1996).

[10]The Guiding Principles on Internal Displacement are premised on the concept of 'sovereignty as responsibility' as developed by Francis Deng, who served as the UN's first Special Rapporteur on the Human Rights of Internally Displaced Persons from 1992 to 2004 (cf. UN Commission on Human Rights, *The Guiding Principles on Internal Displacement*, E/CN.4/1998/53/Add.2 (1998), Principle 3.1).

[11]Upholding the notion of responsible sovereignty, in his renowned article "Two concepts of sovereignty" Annan declared that "States are now widely understood to be instruments at the service of their peoples, and not vice versa" (Annan 1999).

[12]Cf. infra, Chap. 4 para. 5.

[13]ICISS, The Responsibility to Protect. Report of the International Commission on Intervention and State Sovereignty (2001), para. 2.14, 13.

[14]Focarelli (2008), p. 194.

[15]ICISS, The Responsibility to Protect cit., para. 1.34, pp. 7–8.

[16]Cf. Alvarez (2012), p. 26 ff.

international system centred on sovereign States is what we have and is still the most "realistic system for the management of enduring equalities, and of other pathologies of [. . .] international [. . .] law and politics".[17] In this regard, as will be seen, disaster scenarios make no exception.

4.2 The Importance of Sovereignty in Disaster Scenarios

The continuing relevance of sovereignty is particularly evident in disaster scenarios. Indeed, the affected State, as the sovereign authority governing the territory where the disaster has struck, plays a crucial and diverse role in addressing disasters. First of all, it is immediately responsible for taking care of its population, especially those affected by the disaster. Secondly, it has to assess the gravity of the emergency and, based on its capacities, evaluate whether external aid is needed. Last but not least, the territorial State's sovereignty also implies the competence on the one hand to establish the regulatory and legal framework governing international assistance and on the other to monitor and coordinate it.[18]

The situation differs markedly from that prevailing during an armed conflict, where government authorities as parties to the conflict are inevitably biased and thus relief action is generally managed—by substitution—by humanitarian organisations. Instead, in a disaster context the central role of the territorial State cannot be eschewed: concerns about respecting its sovereign role are stronger and apart from situations where the same government is responsible for denying its population's basic needs, generally more legitimate. Nevertheless, for a long time and despite various commitments to building national capacities,[19] both humanitarian actors and donor States have sidelined or even bypassed national and local entities. Even in quite recent emergencies, such as the Indian Ocean tsunami (2004) and the Haiti earthquake (2010), despite the fact that national and local authorities were eager to

---

[17]Kingsbury (1998), p. 625. See also Alvarez (2012), p. 37.

[18]"Sovereignty is even indispensable in international disaster relief operations themselves thanks to the authority of the affected State to manage the disaster's aftermath. No other State can successfully replace the local sovereign in managing the crisis and its long-term consequences" (Focarelli 2013, para. 33). "A state affected by a disaster normally retains the right to coordinate all disaster relief on its territory. This rule reflects the fact that the state is in the best position to understand the needs of its citizens – it knows the infrastructure, understands the habits and special needs of the population, and knows what aid items might be inappropriate to the circumstances" (Benton Heath 2011, p. 436). Benton Heath adds that, even when "a government, out of a failure to realize the gravity of the situation or diplomatic miscalculation, refuses humanitarian aid [. . .] the best-case scenario might be for the government to be convinced (or pressured) to consent to assistance while retaining its local coordinating role" (ibid.). As will be seen, this is what happened in the case of cyclone Nargis in Myanmar (cf. infra, para. 4.3).

[19]Cf. The Sphere Project, Humanitarian Charter and Minimum Standards in Disaster Response, 2004; IFRC, ICRC, Code of Conduct for the International Red Cross and Red Crescent Movement and Non-Governmental Organizations (NGOs) in Disaster Relief, 1994.

collaborate with international relief actors, the latter almost excluded them from most coordination and decision-making activities.

Beside obvious sovereignty concerns, such attitudes clearly risk undermining local capacities and creating dependency from the outside. For instance, the Tsunami Evaluation Coalition review of the response to the 2004 Asian tsunami found that:

> Institutional imperatives of international humanitarian agencies, such as the urgency to spend money visibly, worked against making the best use of local and national capacities. Local contexts, institutions and contributions were frequently neglected. Affected people's will and capacity to move from reliance on handouts to rebuilding their lives were inadequately exploited in the relief and early recovery phases of the international response. They were marginalised, even undermined, by an overwhelming flood of international agencies controlling immense resources.[20]

Along similar lines, in an evaluation report of the Haiti earthquake response it was observed that:

> [m]any government agencies at the national and local levels (*e.g.* ministries, the Directorate for Civil Protection (DPC) and municipalities) felt (and in most cases were) excluded from humanitarian coordination and decision-making. As a result, the relationship between humanitarian organizations and the government has been strained and there is a risk that the humanitarian response will further weaken the government[21]

In addition to the tendency (especially in cases of mega-disasters) to consider the affected country a failed State, a common perception is that recipient countries have ineffective or corrupt institutions. These trends are part of a more generalised trust deficit between affected governments and international aid actors:

> Some states perceive international humanitarian aid as a largely western endeavour. For their part, wealthy states often assume that international assistance is only an issue of poor countries. There are many experiences including Hurricane Katrina in the United States and the Fukushima emergency in Japan that test this assumption.[22]

Only in recent years has an opposite trend concerning both affected States and relief providers (donors and humanitarian actors) been detected. With respect to the affected States, at an ALNAP meeting in 2010 a growing capacity and willingness to

---

[20]Telford, J., & Cosgrave, J. (2006). Joint Evaluation of the International Response to the Indian Ocean Tsunami: Synthesis Report, Tsunami Evaluation Coalition, 93.

[21]Grünewald, F., & Binder, A. (2010), *Inter-agency real-time evaluation in Haiti: 3 months after the earthquake, Final Report*, para. 75.

[22]Harvey and Harmer (2011), p. 6. Such a trust deficit also owes to the frequent lack of independent and public analyses of government responses to disasters:

> [t]he lack of independent and publicly available analysis of government responses to disasters makes it more difficult to establish the trust and credibility donor governments need to confidently directly support governments to respond to their own disasters. The evidence base on the effectiveness, efficiency and impact of government responses to disasters is woefully insufficient (ibid., p. 39).

respond to emergencies was observed.[23] This was partly the result of the DRR agenda, which increasingly recognises the primary role of territorial States in disaster risk management.[24] While the reality on the ground remains far from what it should be according to international commitments, important changes can be observed even in the attitudes of assisting actors as well as in donor funding. The World Bank, which has become increasingly involved in disaster response, in 2006 established the Global Facility for Disaster Reduction and Recovery, a grant-funding mechanism that supports developing countries in understanding, managing and ultimately reducing their risk from natural hazards and climate change.[25] Similarly, different regional organisations are increasingly engaged in DRR and disaster preparedness and thus in the building of national capacities. Apart from the EU and ASEAN, it is worth citing the work undertaken by the Southern African Development Community (SADC), which since 2005 supports national-level vulnerability assessment committees in order to strengthen risk assessments.[26] As regards donor States, the emergence of wealthy developing countries within the previously Western-dominated donor community has caused a paradigm shift, with funding being predominantly addressed to affected governments rather than to humanitarian actors. Such a tendency, "at least in natural disaster responses where the government has the capability and means to manage the response effort, has the effect of supporting and building domestic capacity, rather than circumventing it".[27] All these elements have thus refocused attention on the territorial State as the first and primary actor in disaster response.

4.3 Against Easy Manicheism: Lessons Learned from the Nargis Case

The Nargis case constitutes a perfect testing ground because it epitomises most of the legal and practical issues arising after a disaster when it is evident that the affected State is unable and/or unwilling to cope with the disaster's humanitarian consequences.

---

[23]Cf. ALNAP (2010), The role of national governments in international humanitarian response to disasters, 26th ALNAP Meeting in Kuala Lumpur, 16–17 November 2010, Meeting Background Paper. ALNAP (Active Learning Network for Accountability and Performance) is a global network of NGOs, UN agencies, members of the International Red Cross and Red Crescent Movement, donors, academics and consultants dedicated to learning how to improve response to humanitarian crises.

[24]Cf. United Nations, Sendai Framework for Disaster Risk Reduction 2015–2030, Part III 19(a).

[25]Cf. https://www.gfdrr.org/en.

[26]SADC, Strengthening Vulnerability Assessments and Analysis in the SADC Region, through the SADC Regional Vulnerability Assessment Committee. A Five-Year Programme (2005-09), Gaborone, June 2005.

[27]Harmer and Martin (2010), p. 8.

Immediately after the event, a political and academic debate broke out on the consequences of the inadequate response by Myanmar's military regime. The debate was somewhat biased by the poor reputation that the Burmese regime had gained within the international community. As will be seen, however, a closer examination of the broader context in which the disaster broke out and of the reasons behind the regime's attitude as well as of the diplomatic channels through which the crisis was solved, can help us to identify a list of lessons learned that are potentially applicable to other disasters for which an international response is needed.

Moreover, the Nargis disaster happened at a crucial time, when the ILC was about to analyse the role of the affected State and the conditions for aid refusal. It thus had an invaluable impact on the Commission's work and partially explains its stance on some of the key legal issues involved, starting with the applicability of the R2P.[28]

On 2–3 May 2008, the Category 3 tropical storm Cyclone Nargis hit the southern part of Myanmar on the Irrawaddy Delta and Yangon, leaving behind devastation and death. One of the deadliest storms ever recorded in world history, it affected over 2.4 million in the country and caused the deaths of approximately 138,000 people. Faced with the catastrophe, the authorities appeared overwhelmed and unable to appreciate the extent of the damage. Even ten days after the disaster, the UN estimated that three quarters of the victims were still waiting to be assisted.[29] Indeed, while local aid was generally permitted, international assistance was accepted only very selectively. For example, some relief consignments from China arrived in Yangon on 7 May. By contrast, most relief items coming from Western countries and international organisations were not accepted. Countries like the United States, Britain and France, which already had warships in the area, approached Myanmar's coast to deliver aid. Myanmar's refusal to allow such assistance was outright and explained as follows: "[t]he strings attached to the relief supplies carried by warships and military helicopters are not acceptable to the Myanmar people".[30]

The international humanitarian community and Western countries were outraged by such a stance. France, through its foreign minister Bernard de Kouchner, the founder of *Médecins Sans Frontières*, even proposed that the UN Security Council act on the basis of Chapter VII in application of the R2P doctrine, on the grounds that refusal to humanitarian assistance constituted a crime against humanity. China, Russia and South Africa—as well as Indonesia and Vietnam, Myanmar's fellow ASEAN members on the Security Council—expressed their disapproval towards such a course of action, holding that the R2P doctrine did not apply to natural disasters. Irrespective of the applicability of R2P to the case, it was rightly cautioned by one of its same architects that its application "might be counterproductive for three reasons: (1) it would increase the paranoia of the junta; (2) it could diminish the

[28]Cf. infra, Chap. 9, para. 1.

[29]"Only a quarter of Burma's cyclone victims are receiving aid, UN warns", in Daily Mail, 13 May 2008, available at www.dailymail.co.uk.

[30]Talmadge (2008).

doctrine in the future; and (3) in practical terms, intervention in the form of air drops would probably be ineffective".[31]

The regime's reluctance to accept most of international assistance as well as its blanket refusal to issue visas for foreign workers would seem an obvious consequence of its authoritarianism and closure to the outside world.[32] However, such behaviour should not be considered in isolation from the broader historical context in which it took place. As was rightly remarked, "Myanmar's unpopularity should not preclude analysis of its action. Its refusal of international aid could still be a political act with complex motives".[33]

At the time of the disaster, Myanmar was still ruled by the military junta that had taken power in March 1962. Nonetheless, over the preceding two years, and in particular since the Saffron Revolution, the country had experienced significant internal turmoil, which was harshly repressed by the government. This caused international condemnation and exposed Myanmar to a sanctions regime, which was enacted in particular by the United States and the EU's Member States. It was thus obvious that these countries and their humanitarian aid were viewed with suspicion by the junta. Moreover, Nargis hit an area—the Karen State—inhabited by a major ethnic minority that was in perennial conflict with the government and had received political support from the United States. Last but not least, a referendum on a new constitution, whose main purpose was to attribute more power to the ruling regime, had been scheduled for 10 May, a few days after the cyclone. Against this background, the junta's sovereignty concerns, while not (completely) justifiable compared to the humanitarian needs of the disaster-affected population, were nonetheless understandable.[34]

In the end, the crisis was resolved through international cooperation[35] and in particular thanks to the crucial role played by ASEAN, which acted as a facilitator between the junta and the international community.[36]

---

[31]Haacke (2009), p. 168.

[32]As was notoriously affirmed by Naomi Klein, repressive regimes are terrified by natural disasters: once fear and the aura of total control seem absent or disorganised, "their subjects can become dangerously emboldened" (Klein 2008, p. 2).

[33]Allan and O'Donnell (2013), p. 42.

[34]"[. . .] [D]espite generally offending democratic eyes, Myanmar's resistance to humanitarian aid in 2008 may have been based on paranoid, but genuine, fears of foreign intervention aiming at regime change" (Allan and O'Donnell 2013, p. 1). The regime feared not only direct military intervention but also the smuggling of arms to some ethnic minorities—notably the Karens—through foreign relief workers. According to Nelson, the junta's behavior was also due to the fact that it was a regime in transition (Nelson 2010, p. 398).

[35]As was remarked by Costas Trascasas, "[t]he majority of commentators conclude that the crisis was solved in the best way possible and that the various initiatives pursued led to the desired result: enhanced access to affected areas and close cooperation with national authorities" (Costas Trascasas 2012, p. 238).

[36]"ASEAN was [. . .] a key stakeholder which played a 'bridging' role between Myanmar and the international community" (UN OCHA (2008), *Inter-Agency Real Time Evaluation of the Response to Cyclone Nargis*, 42).

In a region particularly attached to the principles of sovereignty and non-intervention, which not coincidentally feature among ASEAN's main values, ASEAN succeeded in the first place to deploy on 9 May 2008 an Emergency Response Assessment Team to the stricken zones and then to set up a mechanism—the Tripartite Core Group—comprising representatives from the Myanmar Government and the United Nations to coordinate, facilitate and monitor the flow of international assistance into the country. It was thus mainly through its efforts that international assistance and relief actors could finally reach the stricken populations in Myanmar. Interestingly, ASEAN's action was in line with the object and purpose of the regional treaty on disaster management—the ASEAN Agreement on Disaster Management and Emergency Response (AADMER)—although this had not yet entered into force.[37]

By way of conclusion, several lessons learned can be drawn from the Nargis case. First of all, the continued importance of State consent, "whatever the circumstances and however grave the crisis".[38] Indeed, access is practically impossible when logistical challenges are accompanied by State restrictions and/or the wilful denial of authorisation to external aid. Moreover, aerial aid drops or foreign troops may bring more harm than good,[39] further politicising the crisis with inevitable repercussions on the delivery of humanitarian aid.

Secondly, international cooperation and solidarity are much more effective than muscular humanitarianism. As shown, the crisis was resolved not by activating R2P but rather through diplomatic efforts, in primis by the regional economic integration organisation: ASEAN.[40] Certainly, its "less confrontational and more inclusive approach"[41] towards Myanmar, together with its knowledge of the internal dynamics of the ruling elite,[42] proved crucial for obtaining humanitarian access.

Last but not least, disasters can be key drivers of change. In the case of Myanmar, the outright refusal of international assistance after the cyclone showed the blatant inability of the junta to meet the needs of the affected people as well as its corruption

[37]The Agreement was signed on July 26th 2005 and entered into force on December 24th 2009. It has been ratified by all ten Member States.

[38]Harvey (2009), p. 17.

[39]Barber (2009), pp. 32–33.

[40]"The humanitarian response to Cyclone Nargis was unique in constraints and approach. Characterized by uncertainty due to limits on access and communications, distinctive approaches were employed for both coordination and operations. The response to date has been notable in the *regional solidarity* shown by member states of ASEAN, and other neighbors" (UN OCHA (2008), 42, emphasis added).

[41]Thomsen (2015), p. 509.

[42]"[. . .] ASEAN leaders appreciated something that many in the West did not, which was that the mindset of the junta was not uniform, and that different political players, and their shifting power and roles, had direct policy consequences for the relief effort. Nargis exacerbated already existing tensions within the ruling junta between those who favored a degree of liberalization and engagement with the outside world, such as the Prime Minister Chair of the National Disaster Committee Thein Sein and General Thura Shwe Mann, and hardliners, such as Vice Senior General Maung Aye and Secretary-1 Tin Aung Myint Oo" (Shanahan Renshaw 2014, p. 183).

and incompetence. It has been convincingly asserted that the very poor domestic management of the disaster at least contributed to the subsequent democratic change initiated in the country in 2010–2011.[43] Indeed, in those years the regime released Aung San Suu Kyi (the leader of the National League for Democracy), enacted a series of political, economic and administrative reforms and signed ceasefires and peace agreements with Kachin and Karen rebels.

List of Documents

Grünewald F, Binder A (2010), *Inter-agency real-time evaluation in Haiti: 3 months after the earthquake, Final Report*

ICISS, The Responsibility to Protect. Report of the International Commission on Intervention and State Sovereignty, 2001

IFRC, ICRC, Code of Conduct for the International Red Cross and Red Crescent Movement and Non-Governmental Organizations (NGOs) in Disaster Relief, 31 December 1994

Island of Palmas Case (Netherlands v United States of America) (Award), 4 April 1928, Reports of International Arbitral Awards (1928) II

Sphere Project, Humanitarian charter and minimum standards in disaster response, 2004

UN Commission on Human Rights, *The Guiding Principles on Internal Displacement*, E/CN.4/1998/53/Add.2, 1998

Telford J, Cosgrave J (2006). Joint Evaluation of the International Response to the Indian Ocean Tsunami: Synthesis Report, Tsunami Evaluation Coalition

UN GA, Resolution 69/283: Sendai Framework for Disaster Risk Reduction 2015–2030, A/RES/69/283, 23 June 2015

References

Allan C, O'Donnell T (2013) An offer you cannot refuse? Natural disasters, the politics of aid refusal and potential legal implications. Amst Law Forum 5(1):36–63

ALNAP (2010) The role of national governments in international humanitarian response to disasters. 26th ALNAP Meeting in Kuala Lumpur, 16–17 November 2010, Meeting Background Paper

Alvarez JE (2012) State sovereignty is not withering away: a few lessons for the future. In: Cassese A (ed) Realizing utopia: the future of international law. Cambridge University Press, Cambridge, pp 26–37

Anghie A (2004) Imperialism, sovereignty, and the making of international law. Cambridge University Press, Cambridge

Annan K (1999) Two concepts of sovereignty. The Economist 352

[43]Cf. Kovach (2013); Cubie (2017), p. 241.

Arand RP (1986) Sovereign equality of states in international law. In: Recueil des Cours de l'Académie de Droit International, vol 197. Martinus Nijhoff, The Hague
Barber R (2009) The responsibility to protect the survivors of natural disaster: Cyclone Nargis, a case study. J Confl Secur Law 14(1):3–34
Bartelson J (1995) A genealogy of sovereignty. Cambridge University Press, Cambridge
Benton Heath J (2011) Disasters, relief, and neglect: the duty to accept humanitarian assistance and the work of the international law commission. N Y Univ J Int Law Polit 43:419–477
Besson S (2011) Sovereignty. Max Planck Encyclopedia of Public International Law. Oxford University Press, Oxford
Carrillo Salcedo JA (1996) Droit international et souveraineté des Etats. In: Recueil des Cours de l'Académie de Droit International, vol 257. Martinus Nijhoff, The Hague
Cohen JL (2010) Sovereignty in the context of globalization: a constitutional pluralist perspective. In: Besson S, Tasioulas J (eds) The philosophy of international law. Oxford University Press, Oxford, pp 261–280
Costas Trascasas M (2012) Access to the territory of a disaster-affected state. In: De Guttry A, Gestri M, Venturini G (eds) International disaster response law. Springer, New York, pp 221–249
Cubie D (2017) The international legal protection of persons in humanitarian crises. Exploring the Acquis Humanitaire. Hart, Oxford
Deng FM, Kimaro S, Lyons T, Rothchild D, Zartman IW (1996) Sovereignty as responsibility: conflict management in Africa. Brookings Institution Press, Washington DC
Donnelly J (2004) State sovereignty and human rights. Human rights and human welfare working papers, 21
Falk RA (1981) Human rights and state sovereignty. Holmes & Meier, New York
Falk R (1995) On human governance. Pennsylvania University Press, University Park
Focarelli C (2008) The responsibility to protect doctrine and humanitarian intervention: too many ambiguities for a working doctrine. J Confl Secur Law 13:191–213
Focarelli C (2013) Duty to protect in cases of natural disasters, MPEIL. Oxford University Press, Oxford
Haacke J (2009) Myanmar, the responsibility to protect, and the need for practical assistance. Global Responsibility Protect 1(2):156–184
Harmer A, Martin E (eds) (2010) Diversity in donorship: field lessons. HPG Report 30. Overseas Development Institute, London
Hart HLA (1961) The concept of law. Oxford University Press, Oxford
Harvey P (2009) Towards good humanitarian government. The role of the affected state in disaster response. HPG Report, 29
Harvey P, Harmer A (2011) Building trust: challenges for national authorities and international aid agencies in working together in times of disasters, Background Paper 1. Humanitarian Outcomes
Henkin L (1994) The mythology of sovereignty. In: Macdonald RSJ (ed) Essays in honour of Wang Tieya. Martinus Nijhoff, Dordrecht, pp 351–358
Kelsen H (1944) The principle of sovereign equality of states as a basis for international organisation. Yale Law J 53(2):207–220
Kingsbury B (1998) Sovereignty and inequality. Eur J Int Law 9:599–625
Klein N (2008) In the wake of catastrophe comes the whiff of unrest. The Guardian, available at: http://www.guardian.co.uk/commentisfree/2008/may/16/cyclonenargis.chinaearthquake (last accessed on 24 August 2020)
Kovach T (2013) The politics of disaster response: disaster diplomacy and the responsibility to protect after Cyclone Nargis. American University School of International Service Working Paper
Krasner SD (1999) Sovereignty: organized hypocrisy. Princeton University Press, Princeton
Kreijen G (ed) (2002) State, sovereignty and international governance. Oxford University Press, Oxford

MacCormick N (1999) Questioning sovereignty: law, state, and practical reason. Oxford University Press, Oxford

Meron T (2003) International law in the age of human rights: general course on public international law. In: Collected Courses of the Hague Academy of International Law, vol 301. Martinus Nijhoff, The Hague

Nelson T (2010) Rejecting the gift horse: international politics of disaster aid refusal. Confl Secur Dev 10(3):379–402

Reisman WM (1990) Sovereignty and human rights in contemporary international law. Am J Int Law 84(4):866–876

Roth BR (2004) The enduring significance of state sovereignty. Fla Law Rev 56:1017–1050

Schrijver N (1999) The changing nature of state sovereignty. Br Yearb Int Law 70(1):65–98

Shanahan Renshaw C (2014) Disasters, despots, and gun-boat diplomacy. In: Caron DD, Kelly MJ, Telesetsky A (eds) The international law of disaster relief. Cambridge University Press, Cambridge, pp 164–189

Shue H (2004) Limiting sovereignty. In: Welsh JM (ed) Humanitarian intervention and international relations. Oxford University Press, Oxford, pp 11–28

Talmadge E (2008) Myanmar appears to nix US navy help, saying "strings attached". Associated Press, Bangkok, available at https://www.jpost.com/International/Myanmar-appears-to-nix-US-Navy-help-saying-strings-attached (last accessed on 24 August 2020)

Thomsen M (2015) The obligation not to arbitrarily refuse international disaster relief: a question of sovereignty. Melb J Int Law 16:484–521

Warbrick C, Tierney S (eds) (2006) Towards an 'International Legal Community'?: The sovereignty of states and the sovereignty of international law. British Institute of International and Comparative Law, London

Chapter 5
The Legal Framework

Contents

5.1 Offers and Requests of Assistance

The great majority of disasters are entirely managed at the national level. It is thus the exception and not the rule for an affected State to ask for international assistance.[1] This is consistent with the primary role that, as a result of sovereignty, is attributed to States even in disaster contexts.

IDL instruments typically provide for an obligation to notify other States that might be affected by a disaster likely to have transboundary consequences.[2] This obligation is "a corollary to the requirement, recognized by [such] instruments, that States are to ensure that appropriate early warning and information-sharing mechanisms are put into place".[3] Otherwise, most of disaster law treaties emphasise the sovereign role of the affected State to address the disaster as it deems fit and its

[1]"[. . .] [N]early all disasters are addressed domestically. Requests for international assistance are thus normally reserved for the most massive disasters" Fisher (2007a), p. 89.

[2]For an exhaustive list of such instruments cf. ILC Secretariat, Protection of persons in the event of disasters. Memorandum, 11 December 2007, A/CN.4/590, fn. 175.

[3]Ibid., para. 50. This obligation is generally incumbent on the affected State, even though some agreements also impose it on States that are aware of an impending disaster (ibid.).

F. Zorzi Giustiniani, *International Law in Disaster Scenarios*,
https://doi.org/10.1007/978-3-030-50597-4_5

connected discretion to request or allow international assistance.[4] It is only in exceptional cases—primarily when the affected State is unable or unwilling to assist and protect the victims, or when the disaster has a transnational impact, such as by causing mass displacement—that international assistance should intervene.[5]

The mere unsolicited offer of assistance[6] cannot be considered an unlawful intervention in the internal affairs. An early recognition of this principle, which has its origins in the law of armed conflicts,[7] can be found in the Red Cross Declaration of Principles for International Humanitarian Relief to the Civilian Population in Disaster Situations (1969), adopted by the XXI International Conference of the Red Cross and Red Crescent, stating that "the offer of [disaster] relief by an impartial international humanitarian organisation ought not to be regarded as an unfriendly act".[8] It was then notoriously recognised by the ICJ in the Nicaragua judgement,[9] and subsequently reiterated by the Institut de Droit International (IDI) in its resolutions of 1989 and 2003.[10]

The ILC has opted for a low profile in this respect. The Special Rapporteur, building on a progressive interpretation of relevant international instruments, had

---

[4]As remarked by David Fisher, "[t]he situation is thus something of the inverse of [...] human rights instruments [...]", where the focus is on individual human beings and their protection Fisher (2007b), p. 354.

[5]"[I]t seems generally understood that a state must at least request assistance when it is unable or unwilling to help its own population" Benton Heath (2011), p. 470.

[6]Unsolicited offers are those offers which do not follow an appeal or a request from the affected State. According to the ILC Memorandum, such offers are extended "either because the affected State has not made or cannot make a request for international assistance (for example in situations where no functioning government exists), or because no request was directed to the State making the offer" (cf. ILC Secretariat, A/CN.4/590, para. 64).

[7]The possibility of third parties making unsolicited offers of assistance is generally presupposed by the provisions of the Geneva Conventions and their Additional Protocols dedicated to relief actions (contra see Bindschedler-Robert 1979, p. 77, who deems that the Fourth Geneva Convention authorises third States to *only* offer relief directed to civilians of an occupied territory (cf. art. 59, Fourth Geneva Convention)). These treaties, moreover, explicitly recognise a right of initiative to humanitarian organisations like the ICRC or any other impartial humanitarian body (cf. Art. 3 common to the Geneva Conventions and Arts. 9/9/9/10 of the same Conventions; Art. 59, IV Geneva Convention; Art. 9.2, I Additional Protocol) as well as to some national and international relief societies (Art. 125, III Geneva Convention).

[8]XXI International Conference Of The Red Cross, Resolution XXVI, Red Cross Declaration of Principles for International humanitarian relief to the civilian population in disaster situations, Istanbul, September 1969. According to Patrnogic, this instrument, being adopted by an international conference reuniting not only the representatives of the International Movement of the Red Cross and Red Crescent but also the States Parties to the Geneva Conventions, has to be considered "comme une convention de la Croix-Rouge qui doit être respectée et appliquée non seulement par les membres de la famille de la Croix-Rouge internationale mais aussi par les gouvernements" Patrnogic (1977), p. 21.

[9]ILC, Fourth report on the protection of persons in the event of disasters, A/CN.4/643, 11 May 2011, para. 84.

[10]"Humanitarian assistance shall be offered and, if accepted, distributed without any discrimination [...]" (IDI, 2003, Art. II, para. 3).

originally conceived the *right* to offer assistance as “[a]n appropriate point of complementarity between the primary responsibility of the affected State and the interest of non-affected States in the protection of persons in the event of disasters”.[11] Accordingly, he had proposed to recognise a right to offer assistance with “States, the United Nations, other competent intergovernmental organizations and relevant non-governmental organizations”.[12] In the final version of the DAs, however, the said right was turned into a mere faculty, thereby also downsizing the entire role attributed to the international community. Indeed, the various obligations of the affected State are counterbalanced by only one obligation on the part of third States and other assisting actors: that of “expeditiously giv[ing] due consideration to [a] request [of assistance] and inform the affected State of [their] reply”.[13]

Be that as it may, “[t]he offer of assistance is to be distinguished from its concrete delivery”,[14] which requires that aid be requested or at least accepted by the affected State.[15] The pertinent international legal framework, as mainly expressed in IDL treaties, is premised on the circumstance that a State makes an appeal or a request for international assistance after a disaster. While a request is directed to specific addressees—typically the other parties in a treaty framework—appeals have a more general character.

Contrary to outright refusals, which are quite rare, especially in the case of massive disasters, appeals/requests as well as the acceptance of unsolicited offers often come late, with inevitable consequences in terms of the number of persons who can be saved or promptly assisted.[16] This can be due to reasons of national pride, but also in most circumstances to the unpreparedness of the domestic civil protection system.[17] The first scenario is best exemplified by the attitude of India, traditionally very loath to ask for international assistance. It is well known that it publicly refused aid even following the Indian Ocean tsunami as well as after a devastating

---

[11]Cf. A/CN.4/643, para. 84.

[12]Ibid., para. 109.

[13]Cf. Art. 12 para. 2.

[14]The point has been efficaciously made by Focarelli (cf. Focarelli 2013, para. 22).

[15]The latter case is envisaged by the Inter-American Convention to Facilitate Disaster Assistance, which provides: “[. . .] acceptance by a State party of an offer of assistance from another State party shall be considered to be a request for such assistance” (cf. Art. I para. b of the Convention, which was adopted by the General Assembly of the Organisation of American States (OAS) with res. 1101 of 12 June 1991). See also, in similar terms: ASEAN Agreement on Disaster Management and Emergency Response, Art. 3, para. 1 (“external assistance or offers of assistance shall only be provided upon the request or with the consent of the affected Party”); IFRC, ‘Model Act for the Facilitation and Regulation of International Disaster Relief and Initial Recovery Assistance’, March 2013, Art. 7(a) and (e).

[16]Cf. Hardcastle and Chua (1998), pp. 589–590. The authors refer, in particular, to the late appeal of the Iranian government after the earthquake hitting the Gilan province in 1990, affirming that such “delay resulted in the otherwise preventable death of a large proportion of the injured” (ibid., p. 590).

[17]Cf. Fisher (2007a), p. 14.

earthquake levelled villages in the Indian-controlled part of Kashmir in the subsequent year.[18]

The second scenario occurs in most cases as a consequence of unclear or deficient national legislation, which for instance does not establish a clear division of tasks at the national level. These problems trouble not only poor States but also highly developed countries such as the United States and Japan. The United States' poor management of the response to Hurricane Katrina is a case in point. The country, which at first declared its self-sufficiency in addressing the disaster, proved instead to be highly unprepared and generally reacted in an inconsistent and tardy manner to generous offers of assistance coming from all over the globe.[19] As a result, many relief items were left to perish or were withdrawn by the sending State before permission was officially granted.[20] A similar reaction vis-à-vis international assistance came from the Japanese authorities after the Kobe earthquake in 1995. In that case, the reluctance to accept aid was mainly due to the fact that the eventuality to rely on such assistance had not been envisaged in national legislation. It was only after the earthquake that the country decided to amend its domestic legal framework so as to be prepared to welcome incoming external aid.[21]

Typically, IDL instruments require the issuance of a formal request or an appeal.[22] With the notable exception of AADMER,[23] however, these treaties only regulate relationships between States and/or intergovernmental organisations.[24] The role of NGOs in the process of aid delivery is instead mostly regulated by soft law

---

[18]Sengupta (2005). https://www.nytimes.com/2005/10/19/world/asia/pride-and-politics-india-rejects-quake-aid.html.

[19]"[...] 151 countries and international organizations offered cash and in-kind assistance, including equipment, food, and other supplies, as well as response personnel and other technical experts. FEMA and the U.S. government at large had no guidance or systems in place to ensure orderly consideration, acceptance, and utilization of such offers for the benefit of persons impacted by the disaster" Katcha (2015), p. 926.

[20]"[W]ithout proper advance planning of procedures to determine when and how to consent to contributions from the international community, FEMA risked, on the one hand, foregoing potentially essential resources for addressing a catastrophic response and, on the other, an influx of unexpected and unnecessary goods, complicating logistics efforts and serving as an operational distraction and public relations embarrassment" (ibid., 929). On the failures of the U.S.' response to Katrina see *inter alia*: Bannon and Fisher (2006), Katcha (2015), Medina (2006–2007), Richard (2006), Sirkin (2006) and US House of Representatives (2006).

[21]Cf. Nishimoto (2014), p. 305.

[22]See for instance Tampere Convention on the Provision of Telecommunication Resources for Disaster Mitigation and Relief Operations, 1998, Art. 4; and Framework Convention on Civil Defence Assistance, 2000, Art. 3(a). Contrary to requests, appeals are general and not directed to specific addressees.

[23]Cf. Art. 11.

[24]An exception in this regard is constituted by the Cotonou Agreement, which lists NGOs among the possible authors of a request of external assistance: "[h]umanitarian and emergency assistance operations shall be undertaken either at the request of the ACP [African, Caribbean or Pacific] country affected by the crisis situation, the Commission, international organizations or local or international non-State organizations" (Partnership agreement between the members of the African,

documents.[25] Moreover, apart from large organisations, NGOs usually begin to establish official communication with the affected State's authorities only once they have arrived in loco.[26] It is thus a common scenario that, notably following a massive—and hence very mediatised—disaster, affected States find themselves confronted with a huge influx of foreign relief actors, rendering coordination an almost impossible task.[27]

Although IDL treaties envisage the affected State's request of assistance as a *prerequisite* to the delivery by external actors, various soft law instruments instead consider the issuance of a request/appeal as a veritable *obligation* of the affected State when the disaster exceeds its coping capacities.[28]

In this regard the ILC Project, at Art. 11 (Duty of the affected State to seek external assistance) so provides:

> To the extent that a disaster manifestly exceeds its national response capacity, the affected State has the duty to seek assistance from, as appropriate, other States, the United Nations, and other potential assisting actors.

The reference to an obligation *to seek* assistance, which is clearly inspired by the IDI resolution on Humanitarian Assistance and the IFRC Guidelines,[29] was chosen by the Special Rapporteur in order to guarantee a certain amount of leeway to

---

Caribbean and Pacific Group of States of the one part, and the European Community and its member States, of the other part, 23 June 2000, Art. 72(6)).

[25]The 2007 IFRC's IDRL Guidelines e.g. include in the definition of "assisting actors" humanitarian organisations, foreign individuals and private companies providing charitable relief, or other foreign entities responding to a disaster on the territory of the affected State or sending in-kind or cash donation (cf. para. 2, point 14).

[26]"For example, 62 per cent of international humanitarian organizations (predominantly NGOs) responding to the IDRL survey reported that formal agreements they had with governments were normally made during a disaster operation rather than before. Certainly, private citizens shipping aid collectively or to relatives or friends in an affected state, do not generally have prior official contacts and do not necessarily wait for official appeals. Thus, in practice, affected state control over the initiation of disaster response by these actors (if any) is normally exercised in other ways, for example, through visa and customs controls and in regulations on in-country operations [. . .]" Fisher (2007a), p. 92.

[27]See infra, para. 5.3.

[28]Cf. IDI-Institute of International Law, Resolution of the Sixteenth Commission on Humanitarian Assistance, 2 September 2003 (Bruges Resolution), pt. III.3 ("[w]henever the affected State is unable to provide sufficient humanitarian assistance to the victims placed under its jurisdiction or de facto control, it shall seek assistance from competent international organizations and/or from third States"); IFRC, IFRC Guidelines for the Domestic Facilitation and Regulation of International Disaster Relief and Initial Recovery Assistance, 30 November 2007, Guideline 3(2) ("[i]f an affected State determines that a disaster situation exceeds national coping capacities, it should seek international and/or regional assistance to address the needs of affected persons"); OCHA Guidelines on The Use of Military and Civil Defence Assets In Disaster Relief—"Oslo Guidelines", 27 November 2006 ("[i]f international assistance is necessary, it should be requested or consented to by the Affected State as soon as possible upon the onset of the disaster to maximize its effectiveness").

[29]ILC, A/CN.4/643, paras. 41–42.

affected States. Contrary to the obligation to request, which may seem to imply that the assistance offered thereafter should automatically be accepted,[30] he argued that the obligation to seek

> implies the initiation of a process through which agreement may be reached. As such the Special Rapporteur is of the opinion that a duty to seek assistance both ensures the protection of populations and individuals of concern, and is coherent with the core requirement of State consent[31]

ILC's commentary to Art. 11 correctly remarks that such an obligation "derives from an affected State's obligations under international human rights instruments and as such therefore it can be argued that the said obligation reflects customary law, irrespective of the context (peace or wartime) and the type of disaster".[32] The obligation to seek assistance thus "constitutes an important acknowledgement of the broad scope of the primary responsibility of the affected State to protect disaster victims".[33] Moreover, contrary to the rule prohibiting arbitrary refusals of aid offers,[34] its customary character appears uncontested, as confirmed by the fact that it was well received by States parties and supported by the majority of ILC members.[35]

5.2 Access to the Territory

5.2.1 State Consent

5.2.1.1 General Remarks

> For better or worse, the work of international aid actors depends on the consent of States: whether a State is strong or weak, abusive or concerned for its citizen's welfare, it is still the central determinant of whether or not humanitarian actors can be present in crisis.[36]

---

[30] In fact, the ILC Memorandum cautioned that such an obligation would "constrain [the affected State's] ability to decline offers of assistance" (ILC Secretariat, A/CN.4/590, para. 65). For a different opinion, cf. Benton Heath (2011), pp. 454–455, who deems that "[a]n equally reasonable interpretation would be that international law requires an affected state to put out a call for offers of assistance, while leaving it the plenary right to refuse any offer for any reason".

[31] ILC, A/CN.4/643, para. 44.

[32] ILC, A/CN.4/643, para. 40.

[33] Zorzi Giustiniani (2012), p. 78.

[34] On which cf. infra 5.2.1.

[35] See also the debates surrounding the adoption of the corresponding rule of the Bruges resolution, during which several IDI members affirmed that such an obligation reflected customary international law in both armed conflict and disaster scenarios (Institut de Droit International, Annuaire de l'Institut de Droit International 262 (2004), pp. 153–173).

[36] Harvey (2009), p. 1.

As was shown by the Nargis case, providing assistance without the consent of the affected State can prove almost impossible, "whatever the circumstances and however grave the crisis".[37] Indeed, State consent is the only essential precondition to the initiation of assistance, as it derives from State sovereignty and is also a corollary of the primary role that international law assigns to affected States in disaster response.[38] The need for State consent is equally dictated by the (very practical) concern of avoiding that too much, unnecessary and uncoordinated aid flows into the country.[39] Not coincidentally, stricken States "operating an 'open door' policy as regards foreign actors have encountered problems of supply-driven thinking, non-professional relief workers (often with their own particular goals) and the blocking of appropriate aid".[40] It therefore seems necessary from both a legal and a practical point of view, that States maintain a certain margin of discretion in deciding whether and to which international actors to grant access. As will be demonstrated, consent is not only discretionary "by definition [...] [but it] may be withdrawn or be subjected to conditions".[41] Moreover, the provision of international assistance is lawful only to the extent that it respects the consent requirement and only within the limits of such consent.[42]

Contrary to a very common vulgata, the denial of consent to disaster assistance does not necessarily come from autocratic regimes. Democratic countries, as exemplified for instance by the attitudes of the United States and Japan with respect to two major disasters occurring in their respective territories, are no less likely to refuse international aid.[43] At the same time, however, the blanket withholding of consent is quite rare in situations where external assistance is required.[44] It is much more frequent that the consent—as much as the request for assistance—is delayed for various reasons.[45]

---

[37]Ibid., 13.

[38]ILC Secretariat, A/CN.4/590, 42, para. 51.

[39]"In addition to international law principles, there are operational reasons why the affected state's consent to international aid is crucial – and as a practical concern, knowing what entity or officials from within the affected state has authority to consent. While it was presumably no state's intent to infringe on U.S. sovereignty when it made generous offers to aid the United States' response efforts for Hurricane Katrina, there were in fact numerous instances of assistance arriving in the United States where U.S. officials were not clear about who, if anyone, had accepted the assistance" Katcha (2015), p. 7. Cf. also Fidler (2005), p. 471.

[40]Allan and O' Donnell (2013), p. 40.

[41]ILC Secretariat, A/CN.4/590, para. 65.

[42]Instead, a "blanket" or "advance" consent, by which a stricken State announces in general terms that international assistance is welcomed, may prove insufficient to avoiding a violation by assisting actors of state sovereignty and territorial integrity.

[43]Cf. the study conducted by Nelson (2010), p. 395.

[44]Indeed, as argued by Sivakumaran: "[a]ffected States that appear to withhold their consent generally, in fact request or allow very specific forms of assistance from particular actors" Sivakumaran (2015), p. 526.

[45]Cf. Fisher (2007b), pp. 355–356. An example of delayed consent and its dire consequences was the Indonesian government after the Indian Ocean tsunami: "perishable items rotted, medicines

5.2.1.2 Exceptions to the Consent Rule

As international subjects, States are obligated to respect the requirement of consent, under penalty of incurring international responsibility. The same can be said of all those intergovernmental organisations which are committed, through various agencies and bodies, to international relief. The humanitarian community is nonetheless composed to a certain extent by other non-State entities, especially NGOs, which do not possess international personality. Consequently, such entities are not—or at least not formally—subjected to the consent rule.

In this respect, a specific case is the National Societies of the Red Cross and Red Crescent Movement. These societies are set up at the national level in every State party to the 1949 Geneva Conventions and work as auxiliaries in the humanitarian services of their governments. After a disaster, international assistance is frequently provided by the IFRC *through* the competent national society. In such circumstances, State consent is not required, as it is considered pre-approved. Indeed, the State parties to the Geneva Conventions, by universally agreeing on the Statutes of the Movement and on the Principles and Rules of Red Cross and Red Crescent Disaster Relief, have already accepted the roles assigned by the latter instruments to the Movement's national societies.

Quite different is the situation concerning other humanitarian NGOs. As purely private entities, these organisations need to respect—completely but also exclusively—the national laws and regulations of the host State. They are not bound by international rules on sovereignty and non-interference.[46] Even in the absence of State consent, a (necessarily clandestine) humanitarian operation conducted by an NGO, while exposing the organisation's members to the risk of being incriminated by the host State's national courts, would thus not constitute a violation of international law. Conversely, with respect to international subjects like States and intergovernmental organisations, it will be shown that the lawfulness of an unauthorised operation, even when State consent is invalidly withheld, is still highly disputable.

5.2.1.3 The Consent Requirement Under International Law

The consent requirement in disaster response is routinely envisaged by the international applicable instruments. Nonetheless, its formulation is not univocal but varies depending on the type of instrument in which it is contained.

As to IDL treaties, a first reference to the consent requirement can be found in the IRU Treaty, which while creating an intergovernmental organisation specifically charged with the coordination of disaster relief, cautioned that "[a]ction by the

expired, and emergency relief items like clothes, tents, blankets and surgical equipment, which were essential at the start of the relief effort, were redundant by the time they were cleared months later" Bannon et al. (2006), p. 22.

[46]Gillard (2013), p. 369.

International Relief Union in any country is subject to the consent of the Government thereof".[47] Consent has subsequently been inserted into most of the treaties devoted to disaster assistance, which not coincidentally are premised on the primary role of the affected State.[48] When this is not the case, either the stricter requirement of a request is demanded,[49] or consent implicitly takes the form of acquiescence, i.e. the acceptance of an offer.[50]

A different approach is embraced by various non-binding instruments, where consent is still a crucial factor but is not conceived as an absolute requirement. In fact, in these documents sovereignty concerns are either accompanied or almost completely set aside by the needs and rights of disaster victims. In this respect, the first stance is clearly expressed by GA Res. 46/182, which still constitutes the pivotal resolution of the UN humanitarian system and the major point of reference (as far as GA resolutions are concerned) on disaster relief. Herein the General Assembly, after expressing its "deep[...] concern[...] about the suffering of the victims of disasters and emergency situations [...]",[51] affirms in the annexed Guiding Principles that "humanitarian assistance *should* be provided with the consent of the affected country [...]".[52] Similar language is contained in the IDRL Guidelines, which regarding consent take direct inspiration from the resolution just cited.[53]

The second stance, which evokes circumstances in which consent should be due, was first expressed by the IDI in its 1989 resolution, where it is provided that "States in whose territories [the 'life or health of the population is seriously threatened']

---

[47]Cf. Art. 4, IRU Treaty.

[48]Indeed, the fundamental importance of State sovereignty has generally been recalled in such agreements, as epitomised by the ASEAN Agreement on Disaster Management and Emergency Response, which provides:

> [t]he sovereignty, territorial integrity and national unity of the Parties shall be respected, in accordance with the Charter of the United Nations and the Treaty of Amity and Cooperation in Southeast Asia, in the implementation of this Agreement. In this context, each affected Party shall have the primary responsibility to respond to disasters occurring within its territory and external assistance or offers of assistance shall only be provided upon the request or with the consent of the affected Party (cf. Art. 3.1).

[49]Cf. e.g. Convention on Assistance in the Case of a Nuclear Accident or Radiological Emergency, Art. 2.

[50]The Framework Convention on Civil Defence Assistance for instance provides that "[o]nly assistance requested by the Beneficiary State or proposed by the Supporting State and accepted by the Beneficiary State may take place" (cf. Art 3(a)). Likewise, Art. 4(a)(2) provides that "[t]he Supporting State shall send only those Civil Defence Units requested or accepted by the Beneficiary State". See also the Inter-American Convention to Facilitate Disaster Assistance, which regulates the situation in which "a state party furnishes assistance in response to a request from another State party, except as they otherwise agree" (Art. I(a)).

[51]Cf. UN GA Res. 46/182, third preambular paragraph.

[52]Cf. UN GA Res. 46/182, Guiding Principle 3, emphasis added.

[53]Cf. IFRC, IDRL Guidelines cit., Guideline 10 para. 1 ("[d]isaster relief or initial recovery assistance should be initiated only with the consent of the affected State and in principle, on the basis of an appeal. [...]").

should not arbitrarily reject [...] offers of humanitarian assistance".[54] A more cogent formulation is contained in its subsequent Bruges resolution, which affirms:

> Affected States *are under the obligation not arbitrarily and unjustifiably to reject* a bona fide offer exclusively intended to provide humanitarian assistance or to refuse access to the victims. In particular, they may not reject an offer nor refuse access if such refusal is likely to endanger the fundamental human rights of the victims or would amount to a violation of the ban on starvation of civilians as a method of warfare.[55]

Along similar lines, the UN Guiding Principles on Internal Displacement provide that consent (to offers in support of the internally displaced) "*shall not be arbitrarily withheld*, particularly when authorities concerned are unable or unwilling to provide the required humanitarian assistance".[56] Remarkably, all three documents, while formally non-binding, can be said to constitute in some measure a codification effort, as they are based on existing principles and norms. Moreover, the Guiding Principles have also received explicit acceptance by a certain number of States, which have adopted corresponding national legislation on internal displacement.[57]

Implicit limits to the absolute character of the consent rule are then posed by international human rights law and in particular by the obligations of international cooperation in that domain, such as those enshrined in Art. 2.1 of the ICESCR. The latter provision, which will be analysed in depth in Chap. 7, engages State parties "to take steps, individually and through international assistance and co-operation, especially economic and technical, to the maximum of its available resources, with a view to achieving progressively the full realization of the rights recognized" in the treaty. According to the Committee on Economic, Social and Cultural Rights, the phrase "available resources" is meant to embrace "both the resources existing within a State as well as those available from the international community through international cooperation and assistance".[58] Consequently, a State cannot justify non-compliance with its minimum core obligations by invoking incapability for a lack of resources if at the same time it refuses international assistance. In such circumstances, the receiving State would thus be "obligated" to accept external help.

In trying to contemperate the different demands arising from the need to respect State sovereignty in its traditional sense and the protective purpose of the Project, the ILC has opted for a "qualified consent regime",[59] which is expressed in DA 13 (Consent of the affected State to external assistance) as follows:

1. The provision of external assistance requires the consent of the affected State.

---

[54]Cf. IDI Resolution, The Protection of Human Rights and the Principle of Non-Intervention in Internal Affairs of States, Art. 5, emphasis added.

[55]IDI Resolution, Humanitarian Assistance, Art. VIII.1, emphasis added.

[56]Cf. UN Commission on Human Rights, Guiding Principles on Internal Displacement, E/CN.4/1998/53/Add.2 of 11 February 1998, emphasis added.

[57]Cf. Fisher (2010), pp. 45–128.

[58]CESCR, An Evaluation of the Obligation to Take Steps to the 'Maximum of Available Resources' under an Optional Protocol to the Covenant, E/C.12/2007/1, 10 May 2007, para 5.

[59]*Sic* ILC Commentary DA 13, para. 1.

2. Consent to external assistance shall not be withheld arbitrarily.
3. When an offer of external assistance is made in accordance with the present draft articles, the affected State shall, whenever possible, make known its decision regarding the offer in a timely manner.

The concept of arbitrary withholding of consent, which as shown was already embraced by the IDI and by the Guiding Principles of Internal Displacement, finds its roots in the regulation of humanitarian assistance applicable in armed conflicts. When discussing the corresponding provision (Art. 70) of the First Additional Protocol to the Geneva Conventions concerning international armed conflicts, various delegations agreed that relief actions could be refused only for "compelling reasons, not for arbitrary and capricious ones".[60] Despite its clear origins, however, the concrete meaning of "arbitrary withholding" is far from being uncontroversial. Controversies particularly concern disasters. Contrary to war contexts or even mixed situations of disasters occurring in an armed conflict scenario[61]—where for instance imperative considerations of military necessity could be invoked—in disaster situations there are fewer cases in which a refusal of consent can be justified.[62]

Some help, in this respect, comes from the IDI's works during the Bruges session, where the issue was an object of discussion. The Bruges resolution only specifies that the interdiction of arbitrary refusal is particularly cogent when the victims' fundamental rights are at stake or the refusal would violate the prohibition of using starvation as a method of warfare.[63] Nonetheless, during the debates preceding the approval of the resolution, the IDI's members agreed that a refusal could be considered admissible, at least prima facie, if properly justified.[64] Among the reasons suggested as "valid" were inter alia the following ones: the offer is not politically neutral, i.e. it does not respect the principles of non-discrimination, impartiality and neutrality; humanitarianism is only a pretext;[65] the type of aid offered is not useful in the instant case;[66] or vital national interests are invoked to refuse aid.[67] By contrast, reasons like the protection of sovereignty, national law and honour or the interests of the ruling regime were deemed to be arbitrary.[68]

[60]This position was expressed by Germany and supported by the United States, the Netherlands, the Soviet Union and the United Kingdom, while no delegations challenged it (cf. CDDH/II/SR.87, 12 Official Records, p. 336). See also Bothe et al. (2013), p. 485; Henckaerts and Doswald-Beck (2005).

[61]See infra, Chapter IV.

[62]Cf. Sivakumaran (2015), p. 525.

[63]Cf. Art. VIII para. 1.

[64]Cf. the intervention of A. Cassese (see Annuaire de l'Institut de droit international, vol. 70-I, p. 535). Hence the double reference, in Art. VIII of the resolution, to an arbitrary and *unjustified* refusal (emphasis added).

[65]Ibid., p. 420 (Orrego Vicuña).

[66]Ibid., p. 562 (Rapporteur Vukas).

[67]Ibid.

[68]Ibid., p. 563 (Rapporteur Vukas).

According to the ILC's commentary, the provision of reasons "is fundamental to establishing the good faith of an affected State's decision to withhold consent".[69] However, despite the ambiguity surrounding the notion of arbitrary withholding, the Commission has avoided bringing light to the scope, content and meaning of arbitrariness.[70] After acknowledging that the arbitrariness of a refusal has to be evaluated on a case-by-case basis, it limited itself to indicate a contrario a non-exhaustive list of valid (i.e. non arbitrary) reasons for refusal: (1) where an affected State is capable of providing and willing to provide an adequate and effective response with its own resources; (2) if it has accepted appropriate and sufficient assistance from elsewhere; and (3) if the relevant offer is not extended in accordance with the DAs, and particularly with the principles of humanity, neutrality and impartiality, as well as on the basis of non-discrimination ex DA 6.[71]

The first two reasons, which are centred on the needs of the disaster victims, are quite encompassing and find their origin either directly or indirectly in corresponding provisions of international humanitarian law and human rights law. If the victims are adequately provided with appropriate assistance, either by the affected State or thanks to other assisting actors, consent is not due. The conformity of the aid offered on humanitarian principles, which characterises the third reason, is generally provided by a plethora of instruments dealing with humanitarian assistance, applicable in armed conflicts but also more recently in disaster contexts, such as GA Res. 46/182 and the IDRL Guidelines. A reference to humanitarian principles was also made by the ICJ in the Nicaragua judgment, where humanity and impartiality in particular were recalled.[72] These principles can thus be considered as being the fundamental and distinguishing features of humanitarian action *in any situation*.

Humanity requires that assistance respond to a humanitarian purpose and be provided when it is really necessary. It refers to the same essence of humanitarian assistance.[73] Impartiality instead means that humanitarian aid must be provided solely on the basis of need. While humanity and impartiality indisputably apply to any kind of disaster situations, neutrality at first sight could seem a context-specific principle, inextricably connected to the idea of a conflict or contrast among opposing

[69]ILC, DAs commentaries, DA 13, para. 10. See also ILC, Fourth report cit., para 74. The requirement can nonetheless be satisfied simply through "a general publication of the affected State's decision regarding all offers of assistance" (ibid., para. 12). As remarked by Sivakumaran, "[i]t is only through the provision of a reason that the arbitrariness, or not, of the justification can be assessed. [...] A justification also enables a withholding State to demonstrate the validity of its withholding" Sivakumaran (2015), p. 520.

[70]Several States have criticised the Commission's stance, mainly due to the asserted lack of clarity of the term "arbitrarily" in the absence of further explanation (cf. Israel, A/C.6/66/SR.23, para. 33; United Kingdom, A/C.6/66/SR.23, para. 45; Malaysia, A/C.6/66/SR.24, paras. 117 and 119).

[71]Cf. ILC, DAs commentaries, DA 13, para. 8. See also ILC, Fourth Report cit., Part III.

[72]ICJ, I.C.J. Reports 1986, pp. 124–125, paras. 242–243.

[73]On humanity see generally Pictet (1979). Commentary of the fundamental principles of the Red Cross—I. Humanity, available at https://www.icrc.org/en/doc/resources/documents/misc/fundamental-principles-commentary-010179.htm (last visited on 22 August 2020).

parties. Nevertheless, as was noted by the Special Rapporteur, in disaster situations neutrality should be understood as implying that "those responding to disasters should abstain from any act which might be interpreted as interference with the interests of the State".[74] In other words, neutrality should require from assisting actors that they do not take sides in controversies of a political, racial, religious or ideological nature.[75] In addition to the three principles just mentioned, the DAs as approved on second reading make reference to non-discrimination. This addition would seem unnecessary, because non-discrimination can be considered an aspect of the principles of impartiality and neutrality.[76] Its separate mention, however, is a clear acknowledgment of the growing impact of human rights on IDL[77] and more generally on the international legal framework applicable in disaster contexts.

As to the third reason, the ILC has also specified in the Commentaries that towards offers extended in conformity with the DAs "there would be a strong inference that a decision to withhold consent is arbitrary" in the absence of "alternate sources of assistance".[78] As a result, depending on the circumstances of each case and the effective availability of alternatives, the failed respect of the humanitarian principles but even of other norms and principles affirmed in the DAs could be legitimately invoked to justify aid rejection.

An additional valid reason to refuse aid is envisaged, albeit implicitly, by DA 14, which entitles the recipient State to pose conditions on external assistance in accordance with the DAs and applicable rules of international and national law. This right, whose exercise also requires taking account of "the identified needs of the persons affected by disasters and the quality of the assistance",[79] is thus a clear and specific recognition of the affected State's primary role.[80]

Apart from the notion of arbitrariness, another issue is not clarified by the DAs: the identification of the entity entitled to evaluate the non-arbitrary character of the refusal. Following the initial justification provided by the stricken State, the task of

---

[74] A/CN.4/629, paras. 29–30.

[75] In addition, non-conformity with the neutrality principle could probably be invoked vis-à-vis those States and other actors with which the affected State does not have friendly relations. There is a certain practice in this respect concerning disaster response (see e.g. the offer made by Cuba to send doctors to the U.S. following hurricane Katrina and conversely the aid offered by the U.S. to Cuba following hurricane Charley in 2004).

[76] According to the well-known description made by Jean Pictet, impartiality brings together three distinct ideas—non-discrimination, proportionality and impartiality stricto sensu—which constitute three separate principles (cf. Pictet 1979, available at https://www.icrc.org/en/doc/resources/documents/misc/fundamental-principles-commentary-010179.htm, last visited on 22 August 2020).

[77] See in this respect the considerations of Federico Casolari, who explains the potential added-value of what he calls "the mixed approach to non-discrimination" in disaster contexts (cf. Casolari 2018, p. 199 ff).

[78] Cf. ILC, DAs commentaries, DA13, para. 8.

[79] Sic DA 14.

[80] As specified in the Commentaries, "[t]he right to condition assistance is the recognition of a right of the affected State to deny unwanted or unneeded assistance, and to determine what and when assistance is appropriate" (cf. ILC, DAs commentaries, DA 14, para. 7).

determining whether the reasons adduced by the former are valid needs to be assigned to a third impartial entity. Certainly, such a role cannot be played by other States, whose judgement would inevitably be biased by their own partisan interests. An appropriate candidate, as suggested by Sivakumaran, may be either the UN Emergency Relief Coordinator (ERC), who is responsible for the oversight of all emergencies requiring relief by the UN and thus also of the related needs assessments; or alternatively the Inter-Agency Standing Committee (IASC), which was established by GA Res. 46/182 to be the primary mechanism for the inter-agency coordination of humanitarian assistance.[81]

These shortcomings and ambiguities and consequent difficulties of interpretation were highlighted by several States during the ILC's work[82] and helped cast several doubts on the customary status of the consent rule as devised in the DAs. Nonetheless, on the whole DA 13 certainly constitutes an important recognition of the fact that current international law is progressively limiting the discretion of States in disaster response when peoples' lives and rights are at stake.

5.3 Other Corollaries of the Affected State's Primacy in Disaster Response Situations

As a consequence of the affected State's primacy in disaster response, the effective delivery and provision of relief does not rest merely—and automatically—on its initial consent. Indeed, the recipient State has "the primary role in the direction, control, coordination and supervision of such relief assistance".[83] This formula was most recently enshrined in the ILC DAs, but it can be found expressed in similar terms in various IDL treaties[84] as well as in non-binding instruments on humanitarian relief.[85] It reflects the State's general and ultimate right to control the aid operations, including by rejecting the relief that it considers inappropriate on the basis for instance of the population's needs.[86] This primacy was originally affirmed

[81] Sivakumaran (2015), pp. 529–530.

[82] Cf. supra, fn. 69.

[83] Sic ILC, DA 10, para. 2.

[84] Cf. in particular Art. 4.8 of the Tampere Convention, which inspired the DAs. See also Convention on Assistance in the Case of a Nuclear Accident or Radiological Emergency, Art. 3(a); Inter-American Convention to Facilitate Disaster Assistance, Art. IV(a); Agreement Establishing the Caribbean Disaster Emergency Response Agency, Art 16.1; ASEAN Agreement on Disaster Management and Emergency Response, Art. 3.2.

[85] It can thus be said that the affected State's primacy in managing and supervising aid operations is recognised by both States and humanitarian actors (cf. ILC, Third report on the protection of persons in the event of disasters, A/CN.4/629, 31 March 2010, para. 84).

[86] Cf. ILC Secretariat, A/CN.4/590, para. 58; ILC, Fifth report on the protection of persons in the event of disasters, A/CN.4/652, 9 April 2012, para. 30.

in the law of armed conflict, where the consent requirement has a stronger basis.[87] Nonetheless, as highlighted by Rapporteur Valencia-Ospina, outside the war context it now "stems both from [the affected State's] sovereign prerogatives and its responsibility towards the affected population within its territory".[88]

The receiving State can in the first place pose some conditions—and restrictions—on the provision of external assistance.[89] Such a possibility is also envisaged by ILC DA 14, provided that the conditions "be in accordance with the [...] draft articles, applicable rules of international law, and the national law of the affected State" and that they "take into account the identified needs of the persons affected by disasters and the quality of the assistance".[90]

Furthermore, primacy is expressed in the sovereign right and responsibility to coordinate the whole relief effort through national coordination structures. Coordination is obviously implied in and immediately follows the right to supervise the quality and effectiveness of all the external relief machinery. In principle, the receiving State should retain its coordinating role even when it has been pressured to consent to external assistance.

Nevertheless, coordination in disaster response has proved to be quite a challenging task. First, the international legal framework is very fragmented in this respect. A majority of IDL treaties explicitly recognise the primacy of national coordination

[87]"The parties to the conflict must allow and facilitate rapid and unimpeded passage of humanitarian relief for civilians in need, which is impartial in character and conducted without any adverse distinction, *subject to their right of control*" (ICRC, Customary IHL, Rule 55, emphasis added).

[88]ILC, A/CN.4/643, para. 30.

[89]A typical and general condition is that the receiving State "retains overall control over all aspects of the provision and distribution of such assistance on its territory, including determining the moment of commencement and termination of the assistance" (cf. ILC Secretariat, A/CN.4/590, para. 67, referring to Art. 18 of the Draft International Guidelines for Humanitarian Assistance Operations elaborated by Peter Macalister-Smith (Heidelberg, Germany: Max Planck Institute for Comparative Public Law and International Law, 1991).

[90]Cf. DA 14. As far as the conformity with the DAs is concerned, reference is implicitly made to the principles of humanitarian action, good faith and sovereignty.

mechanisms.[91] Several other instruments instead establish a new coordination entity[92] or identify as lead coordinator an existing mechanism.[93]

Second, apart from the applicable treaty rules, which in any case are addressed to States and not to humanitarian actors, the reality on the ground has shown a frequent lack of communication and coordination (!) among the various coordination layers existing at the national and the international level. In numerous cases this situation is due to the unpreparedness of national institutions. Nonetheless, in general the responsibility for a failure to coordinate must be assigned to external assisting organisations, which tend to operate in complete independence from national authorities. Such a scenario is becoming increasingly frequent, especially in large-scale disasters where the number of assisting actors is substantial.[94] Despite their best intentions, international humanitarian agencies generally establish parallel, duplicate structures that ultimately undermine the role of local and national actors.[95] This attitude characterises the behaviour of both NGOs and intergovernmental organisations. An evaluation of the cluster approach, which was launched by the

[91] See e.g. Inter-American Convention to Facilitate Disaster Assistance, 1991, Art. III; Agreement among the Governments of the Participating States of the Black Sea Economic Cooperation (BSEC) on Collaboration in Emergency Assistance and Emergency Response to Natural and Man-made Disasters, 1998, Arts. 6, 8; Convention on the Transboundary Effects of Industrial Accidents, 1992, Arts. 17-18. As to bilateral treaties, see ex pluris: Agreement on Mutual Assistance in the Event of Disasters or Serious Accidents, Denmark-Federal Republic of Germany, 1985, Art. 7; Agreement on Cooperation and Mutual Assistance in Cases of Accidents, Finland-Estonia, 1995, Art. 8; Agreement between the Swiss Federal Council and the Government of the Republic of the Philippines on Cooperation in the Event of Natural Disaster or Major Emergencies, 2001, Art. 9.1; 2001 Convenio entre al Reino de Espana y la Republica Francesa en Materia de Protection y de Seguridad Civil, Art. 6. The ASEAN disaster management agreement, on its part, establishes a coordinating mechanism, but it underlines that such mechanism "shall work on the basis that the Party will act first to manage and respond to disasters" (cf. AADMER, Art. 20).

[92] See e.g. Agreement Establishing the Caribbean Disaster Emergency Response Agency, 1991, Arts. 10 and 11; ASEAN Agreement on Disaster Management and Emergency Response, 2005, Art. 20 and annex; Agreement on Cooperation in Disaster Preparedness and Prevention and Mutual Assistance in the Event of Disasters, Spain-Argentina, 1988, Art. XXI; Agreement between the Government of the Hellenic Republic and the Government of the Russian Federation on Cooperation in the Field of Prevention and Response to Natural and Manmade Disasters, 2000, Art. 5.

[93] Tampere Convention on the Provision of Telecommunication Resources for Disaster Mitigation and Relief Operations, 18 June 1998, Art. 2; International Convention on Oil Pollution Preparedness, Response and Cooperation, 30 November 1990, Art. 12.

[94] "When large-scale disasters requiring such international coordination do occur – such as the Asian tsunami in 2004 – the creation and operation of coordinating mechanisms has indeed exhibited a flexible tendency. [. . .] However, this flexibility may also exacerbate the difficulty in delineating the roles between national and international coordinating mechanisms [. . .]" (ILC Secretariat, A/CN.4/590, para. 189).

[95] Cf. Ferris (2011), pp. 119–123. Bypassing established State structures, foreign humanitarian actors frequently create parallel structures for the provision of goods and services, with the result of duplicating efforts and causing dependency on outside assistance.

UN in 2005 in order to create a more coordinated and effective humanitarian response system,[96] highlights the spread of the phenomenon among UN agencies:

> In their current implementation, clusters largely exclude national and local actors and often fail to link with, build on, or support existing coordination and response mechanisms. Among other reasons, this is due to insufficient analysis of local structures and capacities before cluster implementation, as well as a lack of clear transition and exit criteria and strategies.[97]

A recent guidance released by the IASC acknowledges this problem. In particular, it emphasises both the need to tailor international coordination schemes to the context and the responsibility of cluster coordinators to build the capacity of national counterparts.[98]

Last but not least, the primary role of the affected State entails the obligation to facilitate the entry of relief personnel and the access of goods and equipment to the disaster area. Such an obligation, which is part of the broader duty to cooperate, can also be considered as a corollary of the consent rule.

Having consented to external assistance, the host State must accord a set of administrative and legal facilities to relief actors without which the concrete operation of a relief mission cannot be guaranteed. Access to the disaster area and the whole delivery process should take place in a timely manner in accordance with good faith. For this purpose, the recipient State needs to do all within its power to facilitate the entry of humanitarian personnel (through the issuance of expedited visas and work permits and the recognition of professional qualifications) and goods (e.g. by facilitating customs clearance and applying exemptions from import duties, fees or charges).[99]

A general obligation to facilitate the work of external disaster relief actors is envisaged by soft law documents, such as in primis GA Res. 46/182.[100] Specific

---

[96]The cluster approach was one of the new elements introduced in 2005 by the Humanitarian Reform Agenda, a major reform of humanitarian coordination aimed at enhancing predictability, accountability and partnership.

Cluster leaders are chosen among both UN and non-UN humanitarian organizations designated by the Inter-Agency Standing Committee and have clear responsibilities for coordination in each of the main sectors of humanitarian action, such as water, health and logistics.

[97]Steets et al. (2010), p. 9.

[98]IASC, Inter-Agency Standing Comittee Transformative Agenda Reference Document 4. Reference Module for Cluster Coordination at the Country Level, November 2012.

[99]Cf. Adinolfi (2012), p. 533 ff.

[100]Cf. UN GA, Res. 46/182, para. 6 (where people are "in need of humanitarian assistance", the affected State should "facilitate the work" of humanitarian organizations); GA, Res. 43/131, paras. 4-5 (the humanitarian work of NGOs was to be facilitated by affected states, and the support of all states to such organisations in their endeavours was urged); Guiding Principles on Internal Displacement Guiding Principles, para. 6 ("States whose populations are in need of humanitarian assistance are called upon to facilitate the work of these organizations in implementing humanitarian assistance"). More detailed is the Bruges resolution, whose Art. VII (Duty to facilitate humanitarian assistance) provides:

rules and technical standards are instead contained in various binding instruments of a universal, regional and bilateral character.[101] More recently, a whole set of common regulatory problems, concerning issues like medication, vehicles, food, telecommunications, moorage and registration, were addressed by the IFRC, first in the IDRL Guidelines and later in the 2013 Model Act. These instruments provide technical guidance to States to improve their domestic regulatory frameworks in order to avoid bottlenecks and other types of barriers to the delivery of aid in the early phases of disaster response.

Despite the progress made by several States that have adapted their legal and regulatory frameworks in accordance with the IFRC's suggestions, most countries in the world have not yet adopted comprehensive rules in the field.[102] Moreover, many States have opted for a pick-and-choose approach, side-lining issues that pose difficulties from a legal or political viewpoint.[103] The result is that a patchwork legal framework continues to prevail.

Against this background, it might have been expected that the ILC identify a set of specific standards and measures to be adopted by States for the facilitation of external aid. Nevertheless, regardless of various suggestions in this regard,[104] the DAs have adopted a rather minimalist approach, leaving a broad margin of discretion to States. DA 15, reading "Facilitation of external assistance", simply requires that affected States "take the necessary measures, within [their] national law, to facilitate

1. States shall facilitate the organization, provision and distribution of humanitarian assistance rendered by other States and organizations. They shall accord them, among other things, overflight and landing rights, telecommunication facilities and necessary immunities. Humanitarian assistance missions shall be exempted from any requisition, import, export and transit restrictions and customs duties for relief goods and services. When visas or other authorizations are required they shall be promptly given free of charge.
2. States should adopt laws and regulations and conclude bilateral or multilateral treaties providing for the above-mentioned facilities relative to humanitarian assistance.
3. The affected States shall permit the humanitarian personnel full and free access to all the victims and ensure the freedom of movement and the protection of personnel, goods and services provided.

[101]See e.g. Tampere Convention, the AADMER and Annex 9 to the Chicago Convention on Civil Aviation.

[102]According to the IFRC, by 2019 37 countries had adopted domestic rules and procedures drawing on the IDRL Guidelines, while ten more bills or draft rules were currently pending. (cf. https://rcrcconference.org/app/uploads/2019/10/33IC_12.5-Disaster-Law-background-doc-final-EN.pdf, last visited on 25 August 2020).

[103]Ibid., p. 25.

[104]Cf. Bartolini, G., Natoli, T., & Riccardi, A. (2015). Report of the expert meeting on the ILC's Draft Articles on the Protection of Persons in the Event of Disasters. Roma Tre University Department of Law—8 and 9 June 2015. *International Law and Disasters Working Papers Series*, *3*, 68. See also the comments to the ILC Project formulated by States representatives (A/CN.4/657, 18 January 2013, para. 23; A/CN.4/697, 17 March 2016, para. 323) and the IFRC (A/CN.4/696, 14 March 2016, p. 52).

the prompt and effective provision of external assistance [. . .]"[105] and that they "ensure that [their] relevant legislation and regulations are readily accessible, to facilitate compliance with national law".[106] For more guidance on the matter, the DAs' commentaries merely refer back to the IFRC's IDRL Guidelines and the Model Act.[107]

List of Documents

ASEAN, Agreement on Disaster Management and Emergency Response, 26 July 2005

Bartolini, G., Natoli,T., & Riccardi, A. (2015). Report of the expert meeting on the ILC's Draft Articles on the Protection of Persons in the Event of Disasters. Roma Tre University Department of Law—8 and 9 June 2015. *International Law and Disasters Working Papers Series, 3.*

Convention (III) relative to the Treatment of Prisoners of War, 12 August 1949 (III Geneva Convention)

Convention (IV) relative to the Protection of Civilian Persons in Time of War, 12 August 1949 (IV Geneva Convention)

Convention Establishing an International Relief Union, 12 July 1927

Convention on Assistance in the Case of a Nuclear Accident or Radiological Emergency, or Radiological Emergency, 26 September 1986

Framework Convention on Civil Defence Assistance, 22 May 2000

IASC, Inter-Agency Standing Comittee Transformative Agenda Reference Document 4. Reference Module for Cluster Coordination at the Country Level, November 2012

IDI-Institute of International Law, Resolution of the Sixteenth Commission on Humanitarian Assistance, 2 September 2003 (Bruges Resolution)

IDI-Institute of International Law, Resolution of the Eighth Commission on The Protection of Human Rights and the Principle of Non-intervention in Internal Affairs of States, 13 September 1989

IFRC, Guidelines for the Domestic Facilitation and Regulation of International Disaster Relief and Initial Recovery Assistance, 30 November 2007

IFRC, Model Act for the Facilitation and Regulation of International Disaster Relief and Initial Recovery Assistance, March 2013

ILC, Third report on the protection of persons in the event of disasters, A/CN.4/629, 31 March 2010

ILC, Fourth report on the protection of persons in the event of disasters, A/CN.4/ 643, 11 May 2011

[105] Cf. DA 15, para. 1.

[106] Cf. DA 15, para. 2.

[107] Cf. ILC, DAs commentaries, DA 15, para. 3.

ILC, Fifth report on the protection of persons in the event of disasters, A/CN.4/652, 9 April 2012

ILC Secretariat, Protection of persons in the event of disasters. Memorandum, 11 December 2007,

A/CN.4/590

Inter-American Convention to Facilitate Disaster Assistance, 7 June 1991

Partnership agreement between the members of the African, Caribbean and Pacific Group of States of the one part, and the European Community and its member States, of the other part, 23 June 2000

OCHA, Guidelines on The Use of Military and Civil Defence Assets In Disaster Relief - "Oslo Guidelines", 27 November 2006

Protocol Additional to the Geneva Conventions of 12 August 1949, and relating to the Protection of Victims of Non-International Armed Conflicts (Protocol II), 8 June 1977

Tampere Convention on the Provision of Telecommunication Resources for Disaster Mitigation and Relief Operations, 18 June 1998

UN Commission on Human Rights, Guiding Principles on Internal Displacement, E/CN.4/1998/53/Add.2, 11 February 1998

XXIth International Conference Of The Red Cross, Resolution XXVI, Red Cross Declaration of Principles for International humanitarian relief to the civilian population in disaster situations, Istanbul, September 1969

References

Adinolfi G (2012) In: De Guttry A, Gestri M, Venturini G (eds) Customs obstacles to relief consignments under international disaster response law. T.M.C. Asser Press, The Hague, pp 533–550

Allan C, O'Donnell T (2013) An offer you cannot refuse? Natural disasters, the politics of aid refusal and potential legal implications. Amsterdam Law Forum 5(1):36–63

Bannon V, Fisher D (2006) Legal lessons in disaster relief from the Tsunami, the Pakistan earthquake and Hurricane Katrina. ASIL Insight 10(6)

Bannon V, Andrade D, Abai J (2006) Legal issues from the international response to the Tsunami in Indonesia. IFRC, Geneva

Benton Heath J (2011) Disasters, relief, and neglect: the duty to accept humanitarian assistance and the work of the international law commission. New York Univ J Int Law Politics 43:419–477

Bindschedler-Robert D (1979) Actions of assistance in non-international conflicts – art. 18 of Protocol II. In: European seminar on humanitarian law. Report. Jagellonean University, Krakow, pp 71–83

Bothe M, Partsch KJ, Solf W (2013) New rules for victims of armed conflicts – commentary on the two 1977 protocols additional to the Geneva conventions of 1949. Martinus Nijhoff, The Hague

Casolari F (2018) Addressing discrimination in disaster scenarios. An international and EU law perspective. In: Zorzi Giustiniani F, Sommario E, Casolari F, Bartolini G (eds) Routledge handbook of human rights and disasters. Routledge, London, pp 193–210

Ferris E (2011) The politics of protection: the limits of humanitarian action. Brookings Institution Press, Washington, pp 119–123

Fidler DP (2005) Disaster relief and governance after the Indian Ocean Tsunami: what role for international law? Melbourne J Int Law 6:458–473

Fisher D (2007a) Law and legal issues in international disaster response: a desk study. International Federation of Red Cross and Red Crescent Societies, Geneva

Fisher D (2007b) Domestic regulation of international humanitarian relief in disasters and armed conflict: a comparative analysis. Int Rev Red Cross 89(866):345–372

Fisher D (2010) The right to humanitarian assistance. In: Kälin W, Williams RC, Koser K, Solomon A (eds) Incorporating the guiding principles in on internal displacement into domestic law: issues and challenges. Brookings Institution, Washington D.C., pp 45–128

Focarelli C (2013) Duty to protect in cases of natural disasters, MPEIL. Oxford University Press, Oxford

Gillard E-C (2013) The law regulating cross-border relief operations. Int Rev Red Cross 890:351–382

Hardcastle R, Chua A (1998) Humanitarian assistance: towards a right of access to victims of natural disasters. Int Rev Red Cross 38:589–609

Harvey P (2009) Towards good humanitarian government: the role of the affected state in disaster response. HPG Policy Brief 37

Henckaerts J-M, Doswald-Beck L (2005) Commentary to Rule 55. In: Henckaerts J-M, Doswald-Beck L (eds) Customary international humanitarian law. Cambridge University Press, Cambridge, pp 193–200

Katcha E (2015) Challenges for "Affected States" in accepting international disaster aid: lessons from Hurricane Katrina. Vanderbilt J Transnational Law 48(4):921–940

Medina MI (2006–2007) Confronting the rights deficit at home: is the nation prepared in the aftermath of Katrina? Confronting the myth of efficiency. California Western Law Rev 43:9–20

Nelson T (2010) Rejecting the Gift Horse: international politics of disaster aid refusal. Confl Secur Dev 10:379–402

Nishimoto K (2014) The role of international organizations in disaster response: a case study of recent earthquakes in Japan. In: Caron DD, Kelly MJ, Telesetsky A (eds) The international law of disaster relief. Cambridge University Press, Cambridge, pp 295–313

Patrnogic J (1977) Protection de la personne humaine au cours des catastrophes naturelles. Ann Droit Int Méd 27:16–33

Pictet J (1979) Commentary of the fundamental principles of the Red Cross, Available at https://www.icrc.org/en/doc/resources/documents/misc/fundamental-principles-commentary-010179.htm (last accessed on 24 August 2020)

Richard AC (2006) Role reversal: offers of help from other countries in response to Hurricane Katrina. Center for Transatlantic Relations, Paul H Nitze School of Advanced International Studies, Johns Hopkins University, Washington DC

Sengupta S (19 October 2005) Pride and politics: India rejects quake aid. *New York Times*. https://www.nytimes.com/2005/10/19/world/asia/pride-and-politics-india-rejects-quake-aid.html (last accessed on 24 August 2020)

Sirkin S (2006) The debacle of Hurricane Katrina: a human rights response. Fletcher Forum World Aff 30(1):223–227

Sivakumaran S (2015) Arbitrary withholding of consent to humanitarian assistance in situations of disaster. Int Comp Law Q 64(3):501–531

Steets J, Grünewald F, Binder A, de Geoffroy V, Kauffmann D, Krüger S, Meier C, Sokpoh B (2010) Cluster approach evaluation 2. Synthesis report. In: IASC Cluster Approach Evaluation 2nd Phase. Groupe URD & the Global Public Policy Institute, Berlin/Plaisians, p 9

US House of Representatives (2006) A failure of initiative. Final report of the select Bipartisan Committee to investigate the preparation for and response to Hurricane Katrina

Zorzi Giustiniani F (2012) The works of the international law commission on 'Protection of Persons in the Event of Disasters'. A critical appraisal. In: De Guttry A, Gestri M, Venturini G (eds) International disaster response law. Springer, New York, pp 65–84

Part III
International Cooperation and Solidarity in Disasters

Introduction to Part III

This part investigates in depth the content of the international duties and obligations of third States in disaster contexts—so-called transnational obligations—in order to shed light on the role of the international community with respect to one of the most important common concerns of our time.

The analysis starts by inquiring, in Chap. 6, how the two notions of international cooperation and solidarity have been conceptualised over time in legal thinking as well as how and to what extent they have come to characterise the contemporary international community. Chapter 7 then focuses on the role of international cooperation within the UN human rights treaty system. The objective is to show not only that international cooperation is attributed a central place in some major human rights treaty frameworks, in primis the UN Covenant on Economic, Social and Cultural Rights (ICESCR), but especially that the various transnational obligations underpinning international cooperation in such context have been developed to precisely apply, inter alia, in disaster scenarios. Specific attention in this regard is devoted to two doctrinal constructs—the minimum core approach and the tripartite classification of State obligations—which established themselves in the practice of UN treaty bodies to give practical content to international cooperation. In addition to the ICESCR, two other human rights treaty frameworks are analysed: the Convention on the Rights of the Child (CRC) and the Convention on the Rights of Persons with Disabilities (CRPD). Both instruments recognise various economic, social and cultural (ESC) rights whose protection must be ensured even in emergency situations—like disasters typically are—and assign a special relevance in this respect to international cooperation. The issue of what kind of assistance is or should be provided in disaster contexts and, notably, the difference between humanitarian relief and development aid is subsequently examined. While traditionally this distinction was clear-cut, today the relief-development divide has become blurred. In disaster contexts, the need to build a bridge between relief and development is best exemplified by disaster risk reduction (DRR) measures. This has resulted in a gradual (and ongoing) shift in focus from disaster response to disaster prevention, whose implications invest the same understanding of disaster assistance.

Chapter 8 then examines two different modalities of putting solidarity into practice. The first is represented by the R2P doctrine, which, it is argued, is conceivable as an institutionalised form of solidarity. R2P has been invoked several times in disaster settings and its application in such contexts, despite the persistent opposition of many States, cannot be excluded a priori. By contrast, the second modality concerns the EU legal order. It is within such a regional system that solidarity in disasters has found the most effective and incisive realisation, in both an internal and an external dimension. This success story is certainly attributable, at least in part, to the EU's peculiar features. Nonetheless, there are reasons to believe that it could be replicated in other regional contexts.

Finally, Chap. 9 takes stock of the preceding chapters of this part with a view towards identifying the current scope and challenges of international cooperation and solidarity in disaster scenarios. Before making some general conclusions and suggestions, it critically examines the place assigned to the two concepts in the Draft Articles (DAs) on the Protection of Persons in the event of Disasters.

Chapter 6
International Cooperation and Solidarity in Disaster Response: A General Introduction

Contents

6.1 The Vattelian Imperative

When addressing the role of the international community in disasters, reference is frequently made to the so-called Vattelian imperative. Writing in 1758, the distinguished Swiss international lawyer Emmerich De Vattel formulated a duty to assist States stricken by disasters:

> [. . .] [I]f a nation is afflicted with famine, all those who have provisions to spare ought to relieve her distress, without however exposing themselves to want. [. . .] To give assistance in such extreme necessity is so essentially conformable to humanity, that the duty is seldom neglected by any nation that has received the slightest polish of civilisation.[1]

The Vattelian imperative is generally regarded as an early conceptualisation of the crucial role of international solidarity in addressing the consequences of catastrophes. In fact, a thorough reading of Vattel's work shows that the author never utilised the concept of solidarity, referring instead to duties or offices of humanity ("les devoirs de l'humanité").[2] Nor did he conceive the duty of assistance in absolute terms. Indeed, such a duty was unenforceable and did not give rise to rights on the

[1]De Vattel (2010), p. 263.

[2]Ibid., Book II, §9, p. 266.

F. Zorzi Giustiniani, *International Law in Disaster Scenarios*,
https://doi.org/10.1007/978-3-030-50597-4_6

part of the affected State but merely to legitimate expectations.[3] Moreover, its application was exceptional and it could be superseded unless "circumstances will allow [the offering nation] to grant [relief] consistently with that regard which she ought to pay to her own safety and interests".[4] Additionally, Vattel specified that

> if [the receiving] nation is able to pay for the provisions thus furnished, it is perfectly lawful to sell them to her at a reasonable rate; for they are not bound to furnish her with what she is herself capable of procuring; and consequently there is no obligation of gratuitously bestowing on her such things as she is able to purchase.[5]

Nonetheless, as will be seen later in this chapter, for his time Vattel had a remarkably progressive vision of international relations and ultimately of the necessary unity of the "society of nations", based on the concept of common humanity.[6]

The Vattelian imperative was mentioned by the Special Rapporteur Valencia-Ospina in his Preliminary report on the Protection of Persons in the event of Disasters. However, Valencia-Ospina then remarked that while considerations of humanity have triggered people to assist disaster victims since times immemorial, it was only in the twentieth century that States, finally driven by "enhanced international solidarity", felt the need to properly regulate disaster relief in international law.[7] According to the Rapporteur, even the work of the ILC was based upon principles of international cooperation and solidarity:

> The underlying principles in the protection of persons in the event of disasters are those of solidarity and cooperation, both among nations and among individual human beings. It is in the solidarity inspired by human suffering that the Commission's mandate finds telos, as an expression of our common heritage in a global context.[8]

Today, solidarity is frequently invoked as a fundamental value, a principle or a right connoting the contemporary international community. While those invoking it do not agree as to its normative character (if ever) in international law, they generally concur in considering disaster response as one of the (admittedly few) areas where the concept, however defined, finds application.

---

[3]Cf. Wellens (2010), p. 5.

[4]De Vattel (2010), Book II, § 9, 266. Indeed, Vattel deemed that a Nation has in the first place duties towards itself: "a nation owes *herself in the first instance, and in preference to all other nations*, to do every thing she can to promote her own happiness and perfection" (ibid., Preliminaries § 14, 73, emphasis added).

[5]Ibid.

[6]It thus appears quite ungenerous the treatment that Immanuel Kant reserved to Vattel by dismissing him, along with the fathers of the natural law tradition of international law (Grotius and Pufendorf) as "leidige Tröster", miserable comforters whose principles and doctrines 'cannot have the slightest legal force' Kant (1795).

[7]ILC, Preliminary Report on the Protection of Persons in the Event of Disasters, A/CN.4/598, 5 May 2008, para. 16.

[8]ILC, Second Report on the Protection of Persons in the Event of Disasters, A/CN.4/615, 7 May 2009, para. 50.

6.2 Cooperation and Solidarity As Two Distinct Concepts in International Law

International cooperation and solidarity are two distinct concepts, but it is not infrequent to find them associated in an hendiadys, or otherwise considered as synonymous. This occurs in common parlance but also within international documents or in the works of distinguished authors. Nonetheless, their background, meaning and place in the international legal order are quite different.

6.2.1 International Cooperation

Cooperation has never been defined by an international document, but in modern international law it generally and broadly "describes the voluntary, co-ordinated action of two or more States which takes place under a legal regime and serves a specific objective".[9] Cooperation per se has no inherent value; its significance and value are dependent on the goal to be achieved.[10] It would thus seem obvious that States are under no general obligation to cooperate under international customary law. This is also a consequence of State sovereignty: each State can freely decide to conclude treaties that engage it to comply with *specific* cooperation duties (or not).[11] Nonetheless, in a more specific sense cooperation marks the new historical era of international relations inaugurated by the UN Charter and is conceived by the latter as the main instrument for promoting truly peaceful relations among States. It features the law of cooperation, as opposed to the law of coexistence that prevailed in classic international law and which was mainly based on obligations to abstain as well as the predominance of the egoistic interests of States.[12] In this sense cooperation has not substituted coexistence but rather it has added some new layers of law that aim to improve interstate relations through the realisation of community values such as equality, justice, order and peace.[13] As a result of this paradigmatic change in the structure of international law, the concept of international cooperation has been translated into a wide number of specific binding obligations to cooperate in many different areas of international regulation. One such sector is international human

---

[9]Wolfrum (2006b), para. 2.

[10]Ibid.

[11]Delbrück (2012), pp. 13–14.

[12]On the differences between the international law of coexistence and the international law of cooperation, see generally Friedmann (1964), p. 60 ff. While it is frequently assumed (including by Friedmann) that legal duties of cooperation have characterised the international legal order only since the twentieth century, E. Jouannet has stressed that they already played an important role in the international relations of the two previous centuries Jouannet (2012), p. 86.

[13]Kolb (2016), p. 73.

rights law, which as will be seen in depth in the following chapter (Chap. 7), has a specific relevance for our purposes.

6.2.2 International Solidarity

Solidarity, for its part, first appeared quite recently in international legal thinking and practice. The term originated in Roman civil law, where it indicated in the expression *obligatio in solidum* an obligation that committed each common debtor to pay to the creditor the whole (*solidum*) debt. It was eventually utilised within the French legal order at the end of the seventeenth century to define a certain category of civil obligations.[14] It was not, however, until the nineteenth century that the concept was developed scientifically, initially in social and political theory. Much of its fortune is due to the sociologist Emile Durkheim, who considered solidarity as the constituent principle of every society. In his masterpiece "De la division du travail social",[15] the author drew the well-known distinction between mechanic solidarity and organic solidarity. He argued that mechanic solidarity was typical of early, primitive societies, where individuals were bound together by a feeling of sameness and empathy: they did the same work, were part of the same family and fought against the same natural threats. In modern society, characterised by an increasing specialisation of tasks and consequently a differentiation of life-styles, the nature of ties between people changed and the production cycle became the new source of bonds. Durkheim termed this situation "organic solidarity" to signify that people were bonded together because of their interdependence.

Durkheim's analysis also influence legal discourse thanks to his pupil Léon Duguit. Indeed, Duguit was the first to introduce the concept of solidarity in the legal sphere, in particular in the administrative and constitutional law.[16] His objectivist theory, based on his schoolmaster's works, considered "social solidarity" or "social interdependence"[17] among individuals as the foundation of law:

> une règle de conduite s'impose à l'homme social par la force même des choses, règle qui peut, se formuler ainsi: ne rien faire qui porte atteinte à la solidarité sociale sous l'une de ses deux formes et faire tout ce qui est de nature à réaliser et à développer la solidarité sociale mécanique et organique. Tout le droit objectif se résume en celle formule, et la loi positive

---

[14] Casini (2013), p. 2, Available at https://poseidon01.ssrn.com/delivery.php?ID=741072022102024081078125122098091026016056000029024069069123106076083091009065089108016120111006027011049007065019120103000110123042042011081092088097006018000092070001052041101127094090119102000003104112029000080030080071088105122073089067014099025029&EXT=pdf (last accessed on 22 August 2020).

[15] Durkheim (1893).

[16] Duguit (1921). On French solidarism see generally Koskenniemi (2001), pp. 284–316.

[17] Duguit considered the two expressions as synonyms Duguit (1923), p. 10.

pour être légitime devra être l'expression, le développement ou la mise en oeuvre de ce principe[18]

Georges Scelle then developed the theory in the field of international law. Like Duguit, Scelle deemed State sovereignty a legal fiction.[19] Inasmuch as in national societies, in the international society individuals are the only source and finality of solidarity and law,[20] which in turn are due to biological necessities. "The bonds of solidarity (solidarity as fact, not as a 'feeling' or a moral principle) formed innumerable groups or societies, within and between which different needs give basis to different laws. Such societies were hierarchically related so that the more inclusive ones overrode the less inclusive ones".[21] In other terms, for Scelle global solidarity prevails over local equivalents and international law over municipal law. As a consequence, sovereignty is held by the "universal human society" and the current inexistence of international bodies superior to States is due, he claimed, to a "carence institutionnelle" that could and should be remedied. Albeit suggestive, his theorisation of solidarity did not have the same success as the doctrine of "dédoublement fonctionnel".[22] Moreover, objectivism ended up showing similar criticalities to natural law.[23]

The crucial and growing relevance of solidarity within modern domestic and international societies was also captured by the Chilean jurist Alejandro Alvarez, writing in 1912. An enemy of legal formalism, Alvarez criticised individualism and deemed that an ideal of justice required "the substitution of the old individualist concept with the idea of solidarity".[24] Given that public conscience, which was at the basis of law, was moving away from individualism, he thought that legal science should do the same. During the nineteenth century the international society had been subjected to greater profound changes than ever before. As a result, the notions of State and sovereignty were modified, alongside the notion of justice. The latter in particular was no longer based on individualism and absolute independence but on "the principles of solidarity that also takes into account the interests of the social group, because individuals live in society and in a situation of mutual dependence".[25] An "international regime of solidarity" was being established wherein

[18]Ibid.

[19]The State legislator did not "create" the law, only "declared" it Scelle (1932), p. 42.

[20]And indeed, Scelle did not speak of "droit international" but rather of "droits des gens" (law of *people*, not of *nations*, because individuals, for Scelle, are the only veritable subjects of international law). See generally Scelle (1932).

[21]Koskenniemi (2001), p. 331.

[22][H]is concept of solidarity, based on the 'droit objectif', has not survived. I cannot quote a contemporary French international scholar operating within that legal framework Cot (2010), p. 82.

[23]Le Fur, for instance, had already remarked that drawing the legitimacy of positive law from biological necessities risks becoming an apology of absolutism Le Fur (1935), p. 95 ff.

[24]Alvarez (1912), p. 140.

[25]Ibid., 33.

the general interest of the society was being taken into consideration.[26] This "idea of solidarity", he argued, is "of crucial importance for international law. It must guide its future orientation and at the same time provide objective elements of interpretation; correctly understood, it will bring back international law's lost prestige".[27]

A renewed interest in international solidarity apparently followed the increase in international cooperation, epitomised by the establishment of the brand-new institutionalised international system revolving around the United Nations and the subsequent wind of change brought about by decolonisation. In this new context, Michel Virally was the first to conceptualise solidarity as a veritable legal principle of international law, which finds expression first of all in international development law. According to Virally, solidarity expresses, at the level of legal principles, "les exigences de l'interdépendance, comme la souveraineté exprime celles de l'indépendance".[28] All the provisions of the UN Charter can be read in the light of these two extremes along the same axis. Sovereignty and solidarity, while being naturally in tension, can thus be reconciled: "[c]'est la raison pour laquelle nous avons cru pouvoir les faire figurer aux deux extremités d'un axe unique, sur lequel pourront prendre place, précisément, toutes les solutions de conciliation".[29] Having evolved from a moral duty to a legal principle, solidarity now constitutes the substratum of rights and obligations.[30]

In more recent times, the existence of a principle of solidarity characterising the international legal order has been advocated by some authoritative international jurists like Ronald St. John Macdonald, Karel Wellens and Rudiger Wolfrum. Nevertheless, despite the increasing evocation of the crucial relevance of solidarity in today's globalised world in international fora as well, solidarity remains an elusive concept, whose meaning and status in international law remain contested.

As to its meaning, increasingly frequent references to solidarity in international documents are rarely accompanied by a definition of the concept. This is the case of the Convention to Combat Desertification in Those Countries Experiencing Serious Drought and/or Desertification, particularly in Africa, where the "spirit of solidarity" is evoked in the provision laying down the principles of the Convention, but not defined.[31] A certain definitional effort has instead been made by the General Assembly in its Resolutions 56/151 and 57/213 on the Promotion of a Democratic and Equitable International Order, where the Assembly:

---

[26]Ibid., 47.

[27]Ibid., 128. For a critical reading of Alvarez, see Koskenniemi (2001), p. 302 ff., who remarks: "By directing his attack against an academic enemy that was largely a straw man, Alvarez remained unthreatening for the legal establishment and could be celebrated as a wonderful manifestation of the profession's liberality" (ibid., 304).

[28]Virally (2015), p. 448.

[29]Ibid.

[30]Virally (1968), pp. 531–554.

[31]Convention to Combat Desertification in Those Countries Experiencing Serious Drought and/or Desertification, particularly in Africa, Paris, 14 October 1994, Art. 3.

> [...] *affirms* that a democratic and equitable international order requires, inter alia, the realization of the following:
>
> [...]
>
> (f) Solidarity, as a fundamental value, by virtue of which global challenges must be managed in a way that distributes costs and burdens fairly in accordance with basic principles of equity and social justice and ensures that those who suffer or who benefit the least receive help from those who benefit the most[32]

According to a more general, and structured definition, proposed by the Routledge Encyclopedia of Philosophy, solidarity

> exists among a group of people when they are committed to abiding by the outcome of some process of collective decision-making, or to promoting the wellbeing of other members of the group, perhaps at significant cost to themselves. Many regard solidarity as an important political ideal on the grounds that it is related to community and fraternity, and conducive to social cohesion and stability. (...).

This definition, in line with others provided by general dictionaries, highlights the main features of solidarity: the existence of a group whose members are tied together by some common interests and objectives and who agree to realise them, even if this implies the postponement of *individual* interests and objectives. Unlike pure altruism, it thus requires a degree of group identification.

Applied to international law, a first problem arises. As was remarked by Robert Michels at the beginning of the twentieth century, "in order to establish a group of solidarity it is *a priori* necessary to have a sharp contraposition: one is sympathetic to another only against somebody else [...] a universal solidarity of a society – solidarity in its purest form [...] can exist only before certain natural disasters".[33] Unlike for national societies, for the international society it was long difficult to identify *the other*—the common enemy or threat—against whom the *community of States* should put up a common front.

In fact, as previously mentioned, Vattel was a forerunner in this regard. Indeed, he was the first one to speak of a "society of nations" whose object, similar to that "of the natural society established between all mankind" is that "[nations] should lend each other mutual assistance in order to attain perfection themselves and to render their condition as perfect as possible".[34] However, the fact that such common duties—"offices of humanity"—cannot prevail over the duties of self-preservation and self-perfection should not, as was seen in legal doctrine for a long time, diminish

---

[32]UN GA, Res. 56/151, 8 February 2002, para. 3 f); id., Res. 2002/72, para. 4 f) and following resolutions. A similar definition is contained in the Millennium Declaration, where solidarity—referred as one of the 'fundamental values to be essential to international relations in the twenty-first century'—is so defined:

> Global challenges must be managed in a way that distributes the costs and burdens fairly in accordance with basic principles of equity and social justice. Those who suffer or who benefit least deserve help from those who benefit most (para. 6).

[33]Michels (1914), p. 55.

[34]De Vattel (2010), Preliminaries, 73, para. 12.

their relevance in Vattel's theory.[35] According to the distinguished Swiss author, such common duties of humanity, as much as those of self-preservation, are part of natural law, even though by their very essence, they are not coercible: "Il est du droit naturel conçu sans contrainte externe car il va au-delà de ce que la contrainte externe pourrait arriver à faire plier ou exiger".[36]

Looking at today's world, it would seem that an international *community*—meant "as an overarching system which embodies a common interest of all States and, indirectly, of mankind"[37]—has finally taken form. This fictional grouping in which common interests and values—incorporated notably in erga omnes obligations and jus cogens norms—are prioritised over the individualistic interests of States, coexists with international *society*, with the additional consequence that also "the law of coexistence, the law of cooperation and the law of solidarity continue to 'co-exist' in parallel".[38] In this context, solidarity is precisely and "undoubtedly one of the most interesting witnesses of the transformation of international law into 'a value based international legal order'".[39]

Once it is established that solidarity is applicable even to international relations, a second problem arises: the tendency of many lawyers to its inflationary use, with the risk, already identified earlier, of watering it down into the more general concept of cooperation.[40] Therefore (and unlike cooperation), solidarity at present shapes only a limited number of branches of international law. International solidarity is also different from charity, as it is a relation among formal equals that is based on interdependence and a certain element of mutuality, albeit not strict reciprocity.[41]

[35]Such prevalence of "egoistic duties" is well elucidated by Jouannet: "[l]a primauté des devoirs de conservation et même de perfection résulte du fait que V. était tout simplement confronté à ce qu'on le peut appeler le 'dilemme réaliste': comment prôner la liberté de chaque Etat souverain de décider de son attitude vis-à-vis des autres Etats tout en continuant quand même à leur dicter des règles de comportement? [...] comment rendre contraignants des devoirs envers autrui dans un monde d'Etats souverains et égaux entre eux?" Jouannet (2009), p. 142.

[36]Ibid., 144.

[37]Tomuschat (1993), p. 227. Similarly, for Villalpando "la communauté internationale se caractérise par un degré de cohésion particulier qui découle de la solidarité des membres du groupe social dans la sauvegarde de certains intérêts identiques collectifs" Villalpando (2005), p. 26.

[38]Wellens (2010), p. 36.

[39]Wolfrum (2006a), p. 1087.

[40]For instance, the former UN independent expert on human rights and international *solidarity*, Rudi Muhammad Rizki, affirmed that "The notion of solidarity corresponds to the notion of cooperation, because one could only cooperate in an act of solidarity" (UN Commission on Human Rights, Human rights and international solidarity — Note by the United Nations High Commissioner for Human Rights, 1 February 2006, E/CN.4/2006/96, para. 13).

[41]In this regard, the definition of solidarity provided by R. St. J. MacDonald is particularly illustrative: "Solidarity is neither charity nor welfare; it is an agreement among formal equals that will all refrain from actions that would significantly interfere with the realization of common goals and fundamental interests. Solidarity requires an understanding that every member of the community must consciously and constantly conceive of its own interests as being inextricable from the interests of the whole. No State may choose to use its power to undertake actions that might threaten the integrity of the community" Macdonald (1993), p. 293.

Being an act of justice, providers of solidarity do not necessarily benefit from it in a direct and concrete manner.[42]

Its late affirmation in international law is also due to the fact that the international legal order is premised on the autonomy of its members, which is represented by the concept of State sovereignty and the corollary of *formal* equality. As it was notoriously affirmed by Vattel, "[a] dwarf is as much a man as a giant; a small republic is no less a sovereign state than the most powerful kingdom".[43] In recent times, the growing interdependence among States has rendered sovereign equality even more theoretical.[44] Nevertheless, the fiction of sovereign equality still serves its function of guaranteeing a minimum level playing field for weaker States. In this respect, solidarity should not be considered as opposed to sovereignty. Rather, the interrelationship between solidarity and sovereignty is a mutually reinforcing one,[45] avoiding as it does the opposite risks of absolutism and imperialism.[46] On the one hand, sovereignty, "removed from the absolute meaning taken in modern political thought (e.g., Hobbes, Rousseau), and re-understood as an expression of the *freedom* of peoples, is paradoxically the condition of a truly human act of solidarity";[47] on the other hand, solidarity is functional to effectively establish not just formal but *substantial* equality among States.

[42]"Solidarity involves long-term and short-term aspects. Of course, in the short run, you do not derive any benefits if you give a loan of 10 million or even 10 billion dollars to one specific country. But in the long run, the lender does it in order to derive some benefits from that kind of operation. The transaction cannot be described as pure altruism. The lender expects something, but not immediately. So there is no immediate consideration but in a long-term perspective, even development assistance is based on reciprocity" (Tomuschat, T., Discussion Following the Presentation by L. Boisson de Chazournes, in Wolfrum, R., Kojima, C. (Eds.)., *Solidarity: A structural principle of international law* (p. 112). Heidelberg: Springer).

[43]De Vattel (2010), Preliminaries, para. 18.

[44]Kokott (2011), p. 6.

[45][O]nce we admit that solidarity implies a mutual relationship, with rights and obligations on both sides, we should also recognize that States are relinquishing part of their sovereignty. Therefore, the ambiguity is due to the fact that on one hand, solidarity as such enhances sovereignty, because it seeks equality and strengthens the position of the weaker States; on the other, once the principle of solidarity evolves into something more complex, through the establishment of institutions, norms, and procedures, States are less powerful and may be subjected to legal consequences (Casini 2013, p. 14).

[46]Considering sovereignty and solidarity as the main manifestations of autonomy and community, respectively, the following considerations by Koskenniemi explain our point:

> Neither community nor autonomy can be exclusive goals. To think of community as the ultimate goal seems utopian: as there is no agreement on the character of a desirable community, attempts to impose it seem like imperialism in disguise. To think of autonomy as the normative aim seems apologist: it strengthens the absolutist claims of national power-elites and supports their pursuits at international dominance Koskenniemi (2006), p. 476.

[47]Carrozza and Crema (2014), p. 19, Available at http://www.fciv.org/downloads/Carozza%20Crema.pdf (last accessed on 22 August 2020).

A final and fundamental problem needs to be answered: what is the status of solidarity in the international legal order? Is it a fact, a value, a right or a principle? Each of these options has indeed been advocated.

Conceived as a fact, solidarity resembles to interdependence and is generally invoked to require a certain behaviour that is considered obligatory. This conception, as can be seen, risks either reducing solidarity to the mere factual condition that exists at the basis of international cooperation, or imposing a particular conduct as 'naturally' binding, thereby bypassing spontaneity, which is instead a typical feature of solidarity and derives from the group identification.

As a value or as a principle, solidarity is intended as a (moral or legal) standard of action through which common interests or issues of common concern should be managed by the international community. According to Wolfrum, one of its most refined and convinced theorists, solidarity is a structural principle of international law and hence it "reorients international law from a set of rules for preserving the present state of existing international relations, into a regime for fulfilling a certain mission, namely the promotion of international social justice among states".[48] The same author, however, is ready to acknowledge that solidarity does not yet inform the whole system, but only certain areas of international law and the respective regulatory regimes, such as those concerning the preservation of peace, the protection of human rights and the environment.

Finally, solidarity has also been considered as a right. Such a conceptualisation can be found, inter alia, in the works on solidarity undertaken by the UN Commission on Human Rights and its successor the Human Rights Council (HRC). For instance, in the Draft Declaration on the Right to International Solidarity, finally presented in June 2017 by Virginia Dandan as Independent Expert on human rights and international solidarity, solidarity was framed both as an international principle and as a *human right*. As a human right, it is defined as follows:

1. The right to international solidarity is a human right by which individuals and peoples are entitled, on the basis of equality and non-discrimination, to participate meaningfully in, contribute to and enjoy a social and international order in which all human rights and fundamental freedoms can be fully realized.
2. The right to international solidarity is grounded in the codification and progressive development of freedoms and entitlements contained in international human rights treaties reflecting civil and political rights, economic, social and cultural rights, the right to development and international labour standards, and complemented by other responsibilities arising from voluntary commitments undertaken in the relevant fields at the bilateral, multilateral, regional and international levels.[49]

---

[48]Wolfrum (2013), p. 338.

[49]Cf. Art. 4 of the Draft Declaration, annexed to the report of the Independent Expert on human rights and international solidarity of 25 April 2017, A/HRC/35/35.

As appears evident, the proposed definition is too general and ambiguous to bring any added-value to the current international human rights framework. Moreover, as hinted by the reference to the right to development, solidarity seems to be utilised as a justificatory basis of the latter right.[50] Not coincidentally, the works of the HRC have revealed the continued clivage between developing States, which strongly supported them and their final outcome, and developed States, which instead expressed their opposition towards the recognition of a human right to international solidarity.[51]

In conclusion, the most convincing readings of solidarity appear to be those that consider it either as a value or as a structural principle of international law. Nonetheless, the complex and multifarious nature of the international legal order—as well as the very diverse stages of development that the law of cooperation and the law of solidarity have attained in each specific area of international law—do not allow us to conceive it as a fundamental basis of the *whole* system. At the end of the inquiry that will be undertaken in this part, we will thus try to assess the scope and status of solidarity in the field of disaster response.

List of Documents

ILC, Preliminary Report on the Protection of Persons in the Event of Disasters, A/CN.4/598, 5 May 2008

ILC, Second Report on the Protection of Persons in the Event of Disasters, A/CN.4/615, 7 May 2009

Convention to Combat Desertification in Those Countries Experiencing Serious Drought and/or Desertification, particularly in Africa, Paris, 14 October 1994

UN GA, Resolution 56/151, 8 February 2002

UN Commission on Human Rights, Resolution 2002/72, 25 April 2002

UN Commission on Human Rights, Human rights and international solidarity—Note by the United Nations High Commissioner for Human Rights, E/CN.4/2006/96, 1 February 2006

UN Human Rights Council, Draft Declaration on the Right to International Solidarity, annexed to the report of the Independent Expert on human rights and international solidarity of 25 April 2017, A/HRC/35/35

[50] Sic Carrozza and Crema (2014), p. 11. The authors also remark that in this latter sense solidarity, while being qualified as a right, actually plays the role of a principle.

[51] Dandan (2016), available at https://www.sef-bonn.org/fileadmin/Die_SEF/Publikationen/Foreign_Voices/fv_2016-02_dandan.pdf (last accessed on 22 August 2020).

References

Alvarez A (1912) La codification du droit international – ses tendances, ses bases. Pedone, Paris

Carrozza P, Crema L (2014) On solidarity in international law. Caritas in Veritate Foundation, Fort Worth. Available at http://www.fciv.org/downloads/Carozza%20Crema.pdf. Last accessed on 22 August 2020

Casini L (2013) Solidarity between States in the global legal space. Paper presented at the Annual Meeting of the European Group of Public Law, Available at https://poseidon01.ssrn.com/delivery.php?ID=741072022102024081078125122098091026016056000029024069069123106076083091009065089108016120111006027011049007065019120103000110123042042011081092088097006018000092070001052041101127094090119102000003104112029000080030080071088105122073089067014099025029&EXT=pdf. Last accessed on 22 August 2020

Cot J-P (2010) Discussion following the presentation by Philip Dann. In: Wolfrum R, Kojima C (eds) Solidarity: a structural principle of international law. Springer, Heidelberg, pp 81–82

Dandan VB (2016) The path to a right to international solidarity. Foreign Voices, 2, Available at https://www.globalpolicy.org/home/271-general/52913-the-path-to-a-right-to-international-solidarity.html. Last accessed on 22 August 2020

De Vattel E (2010) The law of nations, or, principles of the law of nature, applied to the conduct and affairs of nations and sovereigns, with three early essays on the origin and nature of natural law and on luxury, Edited and with an Introduction by B. Kapossy and R. Whatmore. Liberty Fund, Indianapolis

Delbrück J (2012) The international obligation to cooperate – an empty shell or a hard law principle of international law? – A critical look at a much debated paradigm of modern international law. In: Hestermeyer HP, König D, Matz-Lück N, Röben V, Seibert-Fohr A, Stoll P-T, Vöneky S (eds) Coexistence, cooperation and solidarity. Liber Amicorum Rüdiger Wolfrum, vol I. Martinus Nijhoff Publishers, Leiden, pp 3–16

Duguit L (1921) Traité de droit constitutionnel, vol 1, 2nd edn. Boccard, Paris

Duguit L (1923) Manuel de droit constitutionnel: théorie générale de l'Etat, le droit et l'Etat - les libertés publiques, l'organisation politique de la France. 4e ed. rev. et mise au courant. Boccard, Paris

Durkheim E (1893) De la division du travail social. Félix Alcan, Paris

Friedmann W (1964) The changing structure of international law. Columbia University Press, New York

Jouannet E (2009) Les dualismes du Droit des gens. In: Haggenmacher P, Chetail V (eds) Le droit international de Vattel vu du XXIe siècle/Vattel's international law in XXIst century perspective. Martinus Nijhoof, Genève, pp 133–150

Jouannet E (2012) The Liberal-Welfarist law of nations: a history of international law. Cambridge University Press, Cambridge

Kant I (1795) Zum ewigen Frieden. Ein philosophischer Entwurf. Friedrich Nicolovius, Königsberg

Kokott J (2011) States, sovereign equality. In: Max Planck encyclopedia of public international law. Oxford University Press, Oxford

Kolb R (2016) Theory of international law. Hart, Oxford

Koskenniemi M (2001) The Gentle Civilizer of Nations. The rise and fall of international law 1870–1960. Cambridge University Press, Cambridge, pp 284–316

Koskenniemi M (2006) From apology to utopia. The structure of international legal argument. Reissue with a new Epilogue. Cambridge University Press, Cambridge

Le Fur L (1935) Règles génèrales du droit de la paix. Recueil des Cours de l'Académie de Droit International, 54(IV). Martinus Njihoff, Leiden

Macdonald RSJ (1993) The principle of solidarity in public international law. In: Dominicé C, Patry R, Reymond C (eds) Etudes de droit international en l'honneur de Pierre Lalive. Helbing & Lichtenhahn, Bâle/Francfort-sur-le-Main, pp 275–308

Michels R (1914) Zum Problem: Solidarität und Kastenwesen. In: Probleme der Sozialphilosophie. Teubner, Leipzig, pp 44–53

Scelle G (1932) Précis de droit des gens. CNRS, Paris

Tomuschat C (1993) Obligations arising for states without or against their will. In: Recueil des Cours de l'Académie de Droit International, 241. Martinus Nijhoff, Leiden

Villalpando S (2005) L'émergence de la communauté internationale dans la responsabilité des Etats. PUF, Paris

Virally M (1968) Le rôle des 'principes' dans le développement du droit international. In: Recueil d'études de droit international en hommage à Paul Guggenheim. Institut Universitaire de Hautes Études Internationales, Geneva, pp 531–554

Virally M (2015) Le droit international en devenir: essais écrits au fil des ans. Graduate Institute Publications, Geneva

Wellens K (2010) Revisiting solidarity as a (re-)emerging constitutional principle: some further reflections. In: Wolfrum R, Kojima C (eds) Solidarity: a structural principle of international law. Springer, Heidelberg, p 5

Wolfrum R (2006a) Solidarity amongst States: an emerging structural principle of international law. In: Dupuy P-M, Fassbender B, Shaw MN, Sommermann K-P (eds) Common values in international law: essays in Honour of Christian Tomuschat. N.P. Engel Verlag. Kehl, p 1087

Wolfrum R (2006b) International law of cooperation. In: Max Planck Encyclopedia of Public International Law. Oxford University Press, Oxford

Wolfrum R (2013) Solidarity. In: Shelton D (ed) The Oxford handbook of international human rights law. Oxford University Press, Oxford, pp 401–416

Chapter 7
The Role of International Cooperation Within the UN Human Rights Treaty System

Contents

7.1 Art. 2(1) of the ICESCR

When looking at international cooperation obligations in disasters, the major reference point remains the general implementation article of the 1966 ICESCR, which commits States parties to "take steps, individually and through international assistance and cooperation, especially economic and technical, to the maximum of [their] available resources, with a view to achieving progressively the full realization of the rights recognized" therein.[1]

[1]This is not the only article which contains a reference to international assistance and cooperation. A specific obligation in this respect is posed, in particular, by Art. 11.2 which affirms that States parties, "recognising the fundamental right of everyone to be free from hunger, shall take, individually and through international cooperation" the measures enumerated therein. The notion of international assistance and cooperation is then mentioned in Art. 15.4, on international contacts and cooperation in the scientific and cultural fields, as well as in Arts. 22–23 of Part IV, related to measures of implementation.

F. Zorzi Giustiniani, *International Law in Disaster Scenarios*,
https://doi.org/10.1007/978-3-030-50597-4_7

As is well known, the ICESCR was a product of the West-East cleavage and of the different relevance and status accorded by the two blocs, respectively, to civil and political rights on the one hand and economic, social and cultural (ESC) rights on the other. The very existence of two covenants dedicated to the two sets of rights has long been regarded as proof that such categories were also different in character.

ESC rights especially were considered by many as essentially aspirational and non-justiciable.[2] However, this opinion, which ended up denying the binding nature of the Covenant, would not have been sustainable even at the time of the drafting. As was highlighted by Alston and Quinn, the ICESCR "is a treaty that gives rise to formal obligations on the part of ratifying or acceding states and, as such, it must be interpreted in the light of the customary rules to treaty interpretation",[3] which are now enshrined in the Vienna Convention on the Law of Treaties (VCLT). Emphasising in particular the principle of good faith, they then argued, quite paradoxically, that "the reasoning of many of the Covenant's detractors would seem to lead ineluctably to the conclusion that in signing and ratifying the Covenant states parties have not acted in good faith".[4] Moreover, the preparatory work proved unequivocably that when States agreed that a given provision did not trigger legal obligations, this was clearly stated, as was the case for Art. 15.[5]

Nowadays it is almost undisputed that in its international dimension, Art. 2.1 implies some obligations on States parties. Such an international dimension could not be underrated in a treaty that does not contain any territorial or jurisdictional limitations, and indeed is essential for the realisation of ESC rights. Nonetheless, what remains unclear is the exact scope and meaning of so-called 'transnational' or 'extraterritorial' obligations,[6] especially those of a positive character.[7] And this, unfortunately, is not a trivial matter. We cannot but agree that "(i)n the context of the

---

[2]As a consequence, it was assumed that the nature of the obligations posed by ESC rights was substantially different from the one typical of civil and political rights (cf. Craven 1995, p. 9). Remarkably, still in 1993 it was remarked that:

> [t]he shocking reality . . . is that States and the international community as a whole continue to tolerate all too often breaches of economic, social and cultural rights which, if they occurred in relation to civil and political rights, would provoke expressions of horror and outrage and would lead to concerted calls for immediate remedial action. In effect, despite the rhetoric, violations of civil and political rights continue to be treated as though they were far more serious, and more patently intolerable, than massive and direct denials of economic, social and cultural rights (Statement to the World Conference on Human Rights on behalf of the Committee on Economic, Social and Cultural Rights, E/1993/22, Annex III).

[3]Alston and Quinn (1987), p. 160.

[4]Ibid.

[5]Ibid., 186.

[6]"The key question under this Covenant [. . .] is not whether parties have extraterritorial obligations but what is the precise nature and content of those obligations" (Coomans and Kamminga 2004, p. 2). Additionally, Craven remarks that Art. 2.1 is "fairly unsatisfactory [. . .], making it virtually impossible to determine the precise nature of the obligations" (Craven 1995, p. 151).

[7]"For those States pursuing technical or economic assistance in conjunction with another State Party to the Covenant there is [. . .] a question, to our knowledge undertheorized at this point, as to

human rights responsibility of international assistance and cooperation, the devil is *not* in the detail, but in sweeping generalisations of an entirely abstract nature".[8]

In order to shed some light on the scope and meaning of Art. 2.1 ICESCR, limited assistance can be provided by the preparatory works,[9] which nevertheless offer an interesting insight into the views of States at the time of drafting. Despite inevitable differences of opinion, all States representatives agreed on the *need* for international cooperation and assistance.[10] More contentious is the view, advanced by Skogly, that they also concurred that "wealthier states had a duty to assist less well-off states to realise economic, social and cultural rights".[11] In any case, no agreement emerged as to the existence of a *legal* obligation, or of a corresponding right in this respect.[12] Regardless, it now appears difficult to argue that "the commitment to international cooperation contained in the Covenant can accurately be characterized *as a legally binding obligation upon any particular state to provide any particular form of assistance*".[13] Nonetheless, as will be shown, the significance of the Covenant has evolved over time, especially thanks to the active engagement of the Committee on Economic, Social and Cultural Rights (CESCR), to the point of becoming an invaluable tool in achieving international cooperation.

Equally unsatisfying for an understanding of the concrete meaning of "international assistance and cooperation" is the contribution of the travaux préparatoires. The issue was the object of some discussion, which focused in particular on whether the expression was meant to refer only to financial and technical assistance, to which no clear consensus emerged.[14] The legislative history only tells us that the term 'assistance' was not present in the first draft of the article and that it was inserted in 1952,[15] probably in order to underline its importance as a form of cooperation.[16]

---

the nature of the obligation of a State in a position to provide this assistance" (Desierto and Gillespie 2013, pp. 584–585).

[8]Bueno de Mesquita et al. (2010), pp. 128–129.

[9]As a supplementary means of interpretation ex Art. 32 VCLT, the preparatory works can be used either to "confirm" the meaning resulting from the application of the general rule of interpretation ex Art. 31, or to "determine" the meaning when the interpretation according to Art. 31 leaves the meaning ambiguous, obscure, or leads to a result that is manifestly absurd or unreasonable.

[10]Alston and Quinn (1987), pp. 188–189.

[11]Skogly (2006), p. 87.

[12]The only clear affirmation as to the existence of a binding obligation to assist developing countries was made by the Chilean representative, who argued: "international assistance to under-developed countries had in a sense become mandatory as a result of commitments assumed by States in the United Nations" (A/C.3/SR.1203 (1962), para. 10).

[13]Alston and Quinn (1987), p. 191. Vandenhole remarks that "[t]his position focuses on the obligation to fulfil, and does not exclude third State obligations to respect and to protect" (Vandenhole 2009, p. 51).

[14]Craven (2012), pp. 146–147; Skogly (2006), pp. 84–89.

[15]Commission on Human Rights, Report, 8th session (14 April to 14 June 1952), ECOSOC Official Records, 14th session, Supp. No. 4, Annex I.

[16]Karimova (2016), p. 145 fn 123. More generally, Craven affirms that international cooperation may be broader than international assistance, "providing for mutual action directed towards a

This element thus reinforces what already emerges from a literal and systemic analysis of the treaty: international cooperation as a whole is a broad and multifaceted notion that can assume various forms, hence it applies to the implementation of *all* the provisions of the ICESCR.

Due to their *special* character—geared as they are towards third-party beneficiaries—alongside the high degree of abstraction and vagueness that typically characterises their provisions, human rights treaties are generally considered as a "living instrument which must be interpreted in the light of present-day conditions".[17] This is all the more true for the ICESCR obligations, whose "normative design [. . .] stands out for being purposely evolutive and dynamic.[18] Article 2.1, in particular, best capsulizes the evolutive nature of the Covenant".[19]

A crucial effort in interpreting and clarifying the ambiguities of the Covenant was made by the CESCR through its General Comments.[20] Before examining in depth the concepts advanced in such documents with respect to Art. 2.1, it is nevertheless essential to try to elucidate the Committee's role in the interpretation and the development of the Treaty's obligations.

The CESCR was established as a supervisory mechanism by the UN Economic and Social Council (ECOSOC) in 1985[21] and comprises 18 independent experts, who are elected by the same Council on the basis of an equitable geographical distribution and the representation of different forms of social and legal systems.[22] The members of the Committee must have a "recognized competence in the field of human rights",[23] although it is not necessary for them to also have a legal background. As a consequence, the CESCR's composition is interdisciplinary, even though legal experts are generally the majority.[24]

common goal [. . .][w]hereas 'assistance' implies the provision or transfer of some 'good' from one state to another" (Craven 2012, p. 147).

[17]Cf. ECtHR, Tyrer v. United Kingdom, judgment of 25 April 1978, Series A No. 26, pp. 15–16, para. 31. The living instrument doctrine was conceptualised by the European Court of Human Rights with respect to the ECHR, but subsequently it has been considered applicable and indeed applied (additionally under the name of "evolutive interpretation") to the interpretation of human rights treaties in general (see for all Human Rights Committee, Judge v Canada, Communication No. 829/1998, Views Adopted on 5 August 2003, para. 10.3). Accordingly, a lesser value is attributed to the preparatory work and more generally to the intention of the parties (Kälin and Künzli 2009, p. 38).

[18]Desierto and Gillespie (2013), p. 562.

[19]Ibid.

[20]"Interestingly, the bulk of pronouncements on the 'disaster proper phase' has been elaborated in 'General Comments' by the CESCR, rather than in 'Concluding' Observations on specific States' reports and disaster settings" (Hesselman 2013, p. 121).

[21]Cf. ECOSOC, Resolution 1985/17, May 1985.

[22]Ibid., at 2.

[23]Ibid.

[24]Currently, legal experts account for 60% of the CESCR (cf. Geneva Academy of International Humanitarian Law and Human Rights 2018). This stands in stark contrast to the Human Rights Committee, whose membership was always composed almost exclusively by jurists.

While the ICESCR only provided for a mechanism of supervision of States compliance, consisting in the submission of State reports (Art. 16 ICESCR), once created the CESCR was also assigned the competence to draft General Comments (GCs). Following the adoption of the ICESCR's Optional Protocol,[25] the Committee's main tasks are analogous to those of the other UN human rights treaty bodies, consisting mainly in the periodic review of State reports and the formulation of Concluding Observations on them, the adoption of views on individual communications and the drafting of GCs. Unlike the other treaty bodies, however, the CESCR's authority to issue GCs is more firmly established, as it is not derived implicitly from the constituent treaty but from an explicit invitation by the ECOS OC.[26] This is also confirmed by the behaviour of States parties: up to 2005, very few of them remarked that GCs are not binding, thereby expressing an indirect disapproval of the CESCR's work.[27]

As the only body charged with the supervision and the interpretation at the international level of the ICESCR, the CESCR and its documents—in primis the GCs—are the main point of reference when interpreting the Covenant. GCs are official, non-binding statements in which human rights monitoring bodies try to clarify the interpretation of States parties' obligations with respect to a specific right or a cross-cutting issue, in order to facilitate implementation and compliance.[28] They thus have a general and necessarily abstract character. However, despite frequent assumptions as to the overall authoritativeness of the GCs,[29] the reality presents a rather more complex and nuanced picture.

In the case of the CESCR's GCs, several times the Committee went beyond a mere norm-filling function. Admittedly, the boundaries between evolutive interpretation and lawmaking are frequently blurred, especially as far as ESC rights are concerned. Nonetheless, when addressing issues like the concept of "core obligations", the CESCR was accused of engaging in a quasi-legislative approach.[30] Additionally, an overall examination of the GCs adopted sofar shows that the Committee has not always been consistent over time with respect to the same

---

[25]The competence to adopt views on individual communications was instead attributed to the CESCR only quite recently, following the adoption on 10 December 2008 of the Optional Protocol to the International Covenant on Economic, Social and Cultural Rights, which entered into force on 5 May 2013. As of 22 August 2020, the Protocol was ratified by 24 States Parties.

[26]ECOSOC, Resolution 1987/5, 26 May 1987, in E/C.12/1989/4, 27, para. 9.

[27]Cf. Mechlem (2009), p. 921, who cites in support Eibe Riedel (2005), Allgemeine Bemerkungen zu Bestimmungen des Internationalen Paktes über Wirtschaftliche, Soziale und Kulturelle Rechte der Vereinten Nationen, in *Die general comments zu den vn-menschenrechtsverträgen — Deutsche Übersetzung und Kurzeinführung* 160, 165.

[28]According to Alston, GCs are "means by which a UN human rights expert committee distils its considered views on an issue which arises out of the provisions of the treaty whose implementation it supervises and presents those views in the context of a formal statement of its understanding to which it attaches major importance" (Alston 2001, p. 769).

[29]Ben Saul, David Kinley and Jacqueline Mowbray for instance define the CESCR's GCs as "authoritative statements of its opinions and practice" (Saul et al. 2014, p. 5).

[30]See e.g. the remarks of Khaliq and Churchill (2012), p. 207 ff.

issue. Such inconsistencies can be explained—albeit only in part—by the particular drafting process of GCs, which is open to multiple inputs coming inter alia from NGOs and academia.[31]

Be it as it may, per se GCs are not authoritative. Akin to the other documents issued by the CESCR, they *can* acquire authoritativeness—and hence legitimacy[32]—to the extent that the reasoning utilised to advance a certain interpretation is persuasive.[33] In this respect, it bears noting that the application of the rules of interpretation enshrined in the VCLT, while not obligatory for the CESCR, can surely help to better establish a particular construct and ultimately to convince States parties to follow it.[34]

Furthermore, the GCs alone cannot qualify as subsequent practice in the sense of Art. 31.3(b) VCLT.[35] However, a positive response by States or their acquiescence to these statements might constitute such a practice.[36] Moreover, outside the treaty context, GCs can indirectly contribute, through their influence on the opinio juris and the practice of international subjects, to the formation of customary international law.

Now that we have clarified that the legal or practical authoritativeness of a given GC, as well as of any specific pronouncement of the CESCR cannot be established a priori, we will consider two major doctrinal constructs—the minimum core obligations and the tripartite classification of State obligations—which were developed by the CESCR in interpreting Art. 2.1. Such concepts, which were originally devised by authoritative jurists like Henry Shue and Asbjorn Eide, have had a major impact on the theorisation and application of international human rights obligations in the UN treaty system more broadly. Moreover, as will be shown, they have a specific relevance for our purposes as they were applied, in primis by the CESCR, even in disaster contexts.

---

[31]"The adoption of a General Comment is a cumbersome, contested, and competitive process and obviously some committee members, academics, and NGOs exert greater influence than others and shape the quality and content of the outcome. The particular nature of the drafting procedure helps to explain why different General Comments from the same committee can vary in their treatment of an issue, as the example of the CESCR's conceptualization of core obligations" (Mechlem 2009, p. 928).

[32]Borrowing from Khaliq and Churchill, for our purposes we consider legitimacy "as being primarily concerned with the competence of the [CESCR] to address economic and social rights in the manner that [it has]" (Khaliq and Churchill 2012, p. 202).

[33]"In addition to procedural improvements, the legitimacy of treaty bodies' findings can be greatly enhanced by strengthening the reasoning underlying them" (Keller and Ulfstein 2012, p. 422).

[34]Cf. Seatzu (2012), p. 350. According to Mechlem, the CESCR would instead be obligated to apply such rules since it interprets the Covenant in lieu of the States parties (Mechlem 2009, p. 919).

[35]Nolte (2013), p. 384.

[36]International Law Association, Berlin conference (2004) International human rights law and practice, Final report on the impact of findings of the United Nations human rights treaty bodies, para. 21.

7.1.1 The "Minimum Core" Approach

The "minimum core" approach was issued by the CESCR in 1990, in its General Comment 3 on "The nature of States' parties obligations". The concept of a minimum core was developed by the Committee in order to give some determinacy to ESC rights and to establish a correlation between the rights proclaimed in the Covenant and the obligations that States parties cannot postpone by invoking the notion of progressive realisation. Such an approach was based on a teleological interpretation of the treaty and was considered essential by the CESCR to giving effect to the latter's object and purpose. Otherwise, the Committee argued, the Covenant "would be largely deprived of its raison d'être".[37]

As originally formulated in GC 3, the doctrine affirmed that "a minimum core obligation to ensure the satisfaction of, at the very least, minimum essential levels of each of the rights is incumbent upon every State party". This general affirmation was followed by a few examples that should have helped to determine the core content of some rights: depriving a *significant* number of individuals "of essential foodstuffs, of essential primary health care, of basic shelter and housing, or of the most basic forms of education". By contrast, the Committee did not provide general criteria to ascertain the minimum core content. Rather, in its practice it relied on the reports of States parties and the constructive dialogue engaged with them in order to establish such a minimum core.[38]

It was only in 1999 (while adopting GC 12 on the right to adequate food) that the CESCR tried to elaborate on the elements of the core content with respect to a specific right. According to the Committee, the core content of the right to adequate food implies:

> The availability of food in a quantity and quality sufficient to satisfy the dietary needs of individuals, free from adverse substances, and acceptable within a given culture;
>
> The accessibility of such food in ways that are sustainable and that do not interfere with the enjoyment of other human rights[39]

However, the inherent difficulties in concretely identifying the minimum essential level of each right have compelled the Committee to abandon this effort almost immediately and to instead focus, since GC 13, on a more pragmatic approach:[40] to

---

[37]GC 3, para. 10. The idea of a "minimum core" was originally developed by Philip Alston—who then became the first chairperson of the CESCR—in a seminal article published in 1987 (Alston 1987, pp. 332–381) and was meant to apply to all human rights indistinctly.

[38]The reliance on State practice was also at the basis of the minimum core approach. Indeed, in General Comment 3, the CESCR established its new doctrine on "the extensive experience gained by the Committee, as well as by the body that preceded it, over a period of more than a decade of examining States parties' reports" (GC 3, para. 10).

[39]GC 12, para. 8.

[40]Sepulveda (2003), p. 368.

define the "core obligations" of substantive rights.[41] Sofar, the Committee has defined core obligations more or less extensively with respect to multiple rights contained in the Covenant.[42] In GC 14, on the right to health, these obligations are very extensive and are followed by obligations "of comparable priority". In other GCs, like that on the right to work, core obligations are instead much more general and essential.

As will be seen in greater depth in the following paragraph, the CESCR has also identified international responsibilities, for developed States as well as those that are "in a position to assist", to ensure the minimum core of ESC rights[43] of all in a disaster situation.[44]

Minimum core obligations have been defined by Tasioulas as "obligations of 'immediate effect' to which the doctrine of 'progressive realisation' is inapplicable".[45] According to this author, their value consists in "help[ing] address the problem of how to prioritize compliance with human rights obligations in the context of resource limitations by setting a minimum standard that applies to all states irrespective of differences among them".[46] As a whole, this reading can be said to correctly describe (despite minor inconsistencies) the CESCR's minimum core approach.

When first devising its approach in GC 3, the Committee conceded that "any assessment as to whether a State has discharged its minimum core obligation must also take account of resource constraints applying within the country concerned",[47] but that in the case of inability to comply with its minimum core obligations, the State party "must demonstrate that every effort has been made to use all resources that are at its disposition in an effort to satisfy, as a matter of priority, those minimum obligations".[48] The CESCR then clarified that the phrase "to the maximum of its available resources" was intended by the drafters to additionally cover the resources that are "available from the international community through international cooperation and assistance".[49] The same reasoning was reproposed in GC 12. Here the CESCR, after affirming that "States have a core obligation to take the necessary

---

[41]Young argues that "[t]he Committee now uses the 'core obligations' list to outline the necessary steps of 'operationalizing' rights and attempts to circumvent the difficult questions of form and content of legal entitlement" (Young 2008, p. 152).

[42]The different extent of these obligations has been questioned by various authors, such as K. Mechlem and K.G. Young.

[43]CESCR, Substantive issues arising in the implementation of the International Covenant on economic, social and cultural rights: poverty and the International Covenant on economic, social and cultural rights—Statement adopted by the Committee on economic, social and cultural rights on 4 May 2001, E/C.12/2001/10, 10 May 2001, para. 16.

[44]GC 12, para. 38.

[45]Tasioulas (2017).

[46]Ibid.

[47]GC 3, para. 10.

[48]Ibid.

[49]GC 3, para. 13.

action to mitigate and alleviate hunger [...] even in times of natural or other disasters",[50] allowed that "[a] State claiming that it is unable to carry out its obligation [to provide access to food] for reasons beyond its control [...] has the burden of proving that this is the case and that it has unsuccessfully sought to obtain international support".[51]

At the beginning of the 2000s, however, the tones utilised by the Committee became more categorical. In its GCs 14 and 15—related to rights to health and water, respectively—as well as in the Statement on poverty, the Committee stated that core obligations are absolutely *non-derogable*.[52] As a result, they continue to apply even "in situations of conflict, emergency and natural disaster".[53] Such uncompromising statements, if applied in practice, would have prevented a State party from justifying its non-compliance even in a case of dire straits. Moreover, the reference to non-derogability appeared excessively rigid and somewhat misplaced in the context of a treaty that does not contain a derogation clause and whose pivotal notion is rather that of "a state's maximum available resources". Additionally, this interpretation was affirmed at a moment in time when the CESCR was developing highly detailed and encompassing lists of core obligations with respect to the rights to health and to water,[54] and could thus become extremely and disproportionately punitive vis-à-vis poor countries.

---

[50] GC 12, para. 6.

[51] GC 12, para. 17.

[52] "If resource constraints render it impossible for a State to comply fully with its Covenant obligations, it has the burden of justifying that every effort has nevertheless been made to use all available resources at its disposal in order to satisfy, as a matter of priority, the obligations outlined above. It should be stressed, however, that a State party cannot, under any circumstances whatsoever, justify its non-compliance with the core obligations set out in paragraph 43 above, which are nonderogable" (GC 14, para. 47). Along similar lines, in GC 15 the CESCR affirms that "a State party cannot justify its non-compliance with the core obligations set out in paragraph 37 above, which are non-derogable" (para. 40).

[53] CESCR, Substantive issues arising in the implementation of the International Covenant on economic, social and cultural rights: poverty and the International Covenant on economic, social and cultural rights—Statement, E/C.12/2001/10, 4 May 2001, para. 18.

[54] For a partially different reading cf. De Schutter (2005). The author, referring to the core obligations related to the right to health affirmed in GC 14, asserts that these obligations are either of a procedural character or "de nature substantielle mais définies à un niveau tel que l'on peut présumer que même les pays les moins avancés devraient pouvoir s'en acquitter" (ibid., p. 16). Immediately afterwards, however, he adds that the categorical formulation utilised by the CESCR cannot be taken literally with the result of totally excluding situations of non compliance. Rather, "il doit demeurer possible à l'Etat de faire valoir que des circonstances échappant à son contrôle (telles, par exemple, qu'une catastrophe naturelle ou un conflit armé, combiné au refus de l'assistance ou de la coopération internationale d'autres Etats) ont fait obstacle à ce qu'il puisse respecter même ce niveau minimum d'obligation" (ibid.). According to various authors, non-compliance with ESC rights in disaster settings could also be excused by invoking either Art. 61 of the VCLT ("supervening impossibility of performance") or force majeure (cf. e.g. Sepulveda 2003, pp. 297–298; Sommario 2012, p. 344). *Force majeure* as an excuse for non-performance is also recognised by the Maastricht Guidelines on Violations of Economic, Social and Cultural Rights (cf. Guideline 14(f)).

That the Committee went too far in depicting core obligations as automatically and unequivocally non-derogable has been proved by its subsequent practice.[55] Non-derogability is never mentioned again in the subsequent documents issued by the CESCR, which instead embrace the justification for non-compliance originally admitted in GC 3.[56] Moreover, the qualification of core obligations as inderogable is not supported by State practice.

In sum, it can be said that the Committee, despite the transient inconsistencies just reported, has succeeded over time in delineating a convincing reading of the Covenant that indicates how to guarantee the immediate and universal application of its minimum core without disavowing the concept of progressive realisation. Importantly, in various occasions the CESCR also emphasised the crucial need to apply the treaty even in situations of emergency, like those prevailing after a disaster. At the same time, however, it has recognised that ad impossibilia nemo tenetur. Whenever a State party does not have sufficient resources for complying with its core obligations and it is able to prove that it has sought to acquire resources through international assistance without success, it will not be considered in a situation of non-compliance. The fundamental role of international cooperation and assistance in this respect is highlighted in GC 15, where it is recognised that such cooperation "especially economic and technical [. . .] *enables* developing countries to fulfil their core obligations".[57]

The main criticisms that have been addressed over time at the CESCR's core approach assert that such a doctrine primarily targets developing or poor countries[58] and that it is premised on a universality that does not exist in reality.[59] While there is certainly a need for the Committee to further articulate the notion of minimum core obligations, these criticisms can be rejected. Indeed, it is argued that the CESCR's approach provides an interpretation of the treaty that is apt to guarantee the latter's raison d'être, which consists in the full realisation of the ESC rights recognised therein, by identifying obligations that must be complied with immediately. In other terms, core obligations have the value of preventing States parties from instrumentally invoking the notion of progressive realisation in order to indefinitely postpone the engagement they assumed by signing the Covenant. In the words of Alston, the minimum core is "an absolute minimum entitlement, in the absence of which a state party is considered to be in violation of its obligations".[60]

[55] According to Tasioulas, the CESCR's interpretation was contestable, first of all because it had limited support in practice (Tasioulas 2017, p. 17).

[56] Cf. GC 19 para. 60 on right to social security (Art. 9) and GC 18 para. 32; Statement on 'An Evaluation of the Obligation to Take Steps to the "Maximum of Available Resources" under an Optional Protocol to the Covenant', E/C.12/2007/1, para. 6.

[57] GC 15, para. 38 (emphasis added).

[58] Craven (1995), p. 152.

[59] See generally Young (2008).

[60] Alston (1987), p. 353.

Since the signing of the Covenant, a doctrinal debate has emerged on whether the standard on which to measure compliance should be established at the international level, thus setting a universal and geographically invariant standard, or at the domestic level. In principle, the minimum standard can only be the same for every country on pain of denying that human rights are universal.[61] Moreover, the formulation of country-based thresholds could prove to be "almost an impossible task".[62] The Committee, while embracing a universal standard, has nonetheless 'corrected' it in order to reduce the imbalances that would result from its rigid application as well as to take account of the resources *actually* available to each State party. This flexibility is evident, as already mentioned, from the fact that poorer countries or countries experiencing an emergency are granted the possibility of justifying non-compliance based on a lack of international assistance. Additionally, in its monitoring practice the CESCR has invoked the respect of core obligations equally by lower income and higher income countries, thereby rebutting concerns that the core approach would have ultimately disproportionately focused on poor countries.[63] Evidence of such an attitude can also be found in its practice following the 2008 global financial crisis. Certainly, while recognising the inevitability of austerity measures,[64] the Committee required that such measures neither involved the protec-

[61]"To make the content of human rights obligations, whether they be core or non-core, a function of the resource capacities of state would transgress the 'one world, one standard' idea that animates IHRL" (Tasioulas 2017, p. 23). According to Ssenyonjo "there would be no point in having a minimum core of state responsibility if it were state-specific and not universal" (Ssenyonjo 2009, p. 66). A universal, absolute standard is affirmed in the Limburg Principles on the Implementation of the International Covenant on Economic, Social and Cultural Rights, Annex, E/CN.4/1987/17 (June 2–6, 1986) ("States parties are obligated, regardless of the level of economic development, to ensure respect for minimum subsistence rights for all") and in the Maastricht Guidelines on Violations of Economic, Social and Cultural Rights, E/C.12/2000/13 ("Such minimum core obligations apply irrespective of the availability of resources of the country concerned or any other factors and difficulties").

[62]Toebes (1999), p. 279.

[63]Cf. Warwick (2017), p. 9, who bases himself on the review of the CESCR's Concluding Observations over the time period 1999–2016. The CESCR has thus put in practice its affirmation that "because poverty is a global phenomenon, core obligations have great relevance to some individuals and communities living in the richest States" (E/C.12/2001/10, para. 18).

[64]The attitude of the Committee towards the austerity measures taken by multiple States parties after the 2008 crisis was the object of harsh critiques (see e.g. Warwick 2018, pp. 127–149). Nevertheless, by reminding States of the cruciality of the Covenant's minimum core content the CESCR has reiterated the existence of a basic threshold of protection to be respected at all times.

tion of the minimum core content of rights,[65] nor disproportionately affected "the rights of the disadvantaged and marginalized individuals and groups".[66]

Nevertheless, the function of the minimum core approach does not end with determining what States must accomplish first while taking steps to fully realise the ICESCR's rights.[67] Indeed, at the international level it was utilised by the Committee to additionally affirm a duty upon the international community—or rather "richer countries"[68]—to assist those States parties that do not have sufficient resources internally. As was clearly stated by CESCR's member Paul Hunt, core obligations and obligations pertaining to international cooperation under Art 2.1 "should be seen as two halves of a package".[69]

7.1.2 Tripartite Classification of State Obligations

The second major doctrinal construct developed by the CESCR that has a bearing on the interpretation of Art. 2.1 is typically referred to as the tripartite typology or the tripartite classification of State obligations. In its original formulation, the doctrine was devised by Henry Shue, who notoriously rejected the distinction between

[65]The protection of the minimum core content is one of the criteria laid down by the CESCR in 2012 to examine the permissibility of retrogressive measures following the global crisis (cf. Pillay A.G. (Chairperson of CESCR), Letter dated 16 May 2012 addressed by the Chairperson of the CESCR to States parties to the International Covenant on Economic, Social and Cultural Rights, CESCR/49th/SP/MAB/SW, 4 June 2012, 2). See also CESCR, Public debt, austerity measures and the International Covenant on Economic, Social and Cultural Rights. Statement by the Committee on Economic, Social and Cultural Rights, E/C.12/2016/1, 22 July 2016, para. 4. See also the following Concluding Observations: United Kingdom, E/C.12/GBR/CO/6, 14 July 2016, paras. 18–19; Spain, E/C.12/ESP/CO/6, 25 April 2018 para. 14; Argentina, E.C.12/ARG/CO/4, 12 October 2018, para. 6; Bulgaria, E/C.12/BGR/CO/6, 8 March 2019 para. 9. Additionally, in the Concluding Observations on Germany the CESCR "recommends that the State party make every effort to exercise its great leverage to ensure that all international financial institutions of which it is a State member ensure that the conditionalities attached to a loan do not lead borrowing States to violate their obligations under the Covenant. In particular, these conditionalities should not lead to [. . .] the violation of core obligations required by the Covenant, or have a disproportionate impact on marginalized individuals and groups" (E/C.12/DEU/CO/6, 27 November 2018, para. 17).

[66]Cf. Pillay A.G. (Chairperson of CESCR), Letter cit. See also the following Concluding Observations: Spain, 6 June 2012, E/C.12/ESP/CO/5, para. 28; Spain 2018, para. 14; Argentina 2018, para. 6; Bulgaria, 11 December 2012, E/C.12/BGR/CO/4-5, para. 11; New Zealand, 31 May 2012, E/C.12/NZL/CO/3, para. 17.

[67]"[A]fter a State party has ensured the core obligations of economic, social and cultural rights, it continues to have an obligation to move as expeditiously and effectively as possible towards the full realization of all the rights in the Covenant" (E/C.12/2001/10, para. 18).

[68]Sic Paul Hunt in E/C.12/2000/SR.10, para. 27.

[69]Ibid. The fundamental link between the two sets of obligations is also recognised by Young, who asserts: "[a] minimalist definition of economic and social rights is needed to mediate the legal, as well as political and philosophical, challenges of holding states accountable for the socioeconomic deprivations experienced by citizens in other states" (Young 2008, p. 123).

negative and positive rights and instead suggested that the fulfilment of each "basic" right[70] implies the following three categories of "duties": to avoid depriving, to protect from deprivation and to aid the deprived.[71] The tripartite classification was then reformulated, with some alterations, by Asbjorn Eide, who referred to the obligations to respect, protect and fulfil.[72] Eide played an important role in the vulgarisation of the typology and in its success as a tool to interpret the right to food as well as ESC rights as a whole. Indeed, his typology was utilised in the Maastricht Guidelines on Violations of Economic, Social and Cultural Rights[73] and then employed by the CESCR in its GCs since 1999.

The tripartite typology was first espoused by the Committee in its GC 12 and has since been used systematically in subsequent GCs.[74] As embraced by the CESCR, the three levels of State obligations can be summarised as follows.[75] The obligation to respect expresses a negative duty of abstention, by requiring States to refrain from any measure that results in denying or limiting access to the enjoyment of the ICE SCR's rights. The obligations to protect and fullfil instead have a positive character. The obligation to protect, in particular, entails the adoption by States of all the necessary measures apt to protect individuals under their jurisdiction from violations of the Covenant's rights committed by third parties. The obligation to fulfill is more composite and includes the sub-obligations to facilitate, to provide and to promote.[76] As a whole this tertiary level can be defined as requiring a series of actions by the State intended to concretely support individuals and communities in the enjoyment of the ICESCR's rights. Contrary to the obligation to protect, the obligation to fulfil is primarily composed of positive obligations with which the State *itself* and *alone* must comply. Despite its inevitable flaws,[77] the doctrine has facilitated the justiciability of ESC rights at both the international and the domestic level[78] and its influence has not been limited to the right to food.

---

[70]Shue distinguished basic rights into three categories, namely security, subsistence and liberty.

[71]Shue (1980), pp. 52–60. Remarkably, the third category of duties has amongs its beneficiaries those "who are victims of natural disasters" (ibid., 59).

[72]UN Commission on Human Rights, Report on the right to adequate food as a human right submitted by Mr. Asbjorn Eide, Special Rapporteur, E./CN.4/Sub.2/1987/23, 7 July 1987.

[73]Cf. Maastricht Guideline No. 6.

[74]To be true, the Outline for drafting general comments on specific rights of the International Covenant on Economic, Social and Cultural Rights, which was adopted by the CESCR during the same session, in the section concerning "State party's obligations" also referred to two other typologies of State obligations, namely "obligations of immediacy; obligations of progressive realisation" and "obligations of conduct; obligations of result" (E/C.12/1999/11, Annex IX, 19 November 1999, pp. 135–136). Nonetheless, the Committee in its practice has preferred to resort to the typology developed by Shue and Eide, which is also "the only one specifically geared to State duties imposed by human rights (and) is widely applied by scholars" (Sepulveda 2003, p. 174).

[75]Cf. GC 12, para. 15; GC 13, para. 46; GC 14, paras. 34–37.

[76]GC 12, para. 15. The obligation to fulfill (promote) was added to the list of States parties' obligations in GC 14, para. 33.

[77]See for all Koch (2005), pp. 81–103.

[78]De Schutter (2010), p. 248.

The tripartite typology has been accordingly applied to States parties' transnational obligations.[79] This practice was inaugurated by the CESCR in the same GC 12, which for the first time included a dedicated section entitled "International obligations". From then on, GCs generally contain such a section, where the Committee variously describe the transnational obligations and responsibilities of (developed) States parties as well as of other actors within the international community.

The obligation to respect, in its international dimension, requires States parties to refrain from actions that interfere, whether directly or indirectly, with the enjoyment of ESC rights in other States.[80] In other words, States parties should evaluate the impact of the measures they take on such rights, to the extent that these measures can affect the enjoyment of rights in other States. Accordingly, States parties should avoid at all times participating in embargoes or similar measures that prevent the supply of food, water or other commodities essential for securing the Covenant's rights.[81] States parties should also take into account these rights when entering into bilateral or multilateral agreements.[82] Furthermore, the CESCR has indicated that the obligation to respect is applicable to development cooperation programmes promoted by developed countries. Observing that "[m]any activities undertaken in the name of development have subsequently been recognized as ill-conceived and even counterproductive in human rights terms",[83] it called for "a human rights impact assessment [. . .] of major development cooperation activities".[84] As will be seen later in this section, though, this early reference to the respect of human rights standards in development activities was for a long time not recalled, as true also of the object of pertinent recommendations to individual States parties. Last but not least, the Committee has remarked on various occasions that the international obligation to respect ESC rights is equally addressed to international organisations,

---

[79]We prefer to utilise the adjective 'transnational' to 'international' or 'extraterritorial'. Indeed, the qualifier 'international', which is used by the CESCR, is too general and thus confusing, while 'extraterritorial' implies an element of control, which is not a feature of all transnational obligations.

[80]CESCR, General Comment 15, para. 31. Ssenyonjo remarks that such obligation of abstention "is consistent with international law, which provides a general duty on states not to act in such a way as to cause harm outside their territories" (Ssenyonjo 2009, p. 73).

[81]"States parties should refrain at all times from food embargoes or similar measures which endanger conditions for food production and access to food in other countries" (GC 12, para. 37). See, similarly, GC 14, para. 41, and GC 15, para. 32. The impact of sanctions on the enjoyment of the ICESCR's rights was the object of General Comment 8, where the Committee inter alia affirms that "these rights must be taken fully into account when designing an appropriate sanctions regime" (GC 8, para. 12).

[82]"[T]he failure of the State to take into account its legal obligations regarding the right to health when entering into bilateral or multilateral agreements with other States, international organizations and other entities, such as multinational corporations" is cited as an example of violations of the obligation to respect (cf. GC 14, para. 50). However, the cited obligation has a positive character and should thus more correctly be classified as an obligation to "protect" (Sepulveda 2003, p. 200).

[83]General Comment 2, International Technical Assistance Measures, 2 February 1990, para. 7.

[84]Ibidem, para. 8. See also Concluding Observations on United Kingdom 2016, para. 15(a).

in primis financial institutions such as the IMF and the World Bank. Since the early 2000s, it has highlighted in particular that such entities "should pay greater attention to the protection of [ESC rights] in their lending policies, credit agreements and structural adjustment programmes".[85]

Under the obligation to protect States parties to the ICESCR, to the extent that they can influence third parties such as "individuals, groups, corporations and other entities as well as agents acting under their authority",[86] must prevent the latter from violating ESC rights in other countries through legal and political means in accordance with the UN Charter and applicable international law.[87] Moreover, they should ensure that their actions as members of international organisations, notably financial institutions, take due account of ESC rights in other countries.[88] The latter obligation is more compelling on those countries with a certain degree of economic and political leverage and it is accordingly recalled by the Committee in its Concluding Observations addressed to developed States like Germany and France.[89] Such countries are encouraged to do "all [they] can to ensure that the policies and decisions of those organisations are in conformity with the obligations of States parties to the Covenant, in particular the obligations contained in article 2, paragraph 1, articles 11, 15, 22 and 23 concerning international assistance and co-operation".[90]

---

[85]GC 14, para. 64. See also GC 12, para. 41; GC 13, para. 60; GC 15, para. 60.

[86]GC 15, para. 23.

[87]Cf. e.g. GC 14, para. 39; GC 15, para. 33; GC 19, para. 54. This level of obligation was defined in the Maastricht Guidelines as follows: "the obligation to protect includes the State's responsibility to ensure that private entities or individuals, including transnational corporations over which they exercise jurisdiction, do not deprive individuals of their economic, social and cultural rights. States are responsible for violations of economic, social and cultural rights that result from their failure to exercise due diligence in controlling the behaviour of such non-State actors" (Maastricht Guidelines, para. 18).

[88]Cf. e.g. GC 19, para. 58.

[89]The different position of developed States is evident, albeit not clearly stated, in the Maastricht Guidelines: "Member States of such organizations, individually or through the governing bodies, as well as the secretariat and nongovernmental organizations should encourage and generalize the trend of several such organizations to revise their policies and programmes to take into account issues of economic, social and cultural rights, especially when these policies and programmes are implemented in countries that lack the resources to resist the pressure brought by international institutions on their decision-making affecting economic, social and cultural rights" (Maastricht Guidelines, para. 19).

[90]Concluding Observations on Germany, E/C.12/1/Add.68, 24 September 2001, para. 31 and E/C.12/DEU/CO/6, 27 November 2018, para. 13. See also Concluding Observations on France, E/C.12/1/Add.72, 30 November 2001, para. 32 and E/C.12/FRA/CO/4, 13 July 2016, para. 11. "States parties that are members of international financial institutions, in particular the International Monetary Fund, the World Bank and regional development banks, should pay greater attention to the protection of the right to work in *influencing* the lending policies, credit agreements, structural adjustment programmes and international measures of these institutions" (GC 18, para. 30, emphasis added). Similar language is utilised by the Maastricht Guidelines: "It is particularly important for States to use their *influence* to ensure that violations do not result from the programmes and policies of the organizations of which they are members" (para. 19, emphasis added).

This clearly implies "a much more active role aimed at the implementation of the Covenant, particularly the obligation to assist and cooperate with other States".[91]

Last but not least, transnational obligations also concern the obligation to fulfil, which in its international dimension has proved to be the most controversial one. As much as for its internal application, the Committee has distinguished between three sub-levels: to facilitate, to provide and to promote.

The obligation to fulfil-facilitate has not been clearly defined, but most plausibly it requires that States parties take active measures aimed at supporting the enjoyment of ICESCR's rights in other countries.[92] For instance, the CESCR has referred to the international obligation of States parties "to take steps [. . .] to facilitate access to food",[93] or to "facilitate access to essential health facilities, goods and services in other countries".[94] Additionally, the transnational obligation to facilitate the right to food implies that food aid "should be organized in ways that facilitate the return to food self-reliance of the beneficiaries".[95] The Committee has sometimes rendered this contingent on the availability of resources, but it has also singled out "economically developed States parties [as] hav[ing] a special responsibility and interest to assist developing States in this regard".[96] Notably, it has stressed that "it is particularly incumbent on all those who can assist, to help developing countries respect this international minimum threshold".[97]

Moreover, with respect to the right to education, the CESCR has affirmed that "[w]here a state party clearly lacks the financial resources and/or expertise required to 'work out and adopt' a detailed plan of action for primary education, the international community has a clear obligation to assist".[98] However, in this case the duty-bearers are not the State parties, but relevant international agencies to which States in need are required to address their requests for assistance.[99]

The obligation to fulfil-promote has not been specifically referred to by the CESCR in its international dimension. An exception in this respect is constituted by Art. 6, related to the right to work. According to the Committee, "[t]o comply with their international obligations in relation to article 6, States parties should endeavour to promote the right to work in other countries as well as in bilateral

[91]Sepulveda (2006), p. 284.

[92]Sepulveda (2006), p. 285.

[93]GC 12, para. 36.

[94]GC 14, para. 39.

[95]GC 12, para. 39.

[96]GC 14, para. 40; GC 15 para. 34; GC 19 para. 55; GC 23, para. 67.

[97]E/C.12/2001/10, para. 17. See also GC 14, para. 40.

[98]GC 11, para. 9.

[99]"[I]n appropriate cases, the Committee encourages States parties to seek the assistance of relevant international agencies, including the International Labour Organization (ILO), the United Nations Development Programme (UNDP), the United Nations Educational, Scientific and Cultural Organization (UNESCO), the United Nations Children's Fund (UNICEF), the International Monetary Fund (IMF) and the World Bank, in relation both to the preparation of plans of action under article 14 and their subsequent implementation" (ibid., para. 11).

and multilateral negotiations".[100] Moreover, they "should respond to [...] requests [for international assistance and cooperation] [...] by promoting transnational dialogue between employer and worker organizations, among other measures".[101]

The Committee has instead devoted most of its attention to the obligation to fulfil-provide. This preferential interest has been evident since General Comment 3, when the CESCR argued that "international cooperation for development and *thus* for the realization of economic, social and cultural rights is an obligation of all States".[102] In subsequent practice the content of the obligation to provide has been developed essentially in reference to disaster and humanitarian relief on the one hand and development cooperation on the other.

A general outline of the respective responsibilities of States parties and the international community as a whole is found in General Comment 14:

> States parties have a joint and individual responsibility, in accordance with the Charter of the United Nations and relevant resolutions of the United Nations General Assembly and of the World Health Assembly, to cooperate in providing disaster relief and humanitarian assistance in times of emergency, including assistance to refugees and internally displaced persons. Each State should contribute to this task to the maximum of its capacities. Priority in the provision of international medical aid, distribution and management of resources, such as safe and potable water, food and medical supplies, and financial aid should be given to the most vulnerable or marginalized groups of the population.[103]
>
> [...][I]t is particularly incumbent on States parties and other actors in a position to assist, to provide 'international assistance and cooperation, especially economic and technical' which enable developing countries to fulfil their core and other obligations.[104]

While General Comment 14 is concerned specifically with the right to health, the cited paragraph clearly takes a broader perspective and can thus be said to elucidate the CESCR's general approach to transnational obligations to fulfil-provide. Of relevance is, in particular, the fact that after having affirmed the existence of both a joint and individual responsibility to cooperate, the position of those actors "in a position to assist" is singled out. This distinction thus furnishes practical application to the criterium of the maximum of available resources. More frequently, the Committee instead refers to developed countries. The existence of a special "responsibility" on those countries having the necessary resources or capacity is reiterated several times in GCs and assumes a particular cogency when the assistance to be provided concerns a disaster situation or a humanitarian emergency.[105] Moreover, in

---

[100] GC 18, para. 30. Lacking indications from the CESCR, Sepulveda argues that "it is safe to say that this level would require that international assistance and cooperation programmes aim to increase the awareness of Covenant rights in the recipient country and empower people to identify and claim their rights" (Sepulveda 2006, p. 289).

[101] GC 23 para. 67.

[102] GC 3, para. 14 (emphasis added).

[103] GC 14, para. 40. See also GC 12, para. 38.

[104] GC 14, para. 45.

[105] GC 12, para. 38; GC 14, para. 40.

these latter situations "priority is to be given to Covenant rights".[106] In its Statement on the World Food Crisis, the CESCR also recommended to donor States to "prioritize assistance to States most affected" by such crisis.[107]

When affirming the obligation to provide, the Committee has generally been quite cautious, preferring recommendatory to mandatory language. One exception may at first sight be found in GC 22, where it posits that "States that are in a position to do so *must respond to requests* [for assistance] in good faith and in accordance with the international commitment of contributing at a minimum 0.7 per cent of their gross national income for international cooperation and assistance".[108] Nonetheless, the obligation to respond does not necessarily imply an obligation to provide and indeed in the following General Comment 23, such obligations are clearly expressed in non-binding terms: "[d]epending on the availability of resources, States parties *should respond to such requests by providing* economic and technical assistance and technology transfer".[109]

More precise indications as to the concrete content of the obligation to fulfil-provide are given by the Committee in its Concluding Observations on the periodic reports submitted by States parties. In these documents, the CESCR focuses on a particular aspect of Official Development Assistance (ODA), i.e. the percentage of gross national product (GNP)—or gross national income (GNI)—that is allocated to the former. In reviewing States reports, the CESCR is indeed used to consider whether developed States parties have reached the UN target of 0.7 per cent of GNP devoted to ODA,[110] or have at least made progress towards its attainment. Accordingly, it has expressed regret towards countries that are well below the 0.7 target[111] or that have decreased the percentage of their GNP allocated to ODA,[112] while conversely exhibiting satisfaction vis-à-vis those (admittedly few) States that have exceeded their targets.[113] In general, it "recommends" or "encourages" developed States parties "to progressively increase the level of [their] official development

[106]GC 15, para. 34.

[107]CESCR, The World Food Crisis. Statement, E/C.12/2008/1, 19 May 2008, para. 11.

[108]GC 22, para. 50, emphasis added.

[109]GC 23, para. 67.

[110]The 0.7 goal was the object of an international (political) commitment, at first declared in December 1961, at the launching of the First United Nations Development Decade, and then constantly reiterated, lastly in the Addis Ababa Action Agenda, the Sustainable Development Goals and the Sendai Framework for Action.

[111]See e.g. CESCR, Concluding Observations: Finland, E/C.12/1/Add.52, 1 December 2000, paras. 13 and 23; Belgium, E.C.12/1/Add.54, 1 December 2000, paras. 16 and 30; Germany, E/C.12/1/Add.68 (24 September 2001), paras. 15 and 33; Iceland, E/C.12/1/Add.89 (23 May 2003), paras. 11 and 20; Italy, E/C.12/1/Add.103, 14 December 2004, para. 15; Spain, E/C.12/1/Add.99, 7 June 2004, paras. 10 and 27; Republic of Korea, E/C.12/KOR/CO/4, 19 October 2017, para. 20; Switzerland, E/C.12/CHE/CO/4, 18 November 2019, para. 17.

[112]France, E/C.12/1/Add. 72, 30 November 2001, para. 14; Italy, E./C.12/ITA/CO/5, 28 October 2015, para. 12.

[113]See e.g. CESCR, Concluding Observations: Denmark, E/C.12/1/Add.34, 14 May 1999, para. 11 and E/C.12/1/Add.102, 14 December 2004, para. 5; Luxembourg, E/C.12/1/Add.86, 23 May

assistance, with a view to achieving the international commitment of 0.7 per cent".[114]

While ODA has become the main focus of attention with respect to the obligation to provide, a parallel concern with regard to the obligation to respect was affirmed only recently by the CESCR. Indeed, references to the need to respect human rights standards in development policies were for a long time quite rare in the CESCR's Concluding Observations.[115] For instance, in 2002, the Committee recommended to Slovakia that human rights, including ESC rights, be reflected in its ODA policy.[116] In 2005, it instead requested that Norway provide information on the measures taken to ensure compliance with the ICESCR obligations in its international development cooperation.[117] A turning point in this regard was the 2012 Statement in the context of the Rio+20 Conference on "the green economy in the context of sustainable development and poverty eradication". In this document, the CESCR highlighted "the importance of raising [. . .] ODA contributions to 0.7 per cent of gross national income and *ensuring that ODA promotes sustainable development by adopting a human rights-based approach to development*".[118] From then on, the Committee has routinely recommended to States parties "to pursue a human rights-based approach, including human rights impact assessments" in their development cooperation policy.[119] In several Concluding Observations, the CESCR has also identified the following key points of such an approach: (1) undertaking of a systematic and independent human rights impact assessment prior to decision making on development cooperation projects; (2) establishing an effective monitoring mechanism to regularly assess the human rights impact of ODA policies and projects in the receiving countries and to take remedial measures when required; (3) ensuring that there is an accessible complaint mechanism for violations of economic, social and

2003, para. 6; Sweden, E/C.12/1/Add.70, 30 November 2001, para. 7; Norway, E/C.12/1/Add.109, 23 June 2005, para. 3.

[114]CESCR, Concluding Observations on Australia 2017, para. 8; Concluding Observations on Netherlands 2017, para. 10; Concluding Observations on Liechtenstein 2017, para. 8; Concluding Observations on Italy 2015, para. 13; Concluding Observations on Spain 2004, para. 27.

[115]Writing in 2011, Coomans affirms that the "actual effect [of development assistance] on human rights [. . .] has, so far, been ignored by the Committee" (Coomans 2011, p. 28).

[116]Concluding Observations on Slovakia, 2002, para. 21.

[117]CESCR, Concluding Observations on Norway 2005, para. 25 See also Concluding Observations on New Zealand 2011, where the CESCR expressed its appreciation towards "the State party's policy of mainstreaming of human rights in its development cooperation programmes" (para. 7).

[118]E/C.12/2012/1, para. 6 (a), emphasis added.

[119]Concluding Observations on Netherlands 2017, para. 10. See also Concluding Observations on Australia 2017, para. 8; Concluding Observations on Liechtenstein 2017, para. 8; Concluding Observations on France 2016, para. 8; Concluding Observations on Canada 2016, para. 12; Concluding Observations on Italy 2015, para. 13; Concluding Observations Ireland on 2015, para. 36; Concluding Observations on Czech Republic 2014, para. 22; Concluding Observations on Japan 2013, para. 32, Concluding Observations on the Russian Federation, E/C.12/RUS/CO/6, 16 October 2017, para. 21.

cultural rights in the receiving countries embedded in the framework for development cooperation projects.[120]

In sum, the tripartite classification of States' obligations has proved to be an invaluable tool in the hands of the CESCR and has benefited from high levels of acceptance by scholarship[121] as well as by States parties.[122] Although it needs further development, its importance cannot be underestimated. Indeed, its application to ESC rights has contributed enormously to clarifying corresponding States' obligations and has the potential to facilitate an expansive interpretation of these obligations. Nonetheless, its relationship with the minimum core obligations and/or the minimum core content of rights should be clarified. Indeed, apart from some scant and vague references,[123] so far the CESCR has utilised the two constructs as distinct categories.[124] Such reluctance to clarify the relationship between the two doctrines makes minimum core obligations "appear incompletely articulated, while also rendering the 'tripartite classification' less clearly articulated than it could be".[125]

7.1.3 Taking Stock of International Cooperation Duties Under the ICESCR

International cooperation plays a key role under the ICESCR and, primarily through Art. 2.1, imposes legal obligations on States Parties. In this respect, Art. 2.1 perfectly epitomises the peculiar character of the Covenant, first of all vis-à-vis the ICCPR, as "an instrument where the full realisation of the rights that it recognises is not exclusively a function of the action or inaction of States parties in isolation, but also of the interaction between States".[126] Even admitting that the position asserting

[120]CESCR, Concluding Observations on UK 2016. See also Concluding Observations on Austria 2013, para. 1; Concluding Observations on China 2014, para. 13; Spain 2016, para. 15.

[121]With her systematic attack on the tripartite classification, Koch is an exception (Koch 2009).

[122]This stands in stark contrast with the strong critiques addressed by some States parties to the ICCPR towards the Human Rights Committee for its approach to States reservations.

[123]"[F]or the avoidance of any doubt, the Committee wishes to emphasise that it is particularly incumbent on States parties and other actors in a position to assist, to provide 'international assistance and cooperation, especially economic and technical' which enable developing countries to fulfil their core and other obligations" (General Comment 14, para. 45). A similar statement appear in General Comment 15, para. 38.

[124]This is shown most clearly by the same structure of General Comments, which generally devote two separate sections to minimum core obligations and the tripartite classification.

[125]Bódig (2016), p. 82.

[126]Are extraterritorial obligations reviewable p. 3. Remarkably, the ICESCR-Reporting Guidelines, in respect of implementing Art. 2.1, ask States parties to "[i]ndicate the impact of international economic and technical assistance and co-operation, *whether received or provided* by the State party, on the full realization of each of the Covenant rights in the State party or, as the case may be, *in other countries, especially developing countries*" (CESCR, Guidelines on treaty-specific

that the human rights responsibility of international cooperation and assistance is not underpinned by legal obligations, and thus "inescapably [it] fundamentally rest upon charity [...] might have been tenable in years gone by, it is unacceptable in the twenty-first century".[127]

As shown, the legal implications of the international dimension of Art. 2.1 have been clarified and progressively developed primarily as a result of the work undertaken by the CESCR. This has happened in particular through two doctrinal constructs—the minimum core approach and the tripartite classification of obligations—which have been successfully utilised by the Committee as a means of bypassing the limits, or better the prejudices that for a long time accompanied ESC rights, pre-empting their full implementation. The two constructs' persuasiveness and success has been proved, inter alia, by their subsequent adoption by the African Commission of Human and Peoples' Rights.[128]

The minimum core approach was developed in order to show that despite the fundamental notion of progressive realisation, there are some obligations that must be complied with by States parties immediately. Although essentially conceptualised to address the national dimension of implementation, it also played an important role with respect to international cooperation and assistance. Indeed, it provided an indispensable theoretical underpinning to the latter, by affirming its legal implications and at the same time by clearly circumscribing them.

However, the contribution of the tripartite typology is still more relevant for our purposes. It is mainly through this tool that the CESCR has progressively elaborated the actual content of the various transnational obligations stemming from Art. 2.1. As shown, its major contribution has concerned the obligation to fulfil, and notably the obligation to fulfil-provide, as the obligations to respect and to protect were already sufficiently investigated by the doctrine and have always been less controversial. More generally, however, the tripartite typology as applied to transnational obligations has had the merit of showing the breadth and the multifaceted nature of international cooperation and assistance under the Covenant. Apart from the obligation to fulfil—and more specifically of the sub-obligation to fulfil-provide, which has a subsidiary character—transnational obligations are generally not only complementary but also apply *simultaneously* to national ones.

A review of the CESCR's practice reveals that international cooperation and assistance is utilised both in a broad and in a restrictive sense. Stricto sensu, it is

---

documents to be submitted by States parties under articles 16 and 17 of the international Covenant on economic, social and cultural rights, Annex, 18 November 2008, in HRI/GEN/2/Rev.6, para. 9, p. 30, emphasis added).

[127]Paul Hunt (2008), A/HRC/7/11/Add.2, 5 March 2008, para. 133.

[128]Cf. African Commission of Human and Peoples' Rights, Principles and Guidelines on the Implementation of Economic, Social and Cultural Rights in the African Charter on Human and Peoples' Rights, in Report of the 48th Ordinary Session of the African Commission on Human and Peoples' Rights (10–24 November 2010, Banjul, The Gambia), para. 244.

practically identified with development cooperation. In so doing, the CESCR has incorporated in Art. 2.1 "a highly contentious element of inter-state economic relations",[129] which traditionally has always been considered too politically sensitive to be conceived in terms of rights and obligations. By now, references to ODA are routinely included in the assessment of States obligations made by CESCR, which is undeniably a success, albeit with some limits. The UN objective of devoting the 0.7 of GNP to ODA is regularly recalled by the CESCR, which has however avoided from qualifying it as an obligation. Nonetheless, from CESCR's practice it can be clearly deduced that developed States cannot unjustifiably reduce the level of their commitments in this respect without incurring in the risk of violating ICESCR's obligations, nor can they provide ODA in a discriminatory manner. Moreover, in recent times the CESCR has strongly and systematically required that States parties apply a human-rights based approach to development assistance.

As far as the obligation to fulfil-provide is concerned, we have remarked that the language utilised by the CESCR has been quite cautious. A clear-cut obligation to assist, in this respect, could be identified at most in exceptional circumstances, like those prevailing when a State party is stricken by a disaster or another humanitarian crisis that it cannot face with its own resources. In these cases, as more generally in situations in which a State party lacks sufficient resources, the CESCR has consistently and strongly required from the affected State to seek international assistance. A parallel obligation to provide for third States has not however been affirmed in equally clear and unambiguous terms. Nonetheless, the CESCR has constantly called upon developed States or those which are in a position to assist to provide aid when required.

When analysing the position of States parties vis-à-vis Art. 2.1, reference is generally made by the doctrine to the official statements pronounced during the negotiations of the Optional Protocol to the Covenant (OP).[130] The OP, which entered into force on 5 May 2013, was stipulated in order to finally provide the IC ESCR with some complaint and inquiry mechanisms analogous to those of the ICCPR. At the beginning of the discussions on the drafting of the OP, in 2005, the representatives of the United Kingdom, the Czech Republic, Canada, France and Portugal publicly affirmed to believe "that international cooperation and assistance was an important moral obligation but not a legal entitlement, and did not interpret the Covenant to impose a legal obligation to provide development assistance or give

[129] Sic Karimova (2016), p. 174.

[130] Consider however what was reported by M. Sepulveda, who represented the ESCR-NET and Steering Committee of the NGO Coalition for an Optional Protocol to the International Covenant on Economic, Social and Cultural Rights in the three sessions of the Open-Ended Working Group:

> From an observer's point of view, it appears that during the debate held at the OEWG sessions, for some government representatives the issue of international cooperation is a real concern that might influence their country support to an OP. However, for others it seems that the debate on the scope and content of the international obligations under Article 2(1) ICESCR is merely a tool to distract the debate trying to further delay any measure to enhance the supervisory procedure of the ICESCR. (Sepulveda 2006, p. 273).

a legal title to receive such aid".[131] At the same time, however, Portugal also remarked that "as a purely procedural instrument, an optional protocol would accommodate different views on the obligation of international assistance".[132] Furthermore, a year later Canada was alone to confirm its conviction that "international cooperation and assistance was a moral obligation, not a legal one".[133] For the rest, the positions expressed were quite mixed. In any case, even considering only the opinions of the richest States, a review of the travaux préparatoires reveals that just a few parties contested the ICESCR posing some *legal* obligations concerning international cooperation and assistance.[134] Moreover, these States were most probably driven by the concern that Art. 2.1, in its international dimension, could become justiciable.[135] Not coincidentally, similar concerns have resulted in the modest attention devoted to the issue of international assistance and cooperation by the OP. In this respect, the Protocol envisages the possibility for the CESCR to transmit, with the consent of the State party concerned, its recommendations to UN entities when international assistance is required. It also provides for the establishment of a trust fund.[136] Such a fund, to be financed through voluntary contributions, is aimed at providing expert and technical assistance for the enhanced implementation of the ICESCR's rights. Overall, therefore, neither the travaux préparatoires nor the text of the OP can be invoked to prove the disagreement of States parties regarding the existence of at least *some* transnational obligations flowing from the Covenant.

Nonetheless, nowadays it is generally agreed that the famous assertion of Alston and Quinn, according to whom the commitment to international cooperation declared in Art. 2.1 cannot be interpreted as imposing "a legally binding obligation upon any particular state to provide any particular form of assistance"[137] is still valid.[138] And this notwithstanding the undeniable advancements made by States parties, under the guidance of the CESCR, to implement ESC rights. At present the obligation to fulfil-provide is still "imperfect",[139] suffering indeed from a limitation which the CESCR could not overcome by itself. This limitation was acknowledged even by the experts authoring the Maastricht Guidelines, whose Principle 30 recommends to States to "coordinate with each other, *including in the allocation of*

[131] UN CHR, Report of the open-ended working group to consider options regarding the elaboration of an optional protocol to the International Covenant on Economic, Social and Cultural Rights on its second session, E/CN.4/2005/52, 10 February 2005, para. 76.

[132] Ibid., para. 78.

[133] E/CN.4/2006/47, para. 82.

[134] Hesselman (2018), pp. 71–73.

[135] In this sense, albeit in more dubitative terms, cf. Karimova (2016), p. 166.

[136] Cf. Art. 14 para. 3, OP.

[137] Alston and Quinn (1987), p. 191.

[138] "It is [. . .] unlikely that the Committee can direct a specific developed state to assist a particular developing state party since there are no criteria for doing so in the Covenant, and it is unlikely that the Committee would develop this in the near future" (Ssenyonjo 2009, p. 80).

[139] De Schutter (2014), p. 222.

responsibilities, in order to cooperate effectively in the universal fulfilment of economic, social and cultural rights".

7.2 International Cooperation Duties in Other UN Treaty Frameworks

Apart from the ICESCR, two other UN human rights treaties assign particular importance to international cooperation for the implementation of the rights they proclaim: the Convention on the Rights of the Child (CRC) and the Convention on the Rights of persons with Disabilities (CRPD). Furthermore, both treaties recognise various ESC rights and, similarly to the ICESCR, do not envisage the possibility of derogations. As a consequence, the rights enunciated therein must be guaranteed at all times, even in situations of emergency.[140] The respective monitoring bodies have thus drawn from CESCR's practice in interpreting and applying the CRC and the CRPD. Separate attention will now be devoted to each of these treaties, whose practice will help us to sketch an overall picture of the obligations of international cooperation that stem from international human rights law.

7.2.1 The Convention on the Rights of the Child

The CRC was signed in 1989—more than two decades after the ICESCR—and entered into force a year later.[141] Within the UN human rights treaty framework, this convention holds special importance, evidenced by the fact that, with the remarkable exception of the United States, it has enjoyed practically universal ratification. After the ICESCR, the CRC is the universal human rights treaty that includes most references to ESC rights.[142]

The CRC contains a general reference to international cooperation in Art. 4, which so provides:

> States Parties shall undertake all appropriate legislative, administrative, and other measures for the implementation of the rights recognized in the present Convention. With regard to economic, social and cultural rights, *States Parties shall undertake such measures* to the

[140]This point was specifically stressed by the Committee on the Rights of the Child: "It is important to emphasize that the Convention and the Optional Protocols thereto apply at all times and that there are no provisions allowing for derogation of their provisions during emergencies" (Committee on the Rights of the Child, General comment No. 16 (2013) on State obligations regarding the impact of the business sector on children's rights, CRC /C/GC/16, 17 April 2013, para. 49).

[141]The CRC was adopted by the UN GA on 2 November 1989 and entered into force on 2 September 1990.

[142]According to Van Bueren, the CRC protects thirteen different ESC rights (see Van Bueren 2008, p. 578).

> maximum extent of their available resources and, *where needed, within the framework of international cooperation.*[143]

As may be noted, contrary to the ICESCR, international assistance is not specifically mentioned and there is no reference to the "full realisation" of ESC rights. Nonetheless, although cooperation, as a broad(er) term, should logically encompass assistance,[144] "the importance of international co-operation for improving the living conditions of children in every country, in particular in the developing countries" is recognised at the end of the preamble.

The multiple references to international cooperation contained in the treaty text[145] were not the object of specific contestations by States during the negotiations,[146] thus implicitly revealing a consensus over their importance within the Convention. As for Art. 2.1 ICESCR, however, the vague and unspecified terms utilised had to be elucidated by the treaty's subsidiary body, the Committee on the Rights of the Child (CtRC). This was done in General Comment 5 (General measures of Implementation), where the CtRC clarified that Art. 4 implies that the implementation of the Convention requires from States parties the performance of both domestic and transnational obligations:

> The second sentence of article 4 reflects a realistic acceptance that lack of resources - financial and other resources - can hamper the full implementation of economic, social and cultural rights in some States [. . .] When States ratify the Convention, they take upon themselves obligations not only to implement it within their jurisdiction, but also to contribute, through international cooperation, to global implementation[147]

This view was confirmed during the "Day of general discussion on Resources for the rights of the child – responsibility of States", when the CtRC affirmed its belief that "children's rights are a shared responsibility between the developed and the developing countries".[148]

Nevertheless, apart from such general assertions, the CtRC has not focused in detail on the nature of transnational obligations, focusing instead almost exclusively

---

[143]Emphasis added. Other references to international cooperation can be found in particular in Art. 23.4 (recalling "the spirit of international cooperation") as well as in Arts. 24.4 and 28.3, which instead proclaim the obligation for States parties "to promote and encourage international cooperation" with respect to the rights to health and education.

[144]Sepulveda (2006), p. 275 fn. 18.

[145]See the 13th para. of the preamble and Arts. 4, 17(b), 23.4, 24.4 and 45.

[146]Cf. the drafting history of such provisions in Vandenhole (2009), pp. 29–34. Only the United States voiced their discomfort with respect to the mentioning of international cooperation in the preamble (ibid., 33).

[147]General Comment No. 5 General measures of Implementation CRC/GC/2003/5, 27 November 2003, para. 7. See also para. 60 of the same GC: "Article 4 emphasizes that implementation of the Convention is a cooperative exercise for the States of the world. This article and others in the Convention highlight the need for international cooperation".

[148]CRC, General Discussion on 'Resources for the Rights of the Child-Responsibility of States', 46th session, 21 September 2007, para. 51.

on development cooperation:[149] "States parties must respect and protect economic, social and cultural rights of children in all countries with no exceptions, and take all possible measures to fulfil these rights – whenever they are in a position to do so – through development cooperation".[150]

In this respect, the CtRC has endorsed the approach first espoused by the CESCR, by: (1) urging State parties "to meet internationally agreed targets including the United Nations target for international development assistance of 0.7 per cent of gross domestic product";[151] (2) highlighting that "programmes of donor States should be rights-based";[152] recommending that (3) children's rights affirmed in the CRC be mainstreamed into such programmes;[153] and that (4) States parties "comply with their obligations under the Convention and the Optional Protocols when engaging in development cooperation as members of international organizations, and when signing international agreements".[154]

However, the CtRC did not fail to affirm—once again in line with what was already called upon several times by the CESCR—that States parties' responsibilities are particularly cogent in cases of disaster or other humanitarian emergency:

> States have individual and joint responsibility, including through United Nations mechanisms, to cooperate in providing disaster relief and humanitarian assistance in times of emergency[155]

7.2.2 The Convention on the Protection and Promotion of the Rights and Dignity of Persons with Disabilities

The CRPD was adopted by consensus by the UN General Assembly on 13 December 2006,[156] becoming the first human rights treaty of the twenty-first century. It was

---

[149] Cf. Skogly (2006), p. 158. "In its concluding observations, the CRC Committee has emphasized some specific obligations under the CRC with regard to development cooperation [. . .] The CRC Committee has largely neglected third State obligations to respect and to protect economic, social and cultural rights of children in developing countries" (Vandenhole 2009, p. 26).

[150] CRC, General Discussion on 'Resources for the Rights of the Child-Responsibility of States', 46th session, 21 September 2007, para. 51.

[151] CRC Committee, General Comment 5, para. 61; GC 15, para. V. International cooperation.

[152] Ibid.

[153] Ibid.

[154] GC 19, para. 39. "Similarly, States parties should consider the potential impact on children's rights when planning and implementing economic sanctions" (ibid.).

[155] GC 15, para. V. International cooperation.

[156] GA res. A/61/611 (2006), entered into force on 3 May 2008. The CRPD does not contain a jurisdiction clause, which is instead included in its Optional Protocol, adopted on the same date as the Convention and which provides for an individual complaint mechanism (Art. 1). On the CRPD see generally Della Fina et al. (2017).

also the first human rights treaty to accept "regional integration organizations"[157] as parties and indeed it has even been ratified by the European Commission/EU.[158] Moreover, its ratification rate is among the highest within the UN human rights conventions.[159]

The Convention is not meant to create entirely new rights, but rather to clarify, taking as a model the CRC, the applicability of internationally recognised human rights vis-à-vis persons with disabilities.[160] Among its various substantive provisions, it bears noting that Art. 11 (Situations of risk and humanitarian emergencies) specifically requires "to ensure the protection and safety of persons with disabilities in situations of risk, including [...] *the occurrence of natural disasters*".[161]

International cooperation features prominently in the Convention. Indeed, it is not only mentioned in the preamble[162] and in Art. 4.2—related to general obligations—but it is also the object of a separate, stand-alone provision: Art. 32. Neither provision specifically mentions "international assistance"; however, as already noted with respect to the CRC, such expression is now commonly considered as an aspect of the broader term "cooperation".

As a preliminary, it must be remarked that international cooperation was one of the most divisive issues discussed during the negotiations of the Convention. In this regard, the North-South divide was particularly pronounciated and this was due inter alia to the fact that the great majority of disabled persons—approximately 80%—live in developing countries.[163] The EU, in particular, initially voiced its opposition to a separate article on international cooperation for several reasons. Its position is worth citing first of all because it comes from the world's largest development donor and additionally because it expresses concerns that were common to various developed countries.[164]

---

[157]Cf. Art. 44 of the CRPD.

[158]The CPRD is the first human rights treaty to which the EC/EU has acceded. Cf. Ferri (2010), p. 4.

[159]At present it has 177 parties.

[160]"[I]t may be affirmed that the aim of the Convention was (and currently is) to give visibility to persons with disabilities, dealing with existing norms and standards of international law of human rights, for the necessity of their effective protection by States and by other subjects of international law" (Bruno 2017, p. 253).

[161]Emphasis added.

[162]The first preambular paragraph recognises the "importance of international cooperation for improving the living conditions of persons with disabilities in every country, particularly in developing countries".

[163]See official UN power point presentation, Convention in Brief, slide no. 5, at http://www.un.org/disabilities/. On the issue cf. Vandenhole (2009), p. 57.

[164]It bears noting that Ireland initially opposed a reference to international cooperation with the argument that in the UN context such expression was often a "code for developmental assistance", and that it had "grave reservations about creating international obligations regarding developmental aid" (Working Group Daily Summary, volume 3, #10 of 16 January 2004, p. 10).

The Union started by remarking that international cooperation, despite its importance, was a means to implement the treaty and not a right of the individual. It then affirmed that:

> A separate article on international cooperation may hinder implementation of this Convention; it would allow States to say the reason they are not respecting the rights of persons with disabilities is because other States have not met their international cooperation obligations. While international cooperation is vital in implementation, the EU does not support a separate article on international cooperation. It supports international cooperation in general obligations which apply to all articles.[165]

Ultimately, a compromise was found, which subordinated the inclusion of a stand-alone article on cooperation to the exclusion of an explicit reference to development cooperation on the one hand and the addition of a without prejudice clause on the other. As a result, Art. 32 ends by cautioning that its provisions are "without prejudice to the obligations of each State Party to fulfil its obligations under the [. . .] Convention".[166] This caveat thus makes it unambiguously clear that the implementation of the CRPD at the national level cannot be conditional upon the provision of international support.

Art. 4.2, similarly to the general obligations provision of the CRC, conceives international cooperation as a means to achieving the full realisation of ESC rights. Indeed, it provides that "with regard to economic, social and cultural rights, each State party undertakes to take measures to the maximum of its available resources and, *where needed, within the framework of international cooperation*, with a view to achieving progressively the full realization of these rights". Nonetheless, international cooperation within the CRPD "goes beyond the traditional focus on economic, social and cultural rights under previous instruments and includes cooperation in the field of all rights including civil and political rights".[167] This broader focus/target is evident in Art. 32.

Art. 32, for its part, emphasises "the importance of international cooperation and its promotion, in support of national efforts for the realization of the purpose and objectives of the [. . .] Convention".[168] It then calls upon States parties to "undertake appropriate and effective measures in this regard, between and among States and, as appropriate, in partnership with relevant [stakeholders]".[169] Such measures

> could include, inter alia: (a) ensure that international cooperation is inclusive and accessible to persons with disabilities; (b) facilitate and support capacity building, through the exchange and sharing of information, experiences, training programs, and best practices; (c) facilitate cooperation in research and access to scientific and technical knowledge; and

---

[165] Daily summary of discussion at the sixth session, August 1, 2005.

[166] Cf. Art. 32, para. 2.

[167] A/HRC/16/38, para. 5.

[168] Cf. Art. 32, para. 1.

[169] Ibid.

> (d) provide technical and economic assistance, by facilitating access to and share of accessible and assistive technologies, and through the transfer of technologies.[170]

This provision presents various distinctive and innovative aspects, which are illustrated by the Office of the United Nations High Commissioner for Human Rights (OHCHR) in its Thematic study on the role of international cooperation in support of national efforts for the realization of the rights of persons with disabilities.[171] The OHCHR remarks, inter alia, that under the Convention, "international cooperation goes beyond States and includes other actors such as international, regional and civil society organizations".[172] As to State-to-State cooperation, it "is not limited to cooperation between developed and developing countries and could include not only north-south, but also north-north and south-south cooperation", as well as cooperation directed towards non-States parties.[173] Furthermore, "international cooperation, while explicitly including international development programmes, is also broader and could include other forms of cooperation such as international humanitarian assistance".[174] A broad understanding of international cooperation, emphasizes the OHCHR, "is important if it is to support the full implementation of the Convention which requires, inter alia, that States parties take all necessary measures to ensure the protection and safety of persons with disabilities in situations of risk, including situations of armed conflict, humanitarian emergencies and natural disasters".[175]

Last but not least, Art. 32 together with Art. 11 has highlighted once again two aspects of development and humanitarian aid programmes that by now seem to be irrepressible: a human rights-based approach and disability mainstreaming.[176]

---

[170] Ibid. As remarked by Della Fina, Art. 32 "provides, for the first time in a core human rights treaty, a legal framework to sustain inclusive development requiring that international cooperation [. . .] be inclusive and accessible to persons with disabilities" (Della Fina 2017, p. 574).

[171] OHCHR, Study on international cooperation to support national efforts for the realization of the purposes and objectives of the Convention on the Rights of Persons with Disabilities Report of the Office of the United Nations High Commissioner for Human Rights, A/HRC/16/38, 20 December 2010.

[172] A/HRC/16/38, para. 7.

[173] Ibid., para. 6.

[174] Ibid., para. 13.

[175] Ibid.

[176] Cf. General Comment No. 6 (2018) on equality and non-discrimination, CRPD/C/GC/6, 26 April 2018, para. 72. The said two aspects have also been highlighted by the CPRD Committee in its Concluding Observations. See e.g. Concluding Observations on the initial report of Germany, CRPD/C/DEU/CO/1, April 17, 2015, para. 60; Concluding Observations Luxembourg, 2017, para. 57;

Concluding Observations on Spain CRPD/C/ESP/CO/2-3 13 May 2019, para. 61.

7.3 The Relief-Development Divide and Its Relevance in Disaster Contexts

When speaking of assistance in disaster contexts, the question arises as to what kind of aid we are referring. Humanitarian action, as a broad umbrella term, is generally subdivided in two categories, which are both relevant in disaster response: humanitarian assistance or relief and development assistance or cooperation.

Humanitarian assistance or relief is intended to alleviate acute suffering, typically after an emergency. Humanitarian assistance activities include the provision of goods and services to fulfil essential needs and to ensure the survival of the victims of human-made catastrophes like armed conflicts and disasters. They may consist in material aid or various humanitarian services provided by specialised personnel[177] and are delivered within a quite defined and short timeframe. Last but not least, humanitarian assistance is guided by the humanitarian principles of humanity, neutrality and impartiality.

Development assistance, on the other hand, operates in a long-term perspective and is designed to address the root causes of poverty. Over time, it has changed from an unbalanced, charity-like model, which was entirely managed by benevolent donor States according to their preferences, into a cooperative one, which instead is based (at least in principle) on mutual partnership.[178] Not coincidentally, nowadays it is generally identified with the expression "development cooperation". Nonetheless, while international development organisations such as the UNDP, the IMF and the World Bank operate on the basis of a binding institutional legal framework made of strict rules and policy guidelines, bilateral development cooperation is still highly discretionary, poorly regulated at the international level and pervaded by asymmetry and paternalism on the part of donor States.[179]

While humanitarian assistance has always been deemed to be dictated by a moral imperative and hence it is undisputed, development assistance has been the target of many critiques for its frequent politicisation, which risks detracting from its overall

[177] A renowned definition of humanitarian assistance was provided by the Institut de Droit International in the homonymous resolution adopted in 2003 during the Bruges Session. Cf. art. I.1, which so provides:

> 'Humanitarian assistance' means all acts, activities and the human and material resources for the provision of goods and services of an exclusively humanitarian character, indispensable for the survival and the fulfillment of the essential needs of the victims of disasters.

[178] Indeed, until the 1980s developing countries were the mere beneficiaries of externally funded projects without any mutuality of rights or obligations (cf. Dann 2010, p. 55 f.). Commenting on the establishment of a new international economic order, promoted by developing countries during the sixth extraordinary session of the General Assembly, Giuliano remarks: "Il far valere l'esigenza di instaurare nel mondo un *nuovo* ordine economico e sociale potrebbe [. . .] addirittura indurre taluno a supporre che gli stessi Stati in via di sviluppo non ritengano eliminabile il suddetto divario di sviluppo economico e sociale con gli Stati sviluppati" (Giuliano 1985, p. 43).

[179] Kotzur and Schmalenbach (2014), p. 84.

effectiveness. In practice, however, both types of aid have manifested some major and often similar critical issues.

As an expression of solidarity, the two types of disaster assistance should be functional to the attainment of *substantial* equality between the affected State and donor States, and hence respect the sovereignty of the former and its primary role-responsibility even in such a situation of dire straits. However, humanitarian and development actors in many cases have failed to sufficiently involve local authorities and have instead acted as a substitute rather than as a complement to the former. Such behaviour is frequently dictated by mistrust, from aid personnel as well as donors towards recipient States, which are not considered capable of properly managing the assistance provided. Nonetheless, with the exclusion of situations where an effective government is (temporarily) lacking, it runs counter to the spirit of solidarity that should inform humanitarian action and that is contrary to the sovereignty principle. Moreover, while it may appear justifiable in some conflict situations, this is not the case in disaster contexts where, apart from exceptional Haiti-like cases, there is generally still a functioning and legitimate government in place.[180] Together with the undermining of national capacities, this attitude also creates an evident dependence of beneficiaries on external aid, rendering a full recovery as well as the attainment of sustainable development even more difficult. The excessive protagonism of international actors thus risks creating an imbalance in the dichotomy between sovereignty and external help in favour of the latter.

If the relief-development dualism has always been more artificial than real, today it is no longer viable at all. Already in the early 1990s there was acknowledgement that relief and development cannot be considered as two watertight regimes. In fact, from that period on, reference has been made to the establishment of a *continuum* between the two regimes and to the need to manage the *transition* from the one to the other accordingly.[181] Furthermore, the latter conception is unsatisfactory, as

[180]As noted by Von Engelhardt, "humanitarian actors make too little differentiation between conflict-related emergencies and natural disasters or prolonged crises, where strong and capable national authorities may be present or emerging" (Von Engelhardt 2011, p. 472). Concerning the Indian Ocean Tsunami, some of the problems of the international response were the following: "brushing aside or misleading authorities, communities and local organisations; [. . .] displacement of able local staff by poorly prepared internationals; 'misrecognition' of local capacities resulting in inefficient implementation; applying more demanding conditions to national and local 'partners' than those accepted by international agencies; 'poaching' of staff from national and local entities; and limited participation of the affected-population" (Telford and Cosgrave 2006, p. 19).

[181]"There is a clear relationship between emergency, rehabilitation and development. In order to ensure *a smooth transition from relief to rehabilitation and development*, emergency assistance should be provided in ways that will be supportive of recovery and long-term development. Thus, emergency measures should be seen as a step towards long-term development" (cf. A/RES/46/182, 19 December 1991, para. 9, emphasis added). See also A/RES/57/152, 16 December 2002, para. 7. In analogous terms, the 2003 Bruges Resolution considers "rapid and efficient assistance" as often "only the first necessary step to rehabilitation, recovery and long-term development" (preamble). From then on, the need to transcend the humanitarian/development divide, and by consequence to enhance coherence has become a leitmotiv (cf. UN, Agenda for Humanity. Annex to the Report of the Secretary-General for the World Humanitarian Summit, A/70/709, 2 February 2016,

development activities need to be programmed from the early stages of a disaster, rendering a certain temporal overlap inevitable and institutional coordination between relief and development actors essential. Unfortunately, in practice we have instead witnessed a "mission creep" and an increasing blurring of the two branches, resulting in a grey legal area and an unclear division of labour between the respective actors.[182]

The blurring of the relief-development divide is particularly evident with respect to disaster assistance. Traditionally, disaster assistance was exclusively associated with the relief-focused phase immediately following the catastrophe. This is no longer the case as a consequence of the recognition of the strong correlation between the level of development of a country and its exposure to natural disasters. As was effectively explained by Seck, "development that is blind to risk increases vulnerability and vulnerability increases the likelihood of destructive events that tend to reverse development gains".[183]

The need to build a bridge between relief and development by reducing vulnerability (and thus risk exposure) as well as to foster resilience is best exemplified in the field of disasters by disaster risk reduction (DRR). If disasters and their connection to development received only scant attention in the Millennium Development Goals (MDGs), henceforth DRR gradually gained prominence and ended up becoming a critical component of sustainable development, as shown by the relevance attributed to it within Agenda 2030.[184] As a result, it can be argued that the moral, or better the solidarity-based imperative surrounding humanitarian assistance, is progressively affecting DRR activities. The latter, however, are essentially a national responsibility. DRR aid measures therefore necessarily imply the active involvement of the affected State as well as the empowerment of the individuals and the communities potentially affected.

This shift in focus from disaster response to disaster prevention through DRR has by now been sufficiently conceptualised at the international level but it has not yet resulted in a corresponding change in the practice of States and the broad international humanitarian community. First, funding for DRR still constitutes "a tiny fraction of overall investments in development aid"[185] and the great majority of countries at high risk receive very little financing compared to the impressive amounts which are devoted to disaster response and recovery. Despite the undeniable progresses made since the adoption of the Hyogo Framework for Action back in

---

Core Responsibility Four, Lett. C, p. 10; UN, Addis Ababa Action Agenda of the Third International Conference on Financing for Development, (Addis Ababa, Ethiopia, 13–16 July 2015, para. 66, p. 32).

[182]Von Engelhardt (2011), pp. 462, 465.

[183]Seck (2007), p. 5.

[184]The 2030 Agenda for Sustainable Development has a significant focus on the issue of DRR (Goal 1 (target 1.5), Goal 2 (target 2.4), Goal 11 (targets 11.5, 11.b) and Goal 13 (target 13.1)). Cf. General Assembly, Transforming our world: The 2030 agenda for sustainable development, A/RES/70/1, 25 September 2015.

[185]Kellet and Caravani (2013), p. 13.

2005, there is still "a pressing need to move DRR out of the realms of rhetoric and theory, and into more definite action supported by adequate funds".[186] The low funding of DRR is mainly due to the "perverse incentives—both political and strategic—that drive donors and aid recipients after the onset of a natural disaster, and how these impact the perceptions and financing of risk reduction strategies. These perverse incentives are usually exposed and aggravated by events that receive extensive media coverage".[187] Second, the funding gap has not been adequately filled by the Sendai Framework for Action, nor by the Addis Ababa Action Agenda on Financing for Development, which continue to rely on voluntary contributions for the funding of DRR policies and programmes.[188] Last but not least, DRR has yet to receive sufficient attention from both relief and development actors. Being a typical cross-cutting issue, it has not been integrated into either's sector.[189] Nevertheless, despite these deficiencies, the importance of DRR within disaster assistance is destined to increase, challenging even further the ongoing relevance of the relief-development divide.

List of Documents

African Commission of Human and Peoples' Rights, Principles and Guidelines on the Implementation of Economic, Social and Cultural Rights in the African Charter on Human and Peoples' Rights, in Report of the 48th Ordinary Session of the African Commission on Human and Peoples' Rights (10–24 November 2010, Banjul)

---

[186]Kellet and Caravani (2013), p. 21.

[187]Seck (2007), p. 3. The author, in order to show the influence of donor priorities on the scarce investments in DRR, provides the example of El Salvador:

> Governments know that the fields of disaster relief and humanitarian aid are event-driven and highly responsive to catastrophic events. This in turn is a powerful incentive against prevention and mitigation programmes, initiatives that tend to be drawn out processes with donors highly reluctant to provide the necessary funds.
>
> El Salvador provides a good example of this. Following hurricane Mitch, the country was in a prime position to focus on DRR. While Honduras and Nicaragua were most affected by the hurricane, El Salvador suffered only relatively marginal damages but benefited fully from the aid allocated for reconstruction. As a result, it was one of the signatories to the Stockholm agreement between aid recipients and donors calling, among other conditions, for the reduction of social and ecological vulnerability in the region. However, [...] a review of the recovery plan elaborated by the government after the 2001 earthquakes shows that none of the lessons learnt from hurricane Mitch were actually implemented (ibid., p. 16).

[188]Cf. in particular Addis Ababa Action Agenda cit., para. 62.

[189]In ODA, "disaster prevention and preparedness" is considered a sub-category of "humanitarian aid", while investments made in reducing risk are also present within wider development programmes but, lacking a code or marker that represents DRR, they are more difficult to detect (cf. Global Humanitarian Assistance 2012, p. 12).

CESCR:
Concluding Observations on United Kingdom of Great Britain and Northern Ireland, E/C.12/GBR/CO/6, 14 July 2016
Concluding Observations on Argentina, E/C.12/ARG/CO/4, 12 October 2018
Concluding Observations on Australia, E/C.12/AUS/CO/5, 23 June 2017
Concluding Observations on Austria, E/C.12/AUT/CO/4, 13 December 2013
Concluding Observations on Belgium, E/C.12/1/Add.54, 1 December 2000
Concluding Observations on Bulgaria: E/C.12/BGR/CO/4-5, 11 December 2012; E/C.12/BGR/CO/6, 8 March 2019
Concluding Observations on Canada, E/C.12/CAN/CO/6, 23 March 2016
Concluding Observations on Czech Republic, E/C.12/CZE/CO/2, 23 June 2014
Concluding Observations on China, E/C.12/CHN/CO/2, 13 June 2014
Concluding Observations on Denmark: E/C.12/1/Add.34, 14 May 1999; E/C.12/1/Add.102, 14 December 2004
Concluding Observations on Finland, E/C.12/1/Add.52, 1 December 2000
Concluding Observations on France: E/C.12/1/Add.72, 30 November 2001; E/C.12/FRA/CO/4, 13 July 2016
Concluding Observations on Germany: E/C.12/1/Add.68, 24 September 2001; E/C.12/DEU/CO/6, 27 November 2018
Concluding Observations on Iceland, E/C.12/1/Add.89, 23 May 2003
Concluding Observations on Ireland, E/C.12/IRL/CO/3, 8 July 2015
Concluding Observations on Italy: E/C.12/1/Add.103, 14 December 2004; E./C.12/ITA/CO/5, 28 October 2015
Concluding Observations on Japan, E/C.12/JPN/CO/3, 10 June 2013
Concluding Observations on Liechtenstein, E/C.12/LIE/CO/2-3, 23 June 2017
Concluding Observations on Luxembourg, E/C.12/1/Add.86, 23 May 2003
Concluding Observations on Republic of Korea, E/C.12/KOR/CO/4, 19 October 2017
Concluding Observations on Netherlands, E/C.12/NLD/CO/6, 23 June 2017
Concluding Observations on New Zealand, E/C.12/NZL/CO/3, 31 May 2012
Concluding Observations on Norway, E/C.12/1/Add.109, 23 June 2005
Concluding Observations on Russian Federation, E/C.12/RUS/CO/6, 16 October 2017
Concluding Observations on Spain: E/C.12/1/Add.99, 7 June 2004; E/C.12/ESP/CO/5, 6 June 2012; E/C.12/ESP/CO/6, 25 April 2018
Concluding Observations on Sweden, E/C.12/1/Add.70, 30 November 2001
Concluding Observations on Switzerland, E/C.12/CHE/CO/4, 18 November 2019
General Comment 3, The nature of States parties obligations (Article 2, para 1), 14 December 1990
General Comment 8, The relationship between economic sanctions and respect for economic, social and cultural rights, E/C.12/1997/8, 12 December 1997
General Comment 11, Plans of action for primary education (art.14), E/C.12/1999/4, 11 May 1999
General Comment 12, The right to adequate food, E/C.12/1999/5, 12 May 1999

General Comment 13, The right to education (article 13 of the Covenant), E/C.12/1999/10, 8 December 1999
General Comment 14, The right to the highest attainable standard of health, E/C.12/2000/4, 11 August 2000
General Comment 15, The right to water (Articles 11 and 12 of the International Covenant on Economic, Social and Cultural Rights), E/C.12/2002/11, 20 January 2003
General Comment 18, Article 6 of the International Covenant on Economic, Social and Cultural Rights, E/C.12/GC/18, 6 February 2006
General Comment 19, The right to social security, E/C.12/GC/19, 4 February 2008
General Comment 23, The right to just and favourable conditions of work, E/C.12/GC/23, 4 March 2016
Guidelines on treaty-specific documents to be submitted by States parties under articles 16 and 17 of the International Covenant on economic, social and cultural rights, Annex, 18 November 2008, in HRI/GEN/2/Rev.6
Statement on 'An Evaluation of the Obligation to Take Steps to the "Maximum of Available Resources" under an Optional Protocol to the Covenant', E/C.12/2007/1, 21 September 2007
The World Food Crisis. Statement, E/C.12/2008/1, 19 May 2008
Substantive issues arising in the implementation of the International Covenant on economic, social and cultural rights: poverty and the International Covenant on economic, social and cultural rights - Statement, E/C.12/2001/10, 4 May 2001
Maastricht Guidelines on Violations of Economic, Social and Cultural Rights. 24 Agenda Item Day of General Discussion Organized in Cooperation with the World Intellectual Property Organization, E/C.12/2000/13, 2 October 2000
The Limburg Principles on the Implementation of the International Covenant on Economic, Social, and Cultural Rights, E/CN.4/1987/17, 8 January 1987
Letter dated 16 May 2012 addressed by the Chairperson of the CESCR to States parties to the International Covenant on Economic, Social and Cultural Rights, CESCR/49th/SP/MAB/SW, 4 June 2012
Public debt, austerity measures and the International Covenant on Economic, Social and Cultural Rights. Statement by the Committee on Economic, Social and Cultural Rights, E/C.12/2016/1, 22 July 2016
Convention on the Rights of the Child of 2 November 1989
CRPD:
General Comment No. 6 (2018) on equality and non-discrimination, CRPD/C/GC/6, 26 April 2018
Concluding Observations on Germany, CRPD/C/DEU/CO/1, 17 April 2015
Concluding Observations on Luxembourg, 10 October 2017, CRPD/C/LUX/CO/1
CtRC:
General Comment No. 5 General measures of Implementation CRC/GC/2003/5, 27 November 2003

General comment No. 16 on State obligations regarding the impact of the business sector on children's rights, CRC /C/GC/16, 17 April 2013
General Discussion on 'Resources for the Rights of the Child-Responsibility of States', 46th session, 21 September 2007
Convention on the Rights of Persons with Disabilities of 13 December 2006
ECtHR, Tyrer v. United Kingdom, judgment of 25 April 1978
International Law Association, Berlin conference (2004) International human rights law and practice, Final report on the impact of findings of the United Nations human rights treaty bodies
International Covenant on Economic, Social and Cultural Rights, 16 December 1966
IDI-Institute of International Law, *Sixteenth Commission: Humanitarian Assistance. Resolution* (Bruges session, 2 September 2003)
Maastricht Guidelines on Violations of Economic, Social and Cultural Rights, Maastricht, 26 January 1997
UN, Addis Ababa Action Agenda of the Third International Conference on Financing for Development, (Addis Ababa, Ethiopia, 13–16 July 2015)
UN, Agenda for Humanity. Annex to the Report of the Secretary-General for the World Humanitarian Summit, A/70/709, 2 February 2016
UN CHR, Report of the open-ended working group to consider options regarding the elaboration of an optional protocol to the International Covenant on Economic, Social and Cultural Rights on its second session, E/CN.4/2005/52, 10 February 2005
UN CHR, Report of the Open-ended working group established with a view to considering options regarding the elaboration of an optional protocol to the International Covenant on Economic, Social and Cultural Rights, E/CN.4/2006/47, 14 March 2006
UN Commission on Human Rights, Report on the right to adequate food as a human right submitted by Mr. Asbjorn Eide, Special Rapporteur, E./CN.4/Sub.2/1987/23, 7 July 1987
UN ECOSOC, Resolution 1985/17 of 28 May 1985
Optional Protocol to the International Covenant on Economic, Social and Cultural Rights of 10 December 2008
UN ECOSOC, Resolution 1987/5, 26 May 1987
UN GA, Resolution 46/182, 19 December 1991
UN GA, Resolution 57/152, 16 December 2002
UN GA, Transforming our world: The 2030 agenda for sustainable development, A/RES/70/1, 25 September 2015
UN HRC, Judge v. Canada, Communication No. 829/1998, 5 August 2003
UN OHCHR, Study on international cooperation to support national efforts for the realization of the purposes and objectives of the Convention on the Rights of Persons with Disabilities Report of the Office of the United Nations High Commissioner for Human Rights, A/HRC/16/38, 20 December 2010
UN OHCHR, Thematic study by the Office of the United Nations High Commissioner for Human Rights on the role of international cooperation in support of

national efforts for the realization of the rights of persons with disabilities, A/HRC/16/38, 20 December 2010

Vienna Convention on the Law of Treaties, 23 May 1969

References

Alston P (1987) Out of the Abyss: the challenges confronting the new UN Committee on economic, social, and cultural rights. Hum Rights Q 9:332–381

Alston P (2001) The historical origins of 'General Comments' in human rights law. In: Boisson de Chazournes L, Gowlland-Debbas V (eds) The international legal system in quest of equity and universality: Liber Amicorum Georges Abi-Saab. Martinus Nijhoff, The Hague, pp 763–776

Alston P, Quinn G (1987) The nature and scope of states parties' obligations under the international covenant on economic, social and cultural rights. Hum Rights Q 9(2):156–229

Bódig M (2016) Soft law, doctrinal development and the General Comments of the UN Committee on economic, social and cultural rights. In: Lagoutte S, Gammeltoft-Hansen T, Cerone J (eds) Tracing the roles of soft law in human rights. Oxford University Press, Oxford, pp 69–88

Bruno GC (2017) Article 11 [situations of risk and humanitarian emergencies]. In: Della Fina V, Cera R, Palmisano G (eds) The United Nations Convention on the Rights of Persons with Disabilities. A commentary. Springer, Cham, pp 253–261

Bueno de Mesquita J, Hunt P, Khosla R (2010) The human rights responsibility of international assistance and cooperation in health. In: Gibney M, Skogly S (eds) Universal human rights and extraterritorial obligations. University of Pennsylvania Press, Pennsylvania, pp 104–129

Coomans F (2011) The extraterritorial scope of the international covenant on economic, social and cultural rights in the work of the United Nations Committee on economic, social and cultural rights. Hum Rights Law Rev 11(1):1–35

Coomans F, Kamminga M (2004) Comparative introductory comments on the extraterritorial application of human rights treaties. In: Coomans F, Kamminga M (eds) Extraterritorial application of human rights treaties. Intersentia, Antwerp

Craven M (1995) The international covenant on economic, social and cultural rights: a perspective on its development. Oxford University Press, Oxford

Craven M (2012) The international covenant on economic, social and cultural rights: a perspective on its development. Oxford University Press, Oxford

Dann P (2010) Solidarity and the law of development cooperation. In: Wolfrum R, Kojima C (eds) Solidarity: a structural principle of international law. Springer, Heidelberg, pp 55–91

De Schutter O (2005) Le protocole facultatif au Pacte internatinal relatif aux droits économiques, sociaux et culturels. CRIDHO Working Paper, 3

De Schutter O (2010) International human rights law. Cambridge University Press, p 248

De Schutter O (2014) International human rights law: cases, materials, commentary. Cambridge University Press, Cambridge

Della Fina V (2017) Article 32 [international cooperation]. In: Della Fina V, Cera R, Palmisano G (eds) The United Nations Convention on the Rights of Persons with Disabilities. A commentary. Springer, Cham, pp 569–589

Della Fina V, Cera R, Palmisano G (eds) (2017) The United Nations Convention on the Rights of Persons with Disabilities. A commentary. Springer, Cham

Desierto DA, Gillespie CE (2013) Evolutive interpretation and subsequent practice. Interpretive communities and processes in the Optional Protocol to the ICESCR. Zeitschrift für ausländisches öffentliches Recht und Völkerrecht 73:549–589

Ferri D (2010) The conclusion of the UN Convention on the rights of persons with disabilities by the EC/EU: some reflections from a constitutional perspective. *I quaderni europei*

Geneva Academy of International Humanitarian Law and Human Rights (2018) Diversity in membership of the UN human rights treaty bodies, 15, available at https://www.geneva-academy.ch/research/publications/detail/352-diversity-in-membership-of-the-un-human-rights-treaty-bodies (last accessed on 25 August 2020)

Giuliano M (1985) Cooperazione allo sviluppo e diritto internazionale. Giuffrè, Milano

Global Humanitarian Assistance (2012) Aid investments in disaster risk reduction – rethoric to action. Briefing Paper by Dan Sparks, http://devinit.org/wp-content/uploads/2012/10/Aid-investments-in-disaster-risk-reduction-rhetoric-to-action.pdf (last accessed on 22 August 2020)

Hesselman M (2013) Establishing a full 'cycle of protection' for disaster victims: preparedness, response and recovery according to regional and international human rights supervisory bodies. Tilburg Law Rev 18(2):106–132

Hesselman M (2018) A right to international (humanitarian) assistance in times of disaster: fresh perspectives from international human rights law. In: Zorzi Giustiniani F, Sommario E, Casolari F, Bartolini G (eds) Routledge handbook of human rights and disasters. Routledge, London/New York, pp 65–83

Kälin W, Künzli J (2009) The law of international human rights protection. Oxford University Press, Oxford

Karimova T (2016) Human rights and development in international law. Routledge, New York

Keller H, Ulfstein G (2012) Conclusions. In: Keller H, Ulfstein G (eds) UN Human Rights Treaty Bodies. Law and legitimacy. Cambridge University Press, Cambridge, pp 414–425

Kellet J, Caravani A (2013) Financing disaster risk reduction. A 20 year story of international aid. Global Facility for Disaste Risk Reduction and Recovery (GFDRR) at World Bank & Overseas Development Institute (ODI), London

Khaliq U, Churchill R (2012) The protection of economic and social rights: a particular challenge? In: Keller H, Ulfstein G (eds) UN Human Rights Treaty Bodies. Law and legitimacy. Cambridge University Press, Cambridge, pp 199–260

Koch IE (2005) Dichotomies, trichotomies or waves of duties? Hum Rights Law Rev 5(1):81–103

Koch IE (2009) Human rights as indivisible rights: the protection of socio-economic demands under the European Convention on Human Rights. Martinus Nijhoff, Dordrecht

Kotzur MT, Schmalenbach K (2014) Solidarity among nations. Archiv des Völkerrechts 52 (1):68–91

Mechlem K (2009) Treaty bodies and the interpretation of human rights. Vanderbilt J Transnatl Law 42(3):905–947

Nolte G (2013) Third report for the ILC study group on treaties over time. In: Nolte G (ed) Treaties and subsequent practice. Oxford University Press, Oxford, pp 308–384

Saul B, Kinley D, Mowbray J (2014) The international covenant on economic, social and cultural rights: commentary, cases and materials. Oxford University Press, Oxford

Seatzu F (2012) Sull'interpretazione del Patto delle Nazioni Unite sui diritti economici, sociali e culturali: regole, criteri ermeneutici e comparazioni. Anuario Mexicano de Derecho Internacional XII:339–364

Seck P (2007) Links between natural disasters, humanitarian assistance and disaster risk reduction: a critical perspective. Human Development Office Occasional Paper, 15, https://ideas.repec.org/p/hdr/hdocpa/hdocpa-2007-15.html (last accessed on 22 August 2020)

Sepulveda M (2003) The nature of the obligations under the international covenant on economic, social and cultural rights. Intersentia, Antwerpen – Oxford – New York

Sepulveda M (2006) Obligations of 'International Assistance and Cooperation' in an Optional Protocol to the international covenant on economic, social and cultural rights. Neth Q Hum Rights 24(2):271–303

Shue H (1980) Basic rights: subsistence, affluence and U.S. foreign policy. Princeton University Press, Princeton

Skogly S (2006) Beyond national borders: States' human rights obligations in international cooperation. Intersentia, Antwerpen/Oxford

Sommario E (2012) Derogation from human rights treaties in situations of natural or man-made disasters. In: De Guttry A, Gestri M, Venturini G (eds) International disaster response law. Springer, Berlin/Heidelberg, pp 323–352

Ssenyonjo M (2009) Economic, social and cultural rights in international law. Hart, Oxford

Tasioulas J (2017) Minimum core obligations: human rights in the here and now. Research Paper. World Bank, Washington, DC, V, https://openknowledge.worldbank.org/handle/10986/29144 (last accessed on 22 August 2020)

Telford J, Cosgrave J (2006) Joint evaluation of the International Response to the Indian Ocean Tsunami. Synthesis Report. Tsunami Evaluation Coalition, 1, https://www.alnap.org/help-library/joint-evaluation-of-the-international-response-to-the-indian-ocean-tsunami-synthesis (last accessed on 22 August 2020)

Toebes BCA (1999) The right to health as a human right in international law. Intersentia, Antwerpen

Van Bueren G (2008) Committee on the rights of the child. In: Langford M (ed) Social rights jurisprudence: emerging trends in international and comparative law. Cambridge University Press, Cambridge, pp 569–587

Vandenhole W (2009) Economic, social and cultural rights in the CRC: is there a legal obligation to cooperate internationally for development? Int J Child Rights 17:23–63

Von Engelhardt M (2011) Reflections on the role of the state in the legal regimes of international aid. Zeitschrift für ausländisches öffentliches Recht und Völkerrecht 71:451–474

Warwick BTC (2017) The minimum core's place in social rights: fixity vs dynamism, Specifying and Securing a Social Minimum. Paper for workshop at IISL Onati 2017, http://www.sps.ed.ac.uk/__data/assets/pdf_file/0020/232427/Warwick_-_paper.pdf (last accessed on 22 August 2020)

Warwick B (2018) A hierarchy of comfort? The CESCR's approach to the 2008 economic crisis. In: MacNaughton G, Frey D (eds) Economic and social rights in a neoliberal world. Cambridge University Press, Cambridge, pp 127–149

Young KG (2008) The minimum core of economic and social rights: a concept in search of content. Yale Int Law J 33:113–175

Chapter 8
International Solidarity: From Theory to Practice

Contents

8.1 The Responsibility to Protect Doctrine: An Institutionalised Form of Solidarity Potentially Applicable to Disasters

When a disaster strikes, one of the first concerns is how to best assist and protect the affected population. It is not infrequent that the territorial State is unprepared at best—or unwilling at worst—to effectively manage the ensuing humanitarian crisis. External aid can thus make a difference, even though it frequently meets with the resistance of national authorities. In such situations, the Responsibility to Protect (R2P) doctrine has often been invoked.[1]

The R2P principle was developed as a result of the initiative of the UN Secretary-General (SG) Annan after the 'humanitarian' intervention in Kosovo in 1999 in order to avoid the recurrence of immense tragedies like those in Rwanda and in the former Yugoslavia. In such situations, Annan argued, "[w]e confront a real dilemma. Few would disagree that both the defence of humanity and the defence of sovereignty are principles that must be supported. Alas, that does not tell us which principle should prevail when they are in conflict".[2] However, faced with the

---

[1] See supra Chap. 4, para. 3, where we discussed the doctrine's invocation after the Nargis cyclone.

[2] Annan (2000), p. 48.

F. Zorzi Giustiniani, *International Law in Disaster Scenarios*,
https://doi.org/10.1007/978-3-030-50597-4_8

resistance of most developing countries, supported by China and Russia, Annan decided to promote the debate outside of the UN. The solicitation was gathered by Canada, which created for that purpose the International Commission on Intervention and State Sovereignty (ICISS). The results of the Commission's work were published in 2001 in a report titled, quite evocatively, "The Responsibility to Protect".

The report presents a modern reading of sovereignty, which is configured no more as control, but rather as responsibility.[3] This conception implies that the State has the task—the "responsibility"—to guarantee the (human) security, the life and the well-being of its nationals. As a consequence, it is first and foremost up to the territorial State to protect its citizens from the effects of conflicts or massive violations of human rights. It is only when the State proves *unable* or *unwilling* to fulfil its responsibilities—or it is itself the source of the abuses—that it will be up to the broader community of States to act on a supplementary basis:[4] in such a case, the principle of non-intervention should give way to the *emerging principle* [sic] of the responsibility to protect.[5] Among the "conscience-shocking situations" that would justify an intervention for humanitarian purposes, reference is made to "overwhelming natural or environmental catastrophes, where the state concerned is either unwilling or unable to cope, or call for assistance, and significant loss of life is occurring or threatened".[6]

Contrary to classical theories of humanitarian intervention, which typically only contemplated the reaction phase to redress human rights violations that had already been committed, the report conceives R2P as composed of three phases, corresponding to the responsibility to prevent, the responsibility to react and the responsibility to rebuild. In particular, ample space is dedicated to the first phase, which is meant to address conflicts and other human-made crises at the root before the latter cause serious humanitarian emergencies. Military intervention was thus just a small part of the whole R2P framework as originally conceived.

A few years later, the debate on R2P was reopened within the United Nations in the context of the organisation's proposals for reform. The UN High-Level Panel on Threats Challenges and Change in its report *A More Secure World: Our Shared Responsibility* and the UN SG in its 2005 report *In Larger Freedom: Towards Development, Security and Human Rights for All*, both endorsed R2P as an "emerging norm".[7] In September 2005, the R2P concept was then included in the Outcome

[3]International Commission on Intervention and State Sovereignty (2001), *The Responsibility to Protect. Report*. Ottawa: International Development Research Centre, para. 2.14.

[4]Ibid., para. 2.31.

[5]In a nutshell, the core idea of the report is that "sovereign states have a responsibility to protect their own citizens from avoidable catastrophe – from mass murder and rape, from starvation – but [. . .] when they are unwilling or unable to do so, that responsibility must be borne by the broader community of states" (ibid., p. VIII).

[6]Ibid., 33.

[7]UN GA, A more secure world: our shared responsibility. Report of the High-level Panel on Threats, Challenges and Change, 2 December 2004, A/59/565, para. 202, p. 106; UN GA, In larger

document of the high-level UN World Summit meeting. Here world leaders recognised on the one hand the responsibility of each individual State to protect its population from genocide, war crimes, ethnic cleansing and crimes against humanity and on the other hand a corresponding responsibility of the international community to help States exercise this responsibility through peaceful means, or collective action as a last resort.[8] In particular, they declared to be "prepared to take collective action, in a timely and decisive manner, through the Security Council, in accordance with the Charter, including Chapter VII, on a case-by-case basis and in cooperation with relevant regional organisations as appropriate, should peaceful means be inadequate and national authorities are manifestly failing to protect their populations from genocide, war crimes, ethnic cleansing and crimes against humanity".[9]

As is evident, consensus within the UN was found at the cost of a sharp downsizing of the R2P principle, coupled with various ambiguities. First of all, ratione materiae the applicability of the doctrine is limited to situations of the outmost gravity, which are identified in four specific categories of crimes. This seems unduly regressive with respect to the practice of the UN Security Council (SC) concerning the latter's enlarged understanding of "threat to the peace" ex Art. 39 of the UN Charter. As a consequence, natural disasters—which are not mentioned at all—risk being excluded. The opposition shown by many States to render R2P applicable to disasters has subsequently resulted in a clear stance by the UN SG, who in 2009 warned that "[t]o try to extend the [R2P] to cover other calamities, such as HIV/AIDS, climate change or *the response to natural disasters*, would undermine the 2005 consensus and stretch the concept beyond recognition or operational utility".[10] For the same reason, as will be seen later in this chapter, the Special Rapporteur Valencia-Ospina and the ILC have deemed it more appropriate to exclude R2P from the scope of the project on the Protection of Persons in the event of Disasters.

Second, the residual or complementary responsibility attributed to the international community, while undoubtedly constituting the most innovative feature of the doctrine, lacks operationalisation. Indeed, the effort to institutionalise R2P through the United Nations is incomplete because the World Summit Outcome (WSO) document does not establish clear parameters against which to assess whether in a given case there was an omission to act by third countries.[11] Furthermore, this lack

---

freedom: towards development, security and human rights for all: report of the Secretary-General, 21 March 2005, A/59/2005, 35.

[8]UN GA, Resolution 60/1 of 16 September 2005, A/RES/60/1. 2005 World Summit Outcome, para. 139.

[9]Ibid.

[10]UN GA, Implementing the responsibility to protect. Report of the Secretary-General, A/63/677, 12 January 2009, para.10 b, emphasis added.

[11]"R2P offers little concrete guidance on what outside states should do for at-risk populations. This, then, is R2P's principal challenge: translating its basic principle into an operational doctrine. To be clear, this doctrine need not be exclusively legal in form. Mere policy proposals might induce certain outside states to act; states might themselves support the proposals or be responsive to

indicates a more general ambiguity that pervades the whole doctrine as presented in the WSO document. The terms utilised, starting with the slippery notion of 'responsibility', are deliberately vague in order to facilitate a consensus among States that requires the exclusion of any language that implies a clear obligation to act.[12]

Third, debates regarding R2P have always been haunted since the beginning by the spectre of humanitarian intervention. This spectre has contributed to the shrinking of its scope within the WSO Document and has also resulted in growing mistrust towards R2P by Non-Aligned Movement (NAM) countries, which have voiced their opposition to the possible application of the doctrine in the context of natural disasters.

All this notwithstanding, R2P's contribution and potential should not be underrated. Most importantly, the notion of the R2P can be regarded as an institutionalised form of solidarity through the United Nations.[13] The mutuality element is shown by the fact that responsibilities are ascribed both to the territorial State and the international community.[14] Moreover, the extremely serious situations of human insecurity that characterise the four R2P trigger-crimes clearly indicate the common interest involved.

Furthermore, the engagement undertaken by the UN Member States (MS) at the World Summit concerns not only the reaction to such conscience-shocking situations; reflecting R2P's holistic nature, it also remarkably extends to their prevention.[15] Indeed, the main objective of R2P is to *avoid* the occurrence of mass

constituents who do. But assigning outside states operative legal duties would mean establishing the expectation that helping at-risk populations is not always discretionary—and that not helping can legitimately trigger an outside state's responsibility" (Hakimi 2014, p. 253).

[12]In this regard, see the considerations of Tomuschat and Wood (2010), pp. 111, 117.

[13]Cf. Campanelli (2011), p. 17. According to Boisson de Chazournes: "In solidarity terms, it can be that an international solidarity action takes place when a State or a group of States intervenes in the context of grave human insecurity in a certain region of the world. In other words, the whole construction of the notion of the responsibility to protect can be seen as an institutionalised (through the UN), and also moral and legal expression of solidarity" (Boisson de Chazournes 2010, p. 104). Along similar lines, Casini asserts: "if we frame the responsibility to protect within the legal declinations of solidarity [...] it may be seen as a form of solidarity among States, which preventively agreed to receive 'assistance' whenever they prove to be unable to deliver one of their fundamental tasks – to protect their own citizens" (Casini 2013). See also Da Costa, who deems that "the main advantage of the R2P doctrine, as accepted in the World Summit Outcome, is to institutionalise the response to the gravest crimes through the UN and in particular the UNSC" (Da Costa 2018, p. 31).

[14]Boisson de Chazournes draws a parallel between R2P and common Art. 1 of the 1949 Geneva Conventions, which she defines as a "double-sided obligation, as it calls on States both *to respect and ensure respect*" (cf. Boisson de Chazournes 2010, p. 104, emphasis in the original).

[15]According to K. Wellens, "the normative contribution of the responsibility to protect lies mainly not in introducing the principle of solidarity and giving it a legal status but with regard to the obligation to prevent" (cf. Discussions Following the Presentation by Laurence Boisson de Chazournes cit., p. 116).

atrocities. In the WSO the world leaders agreed to institute a "culture of prevention"—as called for by K. Annan back in 2001[16]—and in particular to strengthen the UN's early warning capacity.[17] A few years later, in 2009, the debates on R2P that took place at the General Assembly clearly showed that the "Responsibility to Prevent" was the aspect of the doctrine over which "the widest degree of consensus was reached".[18]

More generally, R2P's added value with respect to humanitarian intervention lies in its three-pronged approach as well as in the responsibilities assigned to the international community. As stated by former SG Ban Ki-moon in its first report on the Responsibility to Protect, the international community has two distinct and equally important duties: (1) to assist States in building their capacities to protect their populations; and (2) to take timely and decisive action when a State manifestly fails in its primary responsibility to protect its people.[19] Concerning the "Responsibility to React" and in particular the action of the Security Council, R2P purports "to guide [the SC], trying to limit its discretion with respect to whether and how to act in R2P situations".[20]

As far as disasters are concerned, their a priori exclusion from R2P's scope, while being voiced from many quarters, appears implausible. Indeed, it is not conceivable to exclude tout court the possibility that, as a result of a disaster, serious violations of human rights amounting to one of the four trigger-crimes may be committed, as was arguably the case in Myanmar after cyclone Nargis.[21]

Despite frequent invocations of its character as an 'emerging norm' of international law, R2P does not establish *new legally binding* obligations. Only its first pillar can be said to have genuine legal content, as it codifies existing duties that international law—especially human rights law—assigns to States as "responsible sovereigns". Instead, as enshrined in the WSO document, R2P mainly expresses a *political* commitment by States. Moreover, it provides States and the international community with a *moral* standard of action whose main objective is the prevention

[16]Cf. UN General Assembly- Security Council, Prevention of armed conflict. Report of the Secretary-General, A /55/985–S /2001/574, para. 28; cited in ICISS (2001), 27.

[17]Even though, as underlined by Bellamy, they "chose not define [the culture of prevention] or specify measures that would make it a reality, limiting itself instead to a pledge to strengthen the UN's early warning capacity and to statements endorsing measures already in place" (Bellamy 2008, p. 142).

[18]Cf. Huisingh (2013), p. 5.

[19]UN General Assembly, A/63/677, sections II-IV.

[20]Todeschini (2014), p. 101. According to Anne Peters, instead, the exercise of the veto or inaction by the Security Council with respect to R2P situations would constitute illegal acts (Peters 2012, p. 207).

[21]This position is shared *inter alia* by the ILC member Park, according to whom "R2P will come into play in natural disasters in the situation of a 'complex emergency' and from the point of view of international solidarity" (Park 2018, p. 148).

of mass atrocities from happening.[22] It can thus be argued that R2P has been somewhat significant at the normative level, albeit not yet at the juridical level.

8.2 Solidarity at Work. The Case of the European Union

Any analysis of solidarity in disasters in the international legal order cannot avoid a separate study on its value and scope in the European Union, and this for three reasons. First, solidarity was not only at the foundation of the European integration process, but has over time come to permeate in a transversal way various competence areas of the Union, with the result of being considered as an immanent or structural principle of EU law.[23] While its precise meaning and overall value is still the object of debate, its relevance in the EU order cannot be denied and helps set the Union apart from *any* other international or regional organisation. Second, solidarity in disasters has found explicit—and also implicit—recognition in various provisions of EU primary law as well as in secondary legislation, becoming the most prominent manifestation of its kind at the European and international level. Finally and accordingly, EU practice in the domain has implications that go beyond the European Union context and shall thus be evaluated when taking stock of the significance of solidarity in disasters in the broader international legal order.

---

[22]Cf. Gözen Ercan (2016), p. 83. See also Boisson de Chazournes, who deems that "*the strong moral contour of the notion of the responsibility to protect* may have some influence on the decision-making process leading to the adoption of collective security measures decided upon by the Security Council" (Boisson de Chazournes 2010, p. 103, emphasis added). A distinction between the legal, moral and political dimensions of R2P was recently made by the current UN Secretary-General Guterres, who so affirms:

> 11. Legal accountability relates to obligations under national and international law. Accountability for implementation of the responsibility to protect, however, goes beyond legal obligations and includes a moral and political dimension.
>
> [...]
>
> 16. The moral responsibility of the international community to contribute to protecting populations from harm goes beyond genocide, war crimes, ethnic cleansing and crimes against humanity, and stems from our common humanity and solidarity. However, in addition to moral responsibility, the international community has a political responsibility to contribute to the prevention of those crimes under pillars two and three of the responsibility to protect.
>
> 17. Political responsibility stems from the commitments reflected in paragraphs 138 to 140 of the 2005 World Summit Outcome and subsequent resolutions referencing the responsibility to protect" (Report of the UN Secretary-General, "Implementing the Responsibility to Protect: Accountability for Prevention", A/71/1016 –S/2017/556).

[23]Cf. Boutayeb (2011), p. 5 ff.

8.2.1 The Overall Legal Framework

"Europe will not be made all at once, or according to a single plan. It will be built through concrete achievements which first create a de facto solidarity".[24] These words were pronounced on 9 May 1950 by Robert Schuman, one of the founding fathers of European integration, to propose the creation of a European Coal and Steel Community, which would become the first European community. This clearly shows that solidarity has been present since the first inception of the European communities as one of the main inspirational ideas and founding values of the integration process.

As to the founding treaties, solidarity is evoked several times in various areas and contexts, but with partly diverse meanings and separate disciplines.[25] The situation is complicated by the fact that the European legislator has never defined what solidarity is, nor has it elaborated on its content. Moreover, references in the European Court of Justice (ECJ) case law are scarce and generally quite dated.[26]

Returning to Durkheim's distinction between mechanic and organic solidarity, various authors have suggested that European solidarity should be considered based on the latter, this being typical of modern, differentiated societies. Nonetheless, compared to the notion of solidarity in international law, European solidarity is evidently based more on similarities than on differences as well as a stronger communion of intents and principles plus shared values, without which the European project cannot be sustained.

Admittedly, in recent times European solidarity has been put in question several times and in various domains, notably the common asylum system and the economic monetary union. As a consequence, it has been argued that the concept is nothing more than a rhetorical device devoid of real substance. Improper appeals to solidarity as well as proposals to instead apply a so-called flexible solidarity[27] or solidarity à la carte, inevitably contribute to the watering down of its true significance and value, which is hence reduced to pure political rhetoric, or worse, masked assistentialism. Nonetheless, we cannot but agree that the attempt to dismiss solidarity as a merely

---

[24]Schuman (1950).

[25]On the polysemic notion of solidarity in the European Treaties see inter alia De La Rosa (2011), p. 165 ff.

[26]A recent reference to solidarity among Member States was made by Advocate Kokott in the Pringle case (ECJ, Thomas Pringle v. Government of Ireland, Ireland and the Attorney General, Case C-370/12, View of Advocate General Kokott delivered on 26 October 2012, paras. 142–143), to argue that it cannot be inferred from the concept that "there exists a duty to provide financial assistance of the kind that is to be provided by the [European Stability Mechanism]". Unfortunately, the Court in its judgement did not even mention solidarity.

[27]See the proposal, presented at the Bratislava Summit (16 September 2016), of the so-called Visegrad Group (Poland, Slovakia, the Czech Republic and Hungary) to tackle the migrant crisis on the basis of the principle of "flexible solidarity", according to which each Member State should be able "to decide on specific forms of contribution taking into account their experience and potential. Furthermore, any distribution mechanism should be voluntary".

political concept is "untenable as it stands in contrast to the broad usage of this principle in the treaties, its apparent pivotal role in various stages of the history of European integration when difficulties had to be overcome [. . .]. [I]n addition, the interpretation rule of 'effet utile' or 'ut res magis valeat quam pereat' requires that this concept is taken seriously".[28]

Following the innovations and changes introduced by the Lisbon Treaty, it is impressive to see how many references to the notion now feature primary law. In the TEU, solidarity is mentioned first of all as a common value of the societies of EU MS.[29] It then appears among the Union's objectives (Art. 3.3 TEU) and should hence be applied "as a criterion of interpretation and as a binding instruction to implement EU law in the spirit of solidarity".[30]

Solidarity primarily has a horizontal, inter-State dimension, but it also appears under other forms: solidarity between generations, inserted in Lisbon as a specific objective in Art. 3.3 TEU; and solidarity between MS and individuals.[31] This third dimension finds expression in the Charter of Fundamental Rights of the European Union, whose Title IV is entirely devoted to solidarity and enumerates various economic and social rights that Member States need to guarantee to *any* individual when implementing EU law.[32]

An additional horizontal but external dimension of solidarity—"solidarity and mutual respect among peoples"—is cited in Art. 3.5 TEU and should accordingly guide the Union's action in the international arena.[33] This dimension ratifies the

---

[28]Hilpold (2015), p. 259.

[29]Cf. Art. 2.2 TEU. In a similar sense see also the preamble, which after the addition in Lisbon of a reference to solidarity in Lisbon in substitution of "relations, now reads: "[. . .] desiring to deepen the solidarity between their peoples while respecting their history, their culture and their traditions". It bears noting that already the Nice Charter referred to solidarity as an "indivisible and universal value of the EU" (preamble).

[30]Cf. Blanke and Mangiameli (2013), (p. 176, para. 42). Solidarity is also specifically mentioned in Art. 21 TEU as an objective of EU's external action.

[31]See generally Domurath (2013), p. 459 ff.

[32]The close interrelationship existing between inter-State solidarity and solidarity between MS and individuals has been lucidly highlighted by the Commission in its Communication to the European Parliament, the Council, the European Economic and Social Committee and the Committee of the Regions of 2 July 2008 on "Renewed social agenda: Opportunities, access and solidarity in 21st century Europe":

> Europeans share a commitment to social solidarity: between generations, regions, the better off and the less well off and wealthier and less wealthy Member States. Solidarity is part of how European society works and how Europe engages with the rest of the world. Real equality of opportunity depends on both access and solidarity (COM(2008) 412 final, p. 6 (sub 3).

[33]To these said dimensions some authors add still another one, i.e. the vertical solidarity between MS and the Union which is expressed by the principle of loyal cooperation and which as such applies in normal times and not just in exceptional, emergency situations (cf. Casolari (2014), p. 118 ff.). Vedder instead claimed that the duty of cooperation between the Member States flowing from the general principle of loyalty is a specification of inter-Member State solidarity between

recognition of *international* solidarity in the EU order. However, as will be seen, with the partial and notable exception of disasters scenarios, acts of solidarity towards third countries are not classified as such in the Union legal order and generally assume the name and the content of development cooperation.[34]

More specific references to solidarity, essentially related to its inter-State dimension, are contained in the Treaty on the Functioning of the European Union (TFEU) and concern various subject areas of EU competence: immigration (Art. 67), asylum (Art. 80), financial assistance (Art. 122), energy (Art. 194) as well as terrorist attacks and disasters (Art. 222).[35] In such instances, solidarity gives rise to specific obligations of cooperation and assistance that as a whole share the characteristic of addressing, almost exclusively, "out of the ordinary" situations.[36] The objective is clearly to support a MS in difficulties in order to put it in a position to return to contributing like the others to the goals of the Union. In other words, the role of solidarity-based obligations in the TFEU is that of reestablishing—where needed—substantive equality among MS so that each can again assume its share of responsibility for the attainment of the Union's common interests.[37]

8.2.2 EU Solidarity in Disasters

As was aptly remarked by the Special Rapporteur Valencia-Ospina, Art. 222 TFEU—the so-called solidarity clause—"sets the Union apart from other

(Vedder 2007, para. 18). In any case, it should be noted that the ECJ has considered loyalty as a particular and crucial form of solidarity (ECJ, Judgement of 1 February 1973, Case 39/72 72—Premiums for slaughtering cows, para. 21).

[34]However, as will be seen in the realm of disaster management—or civil protection, as it is usually called in EU law—solidarity has expanded beyond the Union's borders and now additionally concerns some third countries that have a closer relation with EU MS, either because they are candidate countries or because as a consequence of their geographical proximity they have adhered to the Civil Protection Mechanism.

[35]As will be seen, though, Art. 222 TFEU also presents a vertical dimension, inasmuch as it imposes on the Union an obligation to assist a MS in distress.

[36]Casolari (2017), pp. 519–530. However, this is not the case of the common policy on asylum, immigration and external border control (Arts. 67, para. 2 and 80 TFEU), where solidarity is a guiding principle of general application. Such a reading was confirmed by the ECJ in *N.S. and others*, where the judges, after referring to the Temporary Protection Directive (2001/55) as an example of solidarity ex Art. 80 TFEU, reminded that "the solidarity mechanisms which it contains apply only to wholly exceptional situations falling within the scope of that directive, that is to say, a mass influx of displaced persons" (Joined Cases C-411/10 and C-493/10, Judgement of 21 December 2011, para. 93).

[37]According to Klamert solidarity can be seen as "an expression of the fundamental principle of the equality of the Member States in the European Union, exhorting the unity between the Member States by prescribing mutual assistance either in kind or financially" (Klamert 2014, p. 37).

regional coordination schemes".[38] Indeed, it is the only hard-law provision existing at the regional level that imposes an obligation to assist in disaster scenarios.

The solidarity clause was introduced by the Lisbon Treaty, building on an identical provision which was contained in the EU Constitutional Treaty.[39] The clause is part of a broader effort to expand the list of threat scenarios addressed by the Union and to complement the mutual defence clause provided by Art. 42.7 TEU, which applies to situations of "armed aggression" against the territory of a Member State. Contrary to the latter, however, the solidarity clause is not merely intergovernmental in character, instead having a potentially much broader scope. As rightly noted, Art. 222 is "both rather ambitious and somewhat vague".[40] It assigns a clear-cut, legal obligation to both the Union and the Member States "to act jointly in a spirit of solidarity if a Member State is the object of a terrorist attack or the victim of a natural or man-made disaster".[41]

Such an obligation could (at least in theory) become the object of an infringement procedure before the ECJ.[42] Nevertheless, this looks quite improbable, as claims of MS against other MS are very rare. Moreover, it bears noting that Declaration No. 37 on Art. 222 annexed to the Final Act of the Lisbon Intergovernmental Conference allows MS "to choose the most appropriate means to comply with their own solidarity obligation" towards their counterparts.[43] In other words, each MS enjoys a degree of flexibility as to the implementation modalities of the duty.

The original version of the clause, as contained in the Constitutional Treaty, was accompanied by implementing modalities that helped clarify its content. In Lisbon the choice was instead to defer to a Council decision the arrangements for the clause's implementation by the Union.[44] The detected vagueness of Art. 222 has been accordingly filled by Decision 2014/415/EU, but only in part, as the latter is focused on the implementation by the Commission exclusively.[45]

Concerning the invocation of the solidarity clause, Art. 4.1 of the Decision affirms that: "In the event of a disaster or terrorist attack, the affected Member

---

[38] ILC, Sixth report on the protection of persons in the event of disasters, A/CN.4/662, 3 May 2013.

[39] At Art. I-43.

[40] Keller-Noellet (2011), p. 329.

[41] Art. 222, para. 1.

[42] Indeed, according to Art. 275 TFEU the jurisdiction of the CJEU is limited exclusively with regard to the Common Foreign and Security Policy (CFSP) and with respect to acts adopted on the basis of the CFSP provisions.

[43] Official Journal of the European Union, 2007 C 306/261. As an annex to the Final Act of the Lisbon Conference and not to the Treaties, the Declaration does not form an integral part of EU treaty law ex art. 52 TEU. Nonetheless, as remarked by Gestri, it must be considered when interpreting Art. 222 TFEU "as forming part of the 'context' of the EU treaties, in accordance with Article 31(2)(b) of the 1969 Vienna Convention on the law of treaties" Gestri (2012), p. 114. Its relevance is further confirmed by Decision 2014/415/EU, which recalls it in the preamble (para. 1).

[44] Art. 222, para. 3.

[45] Cf. Decision 2014/415/EU of 24 June 2014.

State may invoke the solidarity clause if, after having exploited the possibilities offered by existing means and tools at national and Union level, *it considers that the crisis* clearly overwhelms the response capabilities available to it". The provision thus clarifies once and for all that it is up to the affected State alone to evaluate whether to activate the clause.[46] At the same time, it provides a restrictive reading of the clause's applicability because it considers Art. 222 as a last resort mechanism.

As to the material scope of the clause, the Implementing Decision clarifies that disaster "means any situation which has or may have a severe impact on people, the environment or property, including cultural heritage".[47] In other words, the disaster notion is defined on the basis of its consequences, which have to reach, at least potentially, a certain gravity, while it is not limited to those events that have a cross-border character or that affect more than a Member State.[48] The emphasis on the disaster's impact is also confirmed by the clause's territorial scope. Indeed, the Decision not only confirms that Art. 222 essentially has an EU dimension,[49] but that "irrespective of whether [the crisis] originates inside or outside the territory of the MS", it "shall apply: (a) within the territory of MS to which the Treaties apply, meaning land area, internal waters, territorial sea and airspace; (b) when affecting infrastructure (such as off-shore oil and gas installations) situated in the territorial sea, the EEZ or the continental shelf of a MS".[50]

---

[46] A more explicit position on this point was expressed by the European Parliament in 2012, by remarking that "once a Member State has decided to invoke the clause, it should not be a matter for debate for the others to offer assistance" (European Parliament resolution of 22 November 2012 on the EU's mutual defence and solidarity clauses: political and operational dimensions (2012/2223 (INI)), P7_TA(2012)0456, para. 22). According to Martino, "the decision to leave it exclusively to the discretion of the affected Member State to activate the Clause could lead to false or from a strictly legal point of view questionable activation" Martino (2015), p. 48. In response to such concerns, Gestri remarks "the right to request assistance under Article 222 TFEU should be exercised in good faith by the Member State concerned, taking into account that each Member State has a general responsibility to provide its citizens with adequate protection" Gestri (2012), p. 111.

[47] Art. 3(a).

[48] In this sense cf. Gestri, who also notes that such reading is in line with the definition of disaster embraced by the ILC in the DAs on the Protection of Persons in the Event of Disasters, which does not refer to a transboundary element (Gestri 2016, p. 48). Contra Myrdal and Rhinard (2010).

[49] It may thus seem quite puzzling that the clause is situated at the very end of Part V TFEU, which is dedicated to the Union's external action. According to Konstadinides, "[p]erhaps this reflects the sentiment of the Treaty drafters that such a provision neither dovetails neatly with the EU's external action (Part Five, TFEU) nor does it sit comfortably in Section 2 of the TEU (CSDP), for instance, as an inherent part of Article 42 (7) TEU, which encompasses the collective obligation of Member States to assist one of their counterparts in the event of attack on their territory by deploying their military assets" (Konstadinides 2011, p. 11). More convincinly, Cremona argues that the position is due to the fact that "at the time of the drafting of the Constitutional Treaty the solidarity clause was in fact linked to the requirement of solidarity in foreign policy matters [. . .] and represents a bridge between internal and external security. This dual dimension is also reflected in the institutional arrangements for the implementation of the clause in paragraph 3, which involve both the Commission and the High Representative for Foreign Affairs and Security Policy, and both internal and external security committees" Cremona (2011), pp. 29–30.

[50] Cf. Art. 2.

As for the rest, the Decision envisages response arrangements at the Union level that are managed by the Council. Such arrangements, which can be triggered only as a *last resort* (as confirmed by Art. 4.1), do not however exhaust the multifaceted manifestations of internal, EU solidarity in disasters. This raises the more general question of the relationship between the solidarity clause and other expressions of European solidarity in disasters that have their basis in the EU treaties.

In 2002, following the huge summer floods that struck Central Europe, the Council established the European Union Solidarity Fund.[51] The Fund provides financial support, distinct from that available through the ordinary cohesion funds, in terms of grants to the affected MS (or candidate countries) for activities undertaken in the immediate recovery phase, such as the restoration of infrastructures and damaged areas and the provision of temporary accommodation for the populations involved.[52] It was created to apply mainly to major natural disasters, but has also found application in the case of a technological disaster: the Prestige oil spill that polluted a huge area off the coasts of Spain, France and Portugal in November 2002.[53] Despite its limited material scope and the small financial cover it can provide, the instrument has undeniably proved successful, being activated in 76 cases to the support of 24 different European countries.

The Fund's revision of 2014 has specified the criteria for application to "major and 'regional' natural disasters"[54] and, in order to improve the mechanism's responsiveness, it has also introduced the possibility of making advance payments.[55] What nevertheless remains unclear is the relationship between the Solidarity Fund and Art. 122.2 TFEU.[56] The Regulation establishing the Fund was adopted under ex Art. 159.3 TEC on economic and social cohesion,[57] a legal basis confirmed by Regulation 661/2014, which refers to Art. 175.3 TFEU, the corresponding provision of the

[51]See Council Regulation (EC) No. 2012/2002 of 11 November 2002 establishing the European Union Solidarity Fund, 14 November 2002.

[52]The aim is to contribute to a rapid recovery in the affected country or region after "major natural disasters with serious repercussions on living conditions, the natural environment or the economy" (Art. 2.1, Reg. 2012/2002).

[53]The possibility of applying the Fund to technological disasters is only hinted in the Regulation, where it is said that "The assistance should *mainly* be mobilised in case of natural disasters" (sic the first preambular paragraph of Reg. 2012/2002, emphasis added). So far, the only case of application to a technological disaster has concerned the Prestige oil spill which, due to its magnitude, was nevertheless also classified as a regional disaster (cf. EU Solidarity Fund Interventions since 2002 (last update: 21 June 2017), available at http://ec.europa.eu/regional_policy/sources/thefunds/doc/interventions_since_2002.pdf (last accessed on 25 August 2020).

[54]EU Regulation No. 661/2014 of the European Parliament and of the Council of 15 May 2014 amending Council Regulation (EC) No. 2012/2002 establishing the European Union Solidarity Fund, Art. 2, paras. 2–3.

[55]Art. 4a. The full mobilisation of the Fund in each case indeed requires a budget procedure that lasts several months.

[56]Hilson (2010), p. 139.

[57]Additionally, a second legal basis was found in ex Art. 308 TEC (now Art. 352 TFEU) in order to cover actions addressed to candidate countries.

Lisbon Treaty. However, no mention is made of Art. 122.2 TFEU, a brand-new provision introduced at Lisbon as an addition to ex Art. 100 TEC, and which specifically concerns the recourse to financial solidarity "[w]here a Member State is in difficulties or is seriously threatened with severe difficulties caused by natural disasters".[58] Indeed, under such circumstances the Council could decide to grant, on the proposal of the Commission, financial assistance to the concerned MS "under certain conditions".

Art. 122.2 TFEU has not even been used as a legal basis for Regulation 2016/369. The latter constitutes the most recent EU funding mechanism established to give emergency support "in a spirit of solidarity" to MS in order to address the humanitarian consequences of natural and human-made disasters of exceptional scale and impact. This instrument, adopted with the aim of countering the consequences of the refugee crisis,[59] was intended to provide the Union with an internal humanitarian aid mechanism equivalent to that established by Regulation (EC) 1257/96, which regulates humanitarian assistance to third countries. It is based on the first paragraph of Art. 122, which, "[w]ithout prejudice to any other procedures provided for in the Treaties", allows the adoption of measures of an exceptional and general character to address crises that a MS cannot manage alone. This proviso is confirmed in the text of the Regulation, where it is affirmed that the envisaged emergency support "*can only be provided where* the exceptional scale and impact of the disaster is such that it gives rises to severe wide-ranging humanitarian consequences in one or more Member States *and only in exceptional circumstances where no other instrument available to Member States and to the Union is sufficient*".[60] This raises the question of which tool, between this and the solidarity clause, should be resorted to in the first place. As has been convincingly asserted by Casolari, the without prejudice clause ex Art. 122.1 should imply that measures adopted on the latter's basis prioritise the other mechanisms provided by primary law, including the solidarity clause. Nonetheless, the mechanism conceived by Art. 222, being qualified as a *last resort*, would provide in turn a referral back, thereby requiring that the emergency support be applied as a preliminary.[61]

---

[58]Curiously, the affirmation that "Article 122 of the TFEU [. . .] provides for the establishment of a solidarity fund" can be found in the summary of the Communication from the Commission to the European Parliament and the Council of 26 October 2010—Towards a stronger European disaster response: the role of civil protection and humanitarian assistance (Text with EEA relevance) [COM (2010) 600 final (cf. Summaries of EU legislation, Strengthening the European disaster response capacity, available at http://eur-lex.europa.eu/legal-content/EN/TXT/?uri= LEGISSUM:ah0007). In all probability it is a mistake, considering that the full text of the document contains no comparable affirmation, but even so it highlights the logical link existing between Art. 122.2 and the Solidarity Fund.

[59]Cf. the second and third preambular paras.

[60]Cf. Art 1.1.

[61]Cf. Casolari (2017), p. 528. The author also affirms that his reading is conforted by the practice, as the provision of emergency support to Greece in 2016 was not preceded by a previous request by that country to activate the solidarity clause.

Last but not least, among the existing tools at the EU level, particular importance has to be assigned to the Union Civil Protection Mechanism (UCPM). As will be shown, this mechanism has proved to be the most relevant tool through which solidarity in disaster response takes place inside but also outside the Union. EU MS have coordinated their national civil protection capacities in the case of major natural disasters for a long time.[62] Nonetheless, cooperation in disaster management (DM) has received a quantum leap since the entry into force of the Lisbon Treaty.

The so-called Civil Protection Mechanism (CPM) was launched in 2001 by Council Decision 2001/792/EC with the objective of fostering the mobilisation of assistance in case of disasters and improving preparedness at the national level in collaboration with European institutions. The CPM was first reviewed in 2007 through the adoption of an amending decision (Council Decision 2007/779/CE) and a Civil Protection Financial Instrument (Council Decision 2007/162/EC). However, it was not until the Lisbon Treaty that civil protection became a self-standing policy and that it has been provided with a specific legal basis in the Treaties.[63] By enumerating civil protection among the fields in which the EU has a supporting competence, Art. 6(f) TFUE, in conformity with previous practice, asserts that the role of the European institutions is complementary and cannot go beyond the coordination of MS actions.[64] In other words, it recognises the sovereign prerogatives of the States in this domain. In civil protection as a whole, the Commission thus acts as a facilitator.[65]

Art. 196 TFUE (Civil Protection), which regulates in detail the new competence area, starts by affirming that the Union "shall encourage cooperation between Member States in order to improve the effectiveness of systems for preventing and protecting against natural or man-made disasters".[66] The "spirit of solidarity" between the cooperating entities is not mentioned here, although it is implied.[67] Moreover, the relevance of solidarity and notably of the solidarity clause in civil protection is clearly recognised by Decision 1313/3013 establishing the new Union Civil Protection Mechanism (UCPM) and by its implementing Decision 2014/762/EU on the functioning of the UCPM. Decision 1313/2013 considers the UPCM "a

---

[62] Indeed, civil protection cooperation can be traced back to May 1985, when the first informal meeting on the issue took place in Rome.

[63] Earlier, EU civil protection actions and legislation were based on the catch-all provision of Art. 308 TEC (the so-called flexibility clause).

[64] EU action aims to "support and complement MS's action at national, regional and local level" (Art. 196.1 a) TFEU). Art. 196.2 also reminds that, accordingly, "any harmonisation of the laws and regulations of the Member States" is excluded.

[65] As to the decision-making process, Art. 196.2 renders it more democratic and smoother. It demands indeed that legal acts in subiecta materia be adopted according to the ordinary legislative procedure, which assigns to the Parliament the role of co-legislator and requires a qualified majority within the Council. Moreover, acts adopted under the said legislative procedure have a legislative character ex Art. 289.3 TFEU.

[66] Cf. Art. 196.1 TFEU.

[67] Kotzur (2017), p. 42.

visible expression of European solidarity by ensuring a practical and timely contribution to prevention of and preparedness for disasters and the response to disasters and imminent disasters".[68] Furthermore, it affirms that the Mechanism "should also contribute to the implementation of Article 222 [. . .] (TFEU), by making available its resources and capabilities as necessary".[69]

The UCPM is an operational instrument that can be activated for any kind of natural or human-made disasters "which has or may have a severe impact on people, the environment, or property, including cultural heritage".[70] Its operational hub is the Emergency Response Coordination Centre (ERCC), which is based at the Commission's headquarters in Brussels and ensures the permanent monitoring of and immediate reaction to disasters. Indeed, through its information centre it collects, analyses and disseminate real-time information on disasters.[71]

In accordance with the broad wording of Art. 196, the actions pursued by the Mechanism concern all phases of disaster management, from prevention to recovery, with prevention in general having assumed a stronger focus since the adoption of the 2013 Decision. One of the main innovations of the UCPM concerns disaster preparedness and consists of the creation of a European Emergency Response Capacity (EERC) in the form of a "voluntary pool of pre-committed response capacities of the Member States".[72] The EERC, which includes modules, equipment, relief support and services[73] and is at the disposal of the ERCC, has been established to render the Union's action more predictable and coordinated and ultimately to augment the latter's visibility in its disaster response activity.[74]

Contrary to the solidarity clause, the assistance provided through the Mechanism is purely voluntary and each State is free to indicate "the scope, terms and, where applicable, costs of the assistance it could render".[75] Nevertheless, voluntariness has some limits. While MS can freely determine whether to put their response capacities at the disposal of the EERC, "once made available, the response capacities must be

---

[68]Fifth preambular paragraph.

[69]Fourth preambular paragraph, Decision 1313/2013.

[70]Art. 4, para. 1.

[71]Its voluntary pool includes pre-arranged modules, i.e. specialised emergency response units charged to undertake specific tasks like medical evacuation, emergency shelter, search and rescue and aerial fire fighting.

[72]Decision 1313/2013, Art. 11.1.

[73]European Commission, Implementing Decision (EU) 2018/142 of 15 January 2018 amending Implementing Decision 2014/762/EU laying down rules for the implementation of Decision No 1313/2013/EU of the European Parliament and of the Council on a Union Civil Protection Mechanism, Chapter 5.

[74]Crespi (2014), p. 1132. Previously, EU civil protection response was based on ad hoc offers of assistance from MS, rendering the prior planning of emergency operations very difficult and the availability of appropriate and sufficient assistance in all cases uncertain (European Commission, Communication from the Commission to the European Parliament and the Council. Towards a stronger European disaster response: the role of civil protection and humanitarian assistance, COM (2010) 600 final, Brussels 26.10.2010, p. 6, para. 4.1).

[75]Cf. Art. 15, para. 5.

used to help the requesting State: it is not an option, but an obligation which directly comes from the real nature of the voluntary pool".[76] An eventual refusal by a MS could be justified only by proving the existence of imperative circumstances preventing the deployment of the pre-committed assets.[77]

Another remarkable difference with respect to the solidarity clause concerns the personal, territorial and temporal scopes of application, which are broader. Certainly, the UCPM is a manifestation of solidarity both inside and outside the Union. First, apart from EU MS, it also involves Iceland, the former Yugoslav Republic of Macedonia, Montenegro, Norway, Serbia and Turkey. Second, assistance through the Mechanism can be requested by *any* affected country as well as by the UN and its agencies and international organisations.[78] Lastly, as already mentioned, the UCPM also envisages a range of measures concerning the prevention and preparedness phases.

By and large, the Mechanism has proved its effectiveness in meeting the assigned objectives.[79] Nevertheless, in recent years numerous natural disasters have hit Europe as a result of climate change, straining the EU's response capacity and revealing some structural deficiencies.[80] With a view to adapting the Mechanism to the challenges posed by the increasing frequency of extreme events, the Commission in 2017 proposed the introduction of some targeted changes aimed at developing a more integrated DM approach, where *robust* prevention and preparedness measures stand out.[81] Such a proposal was at the basis of Decision 2019/420, which entered into force in May 2019.

The main innovations introduced to the Union Mechanism by the new legislation are the establishment of RescEU as well as changes made to the EERC, which is to be renamed the European Civil Protection Pool. RescEU creates an additional reserve of capacities to respond to disasters, owned and hosted by Member States. With its establishment, the EU intends to remedy the deficiencies of the UCPM—which notably owe to the voluntary character of MS' contribution—as well of MS'

[76]Villani (2017), p. 137. Indeed, Art. 11.1 provides that "response capacities that Member States make available for the EERC shall be available for response operations under the Union Mechanism following a request for assistance through the ERCC" (emphasis added).

[77]Cf. Art. 11, paras. 7–8.

[78]Cf. Arts. 15.1, 16.1 of Decision 1313/2013.

[79]Cf. European Commission, Interim Evaluation of the Union Civil Protection Mechanism. 2014–2016. Final Report, August 2017, available at https://publications.europa.eu/en/publication-detail/-/publication/eb41bfee-78c3-11e7-b2f2-01aa75ed71a1/language-en/format-PDF (last accessed on 25 August 2020). This evaluation is foreseen in Art. 34 of Decision 1313/2013/EU. Cf also European Court of Auditors, Special Report (2016), Union Civil Protection Mechanism: the coordination of responses to disasters outside the EU has been broadly effective, available at: http://www.eca.europa.eu/Lists/ECADocuments/SR16_33/SR_DISASTER_RESPONSE_EN.pdf (last accessed on 25 August 2020).

[80]"In short, this year's extensive disasters have shown that we have now clearly reached the limits of the Union's Civil Protection Mechanism, as it is structured and functions today" (COM(2017) 772, p. 3).

[81]COM(2017)772, para. 3.2.

national response systems. The RescEU reserve will be established gradually, only being completed in 2025. Nevertheless, its 'transition' fleet was already operational last August in Greece to fight devastating forest fires. RescEU is meant to be utilised as a very last resort, "in overwhelming situations where overall existing capacities at national level and those pre-committed by Member States to the European Civil Protection Pool are not, in the circumstances, able to ensure an effective response".[82] Following a request for assistance, it is the Commission that decides, "in close coordination with the requesting Member State and the Member State owning, renting or leasing the rescEU capacity", on the deployment and demobilisation of the requested capacity.[83] RescEU's added value, as remarked by former Commissioner for Humanitarian Aid and Crisis Management Christos Stylianides after its deployment in Greece, is that it "makes our response more robust, quick and efficient".[84]

Furthermore, the European Civil Protection Pool is being strengthened by the provision of increased Union financing to Member States for the adaptation, repair and operating costs of its capacities.[85] Member States as well as the other Participating States are thus given an additional incentive to commit their own capacities to the Pool and ultimately to help each other when needed. Disaster prevention is equally enhanced, in particular through a simplified reporting framework concerning key risks, while the Commission is additionally empowered to establish specific consultation mechanisms "among Member States that are prone to similar types of disasters, including for cross-border risks and low probability risks with a high impact".[86] Overall, the changes introduced to the civil protection legal framework primarily seek to enhance the collective disaster response capacity of the Union and its MS.

The referred Decision has the merit of envisaging a system that combines solidarity with national responsibility,[87] thus rejecting allegations that European solidarity in disasters invites parasitism from Southern MS, as the latter are inherently more exposed to extreme natural events.[88] To the contrary, the ultimate goal is

[82]Cf. Art. 12.1 of Decision No 1313/2013/EU as modified by Decision (EU) 2019/420.

[83]Ibid., Art. 12.6.

[84]European Commission, RescEU assets mobilised to help Greece fight devastating forest fires, Press release, Brussels, 14 August 2019.

[85]The EU co-finances assets that Member States put in the European Civil Protection Pool at 75% of operational costs when used inside the EU (or a Participating State) and 100% of the same costs for deployment outside EU (cf. Art. 23c), paras. 4b and 4c of Decision No 1313/2013/EU as modified by Decision (EU) 2019/420).

[86]Cf. Art. 6.2 1 of Decision No 1313/2013/EU as modified by Decision (EU) 2019/420.

[87]The Decision, while reiterating MS's primary responsibility in DM, emphasizes that the UCPM "promotes" inter-MS solidarity ex Art. 3.3 TEU (sic Decision (EU) 2019/420, 2nd preambular paragraph). See also the 20th preambular paragraph of the Decision, affirming that "[i]n order to balance national responsibility and solidarity among Member States, a part of the operational costs of deploying rescEU capacities should be eligible for Union financial assistance".

[88]This is however less and less the case, as shown by the numerous wildfires that, as a result of shockingly high temperatures due to climate change, hit the whole Scandinavian peninsula in 2018. Moreover, these catastrophes set in motion the largest civil protection operation ever carried out by

"a situation in which all countries have integrated disaster prevention in all their policies, have made arrangements guaranteeing a satisfactory level of response capacity and *can safely rely on EU assistance in case of disasters that are exceptional in scope or nature, and where EU intervention is justified*".[89] Within this framework, MS are not constrained to act in solidarity; nonetheless, they are strongly *induced* to do so by the various practical and financial incentives provided by the Mechanism.

In conclusion, internal solidarity in disaster scenarios undoubtedly represents one of the most prominent and multiform expressions of European solidarity as a value and also as a principle. Among the various solidarity tools available in disasters, the hub of the system remains the UCPM and not, contrary to what might be expected, the solidarity clause. In fact, the UCPM's centrality will grow in the future, thanks inter alia to the establishment of RescEU. Moreover, the changes recently introduced to the Mechanism emphasise the increasing role that solidarity is assuming in the domain at hand and confirm the crucial role of European institutions in order to make solidarity work.[90]

By contrast, the solidarity clause has never been used. However, this does not mean that it should be deemed superfluous. First of all, it has substantial symbolic value.[91] More fundamentally, it must be emphasised that its implementation was conceived as part of the broader picture of existing tools and measures available to address disasters within the EU. As a consequence, "the main idea behind the solidarity clause is to step up the coordination of these many instruments" under the Commission's guidance.[92] In this system, the solidarity clause has a residual role to play: it aims at addressing "an exceptional situation, that overwhelms the response capacities of a Member State even after using *all* the available instruments at European and national level".[93]

---

the EU (see https://ec.europa.eu/echo/news/largest-eu-civil-protectionoperation-helps-sweden-fight-forest-fires_en).

[89]COM(2017)772, p. 11.

[90]"If solidarity is to work, it needs to come under the oversight of strong institutions; otherwise, if left to the States' discretion, it will continue to exist as a principle of good intentions" (Rossi and Casolari 2017, p. 38).

[91]Olsson and Larsson (2009), p. 161.

[92]Cf. the speech of Hans Das, Head of the Civil Protection Policy Unit, at the joint hearing organized between the SEDE and LIBE committees of the European Parliament on 16th June 2015 (The solidarity clause: one of the most unacknowledged innovations of the Lisbon Treaty. The European Parliament debates its implementation but also its ambiguities, available at www.eu-logos.org).

[93]Ibid., emphasis added.

List of Documents

European Commission, Communication from the Commission to the European Parliament and the Council. Towards a stronger European disaster response: the role of civil protection and humanitarian assistance, COM(2010) 600 final, 26 October 2010

European Commission, Interim Evaluation of the Union Civil Protection Mechanism. 2014–2016. Final Report, August 2017, available at https://publications.europa.eu/en/publication-detail/-/publication/eb41bfee-78c3-11e7-b2f2-01aa75ed71a1/language-en/format-PDF (last accessed on 22 August 2020)

European Commission, Implementing Decision (EU) 2018/142 of 15 January 2018 amending Implementing Decision 2014/762/EU laying down rules for the implementation of Decision No 1313/2013/EU of the European Parliament and of the Council on a Union Civil Protection Mechanism

EU, Decision No 1313/2013/EU on a Union Civil Protection Mechanism of the European Parliament and of the Council of 17 December 2013 on a Union Civil Protection Mechanism

EU, Decision 2019/420 of the European Parliament and of the Council of 13 March 2019 amending Decision No 1313/2013/EU on a Union Civil Protection Mechanism

Council of the EU, Regulation (EC) No 2012/2002 of 11 November 2002 establishing the European Union Solidarity Fund

Council of the EU, Decision 2014/415/EU of 24 June 2014 on the arrangements for the implementation by the Union of the solidarity clause

ECJ, Premiums for slaughtering cows, Case 39/72, Judgement of 1 February 1973

ECJ, N.S. and others, Joined Cases C-411/10 and C-493/10, Judgement of 21 December 2011

ECJ, Thomas Pringle v. Government of Ireland, Ireland and the Attorney General, Case C-370/12, View of Advocate General Kokott delivered on 26 October 2012

EU, Regulation 661/2014 of the European Parliament and of the Council of 15 May 2014 amending Council Regulation (EC) No 2012/2002 establishing the European Union Solidarity Fund

European Commission, Communication from the Commission to the European Parliament and the Council of 26 October 2010 – Towards a stronger European disaster response: the role of civil protection and humanitarian assistance (Text with EEA relevance) [COM(2010) 600 final

European Commission, Communication from the Commission to the European Parliament, the Council, the European Economic and Social Committee and the Committee of the Regions - Renewed social agenda: Opportunities, access and solidarity in 21st century Europe (COM(2008) 412 final, 2 July 2008

European Parliament, Resolution of 22 November 2012 on the EU's mutual defence and solidarity clauses: political and operational dimensions, 2012/2223(INI)

ILC, Sixth report on the protection of persons in the event of disasters, A/CN.4/662, 3 May 2013

International Commission on Intervention and State Sovereignty (2001), *The Responsibility to Protect. Report.* Ottawa: International Development Research Centre

UN GA, A more secure world: our shared responsibility. Report of the High-level Panel on Threats, Challenges and Change, 2 December 2004, A/59/565

UN GA, In larger freedom: towards development, security and human rights for all: report of the Secretary-General, 21 March 2005, A/59/2005

UN GA, Resolution 60/1 of 16 September 2005, A/RES/60/1

UN GA, Implementing the responsibility to protect. Report of the Secretary-General, A/63/677, 12 January 2009

UN GA-SC, Prevention of armed conflict. Report of the Secretary-General, A/55/985–S /2001/574, 7 June 2001

UN SG, Implementing the Responsibility to Protect: Accountability for Prevention. Report, A/71/1016–S/2017/556, 10 August 2017

References

Annan KA (2000) Millennium report: we the peoples: the role of the United Nations in the 21st century. United Nations, New York

Bellamy AJ (2008) Conflict prevention and the responsibility to protect. Global Gov 14(2):135–156

Blanke H-J, Mangiameli S (eds) (2013) The treaty on the European Union. A commentary. Springer, Heidelberg

Boisson de Chazournes L (2010) Responsibility to protect: reflecting solidarity? In: Wolfrum R, Kojima C (eds) Solidarity: a structural principle of international law. Springer, Heidelberg, pp 93–109

Boutayeb C (2011) La solidarité, un principe immanent au droit de l'Union Européenne. Eléments pour une théorie. In: Boutayeb C (ed) La solidarité dans l'Union européenne. Eléments constitutionnels et matériels. Pour une théorie de la solidarité en droit de l'Union européenne. Dalloz, Paris

Campanelli D (2011) Principle of solidarity. Max Planck Encyclopedia of Public International Law. Oxford University Press, Oxford

Casini L (2013) Solidarity between States in the global legal space. Paper presented at the Annual Meeting of the European Group of Public Law. Available at https://poseidon01.ssrn.com/delivery.php?ID=741072022102024081078125122098091026016056000029024069069123106076083091009065089108016120111006027011049007065019120103000110123042042011081092088097006018000092070001052041101127094090119102000003104112029000080030080071088105122073089067014099025029&EXT=pdf (last accessed on 22 August 2020)

Casolari F (2014) EU loyalty after Lisbon: an expectation gap to be filled? In: Rossi LS, Casolari F (eds) The EU after Lisbon. amending or coping with the existing treaties? Springer, Heidelberg, pp 93–133

Casolari F (2017) Lo *strano caso* del regolamento 2016/369, ovvero della fornitura di sostegno di emergenza all'interno dell'Unione ai tempi delle *crisi*. In: Triggiani E, Cherubini F, Ingravallo I, Nalin E, Virzo R (eds) Dialoghi con Ugo Villani, Vol. I. Cacucci, Bari, pp 519–530

Cremona M (2011) The EU and global emergencies: competence and instruments. In: Antoniadis A, Schütze R, Spaventa E (eds) The European Union and global emergencies. Hart, Oxford, pp 11–31

Crespi S (2014) Commento all'articolo 196 TFUE in materia di protezione civile. In: Pocar F, Baruffi MC (eds) Commentario breve ai Trattati dell'Unione europea. Padova, CEDAM, pp 1128–1135

Da Costa K (2018) In: Zorzi Giustiniani F, Sommario E, Casolari F, Bartolini G. (eds) Routledge handbook of human rights and disasters. Routledge, New York, pp 27–42

De La Rosa S (2011) La transversalité de la solidarité dans les politiques matérielles de l'Union. In: Boutayeb C (ed) La solidarité dans l'Union européenne. Eléments constitutionnels et matériels. Pour une théorie de la solidarité en droit de l'Union européenne. Dalloz, Paris, pp 165–190

Domurath I (2013) The three dimensions of solidarity in the EU legal order: limits of the judicial and legal approach. J Eur Integr 35(4):459–475

Gestri M (2012) EU disaster response law: principles and instruments. In: De Guttry A, Gestri M, Venturini G (eds) International disaster response law. Springer, pp 105–128

Gestri M (2016) La risposta alle catastrofi nell'Unione europea: protezione civile e clausola di solidarietà. In: Gestri M (ed) Disastri, protezione civile e diritto: nuove prospettive nell'Unione europea e in ambito penale. Giuffré, Milano, pp 3–62

Gözen Ercan P (2016) Debating the future of the "responsibility to protect". The evolution of a moral norm. Palgrave Macmillan, London

Hakimi M (2014) Toward a legal theory on the responsibility to protect. Yale J Int Law 39 (2):247–280

Hilpold P (2015) Understanding solidarity within EU law: an analysis of the 'Islands of Solidarity' with particular regard to Monetary Union. Yearb Eur Law 34(1):257–285

Hilson C (2010) EU environmental solidarity and the ecological consumer. In: Ross MG, Borgmann-Prebil Y (eds) Promoting solidarity in the European Union. Oxford University Press, Oxford, pp 136–150

Huisingh F (2013) A responsibility to prevent? A norm's political and legal effects. Amsterdam Law Forum 5(1)

Keller-Noellet J (2011) The solidarity clause of the Lisbon Treaty's. In: Fabry E (ed) Think Global – Act European: the contribution of 16 European think tanks to the polish, Danish and cypriot trio presidency of the European Union. Notre Europe, Paris, pp 328–333

Klamert M (2014) The principle of loyalty in EU law. Oxford University Press, Oxford

Konstadinides T (2011) Civil protection in Europe and the Lisbon "solidarity clause": A genuine legal concept or a paper exercise. Uppsal Faculty of Law, Working Paper, 3

Kotzur M (2017) Solidarity as a legal concept. In: Grimmel A, Giang SM (eds) Solidarity in the European Union. A fundamental value in crisis. Springer, Heidelberg, pp 37–45

Martino A-M (2015) The "Solidarity Clause" of the European Union – dead letter or enabling act?. SIAK-Journal– Zeitschri für Polizeiwissenscha und polizeiliche Praxis, 2

Myrdal S, Rhinard M (2010) The European Union's solidarity: empty letter or effective tool? An analysis of article 222 of the Treaty on the Functioning of the European Union. Occasional Papers, 2

Olsson S, Larsson P (2009) The future of crisis management in the European Union. In: Olsson S (ed) Crisis management in the European Union – cooperation in the face of emergencies. Springer, Dordrecht, pp 157–167

Park K-G (2018) Law on natural disasters. From cooperation to solidarity? In: Benvenisti E, Nolte G (eds) Community interests across international law. Oxford University Press, Oxford, pp 136–150

Peters A (2012) The responsibility to protect and the permanent five. In: Hoffmann J, Nollkaemper A (eds) Responsibility to protect. From principle to practice. Pallas, Amsterdam, pp 199–211

Rossi LS, Casolari F (2017) The principle of equality in EU law. Springer, Cham

Schuman R (1950) Discours de l'horloge. Paris. https://www.robert-schuman.eu/fr/declaration-du-9-mai-1950 (accessed on 22 August 2020)

Todeschini V (2014) Collective security, the common interest, and the responsibility to protect Doctrine. In: Benedek W, De Feyter K, Kettemann MC, Voigt C (eds) The common interest in international law. Intersentia, Cambridge, pp 93–108

Tomuschat C, Wood M (2010) Discussion following the presentation by Laurence Boisson de Chazournes. In: Wolfrum R, Kojima C (eds) Solidarity: a structural principle of international law. Springer, Heidelberg, pp 111, 117.

Vedder C (2007) Art. I-5. In: Vedder C, Heintschell von Heinegg W (eds) Europäischer Verfassungsvertrag. Nomos, Baden-Baden

Villani S (2017) The EU civil protection mechanism: instrument of response in the event of a disaster. Revista Universitaria Europea 26:121–148

Chapter 9
International Cooperation and Solidarity in Disasters: Whither International Law?

Contents

9.1 International Cooperation and Solidarity in the ILC Works on the Protection of Persons in the Event of Disasters

Our analysis on the role of international cooperation and solidarity in disaster response cannot fail to consider at the end the brand-new ILC project on the Protection of Persons in the event of Disasters. According to the initial intentions of the Special Rapporteur Valencia-Ospina, the Project should have been informed by a rights-based approach,[1] with a focus on the individual victims of disasters as rights-holders, and by *cooperation and solidarity* "both among nations and among individual human beings" as "[t]he underlying principles".[2] Despite these promising premises, however, the Draft Articles approved in second reading are almost exclusively grounded on horizontal relationships between the affected State and assisting States and organisations. Moreover, the distribution of tasks between the affected State and the international community reveals an asymmetry to the detriment of the

[1]On the failed recognition of a rights-based approach in the Project, cf. Zorzi Giustiniani (2012), p. 69 ff.

[2]ILC, Second report on the protection of persons in the event of disasters, A/CN.4/615, 7 May 2009, para 50.

F. Zorzi Giustiniani, *International Law in Disaster Scenarios*,
https://doi.org/10.1007/978-3-030-50597-4_9

former.[3] Indeed, the concern expressed by several States towards the respect of sovereignty and the principle of non-intervention has been accompanied by a refusal to assign a full complementary role to the international community that is in line with the solidarity evoked.

To begin with, it is worth mentioning that at the urging of the ILC, the Special Rapporteur already in 2009 deemed it necessary to exclude R2P from the scope of the topic. Such a decision was a consequence of the widespread political resistance expressed within the Sixth Committee to apply this doctrine in disaster contexts.[4] Accordingly, the ambiguous term "responsibility", initially used with respect to the affected State, was substituted by the more neutral term "role". Nonetheless, no correspondent term is utilised to describe the role of the international community, which, also probably as a result of the censuring of the R2P, appears fairly modest and sometimes indefinite.

In comparison to the role assigned to the affected State, the one attributed to the international community fails to adequately take account of the developments made by the law of international cooperation in recent decades, analysed in the previous paragraphs.[5] As a matter of fact, the Project starts by recognising the "fundamental value of solidarity in international relations and the importance of strengthening international cooperation in respect of all phases of a disaster".[6] Cooperation is then the object of a distinct DA (DA 7—Duty to cooperate), according to which "States shall, as appropriate, cooperate among themselves, with the United Nations, with the components of the Red Cross and Red Crescent Movement, and with other assisting actors". Importantly, this general duty, which can take forms as various as the possible forms of cooperation,[7] is applicable to the whole scope ratione temporis of the Project and thus also to the prevention phase.[8] It is not, however, accompanied by specific obligations incumbent on third actors. While the affected State has

---

[3]This asymmetry was already denounced by Allan and O'Donnell (cf. Allan and O'Donnell 2013, p. 55), and has not been remedied in the second reading.

[4]Cf. Yearbook of the International Law Commission, 2009, vol. II (Part Two), para. 164.

[5]Very scant and selective references to such developments are made in the commentary to DA7, in particular at para. 2. Some more specific (but quite dated) ones can be found in the Fifth report of the Special Rapporteur (A/CN.4/652, paras. 64–65). This stands in stark contrast with the commentary to DA11 (Duty of the affected State to seek external assistance), where some of the relevant practice of international human rights bodies—particularly the CESCR—is cited quite extensively (cf. paras. 3–4).

[6]Cf. the fourth preambular paragraph.

[7]Such forms of cooperation are exemplified in DA 8 (entitled Forms of cooperation in the response to disasters), which so provides:

> Cooperation in the response to disasters includes humanitarian assistance, coordination of international relief actions and communications, and making available relief personnel, equipment and goods, and scientific, medical and technical resource.

As specified in the commentary, DA 8 "does not create any additional legal obligations" (cf. para. 7).

[8]Cf. commentary to DA 1, para. 4.

different duties consonant with its primary role,[9] no correspondent *role* is assigned to the international community.

The only provision somewhat specifying what is *expected* from the international community is DA 12, titled Offers of assistance. The commentary considers it "an expression of the principles of solidarity and cooperation, highlighted in the preamble [...]".[10] This article *authorises* all external actors, irrespective of their status, to offer assistance ("[...] assisting actors *may offer*"[11]) to the affected State.[12] The obligations attributed to the affected State are thus counterbalanced by a mere expectation of receiving outside assistance. The formulation of DA 12, which appears quite regressive with respect to the existing legal framework (probably envisaging if not an obligation to provide, at least an obligation to offer),[13] was a response to the opinion expressed by several States that had denied the existence of a duty to provide assistance under general international law.[14] Nonetheless, the limited

---

[9]The duties to ensure the protection of its population, to seek assistance, not to arbitrarily withold consent and to protect relief personnel, equipment and goods (cf. DAs 10, 11, 13, 15 and 16).

[10]Cf. commentary to DA 12, para. 1.

[11]Cf. DA 12, para. 1, emphasis added. On first reading, Draft Art. 16 [12] distinguished between the position of international subjects ("States, the United Nations, and other competent intergovernmental organizations"), which were assigned "a right to offer", and "relevant non-governmental organizations", which on their part "may also offer assistance". The unification of the position of all assisting actors in the second reading explains the recourse to the softer, permissive language.

[12]Such offers of assistance, "whether made unilaterally or in response to a request, are essentially voluntary and should not be construed as recognition of the existence of a legal duty to assist. Nor does an offer of assistance create for the affected State a corresponding obligation to accept it" (ILC, DAs commentaries, DA 12, para. 2). Moreover it is specified, with a language borrowed from international humanitarian law, that they "cannot be regarded as interference in the affected State's internal affairs" (ibid., para. 3). The commentary also refers to the 1989 resolution of the Institute of International Law on the protection of human rights and the principle of non-intervention in internal affairs of States, whose Art. 5 so provides:

> An offer by a State, a group of States, an international organization or an impartial humanitarian body such as the International Committee of the Red Cross, of food or medical supplies to another State in whose territory the life or health of the population is seriously threatened, cannot be considered an unlawful intervention in the internal affairs of that State.

[13]See e.g. Art. V of the 2003 Bruges Resolution, according to which "[a]ll States should *to the maximum extent possible* offer humanitarian assistance to the victims in States affected by disasters" (emphasis added). At the regional level, the two major IDL frameworks (the EU civil protection mechanism and the ASEAN Agreement on Disaster Management and Emergency Response (AA DMER) consider cooperation in obligatory terms. Art. 3(3) AADMER provides that "The Parties shall, in the spirit of solidarity and partnership and in accordance with their respective needs, capabilities and situations, strengthen cooperation and co-ordination to achieve the objectives of this Agreement".

More generally, O'Donnell and Allan remark that "pre-existing specialist IDRL instruments [...] (which the ILC already heavily relied on for the provision saying that an affected state 'shall not' arbitrarily withhold its consent to aid) are more definite in their sense of an obligation for external actors to assist" (Allan & O'Donnell 2016, p. 474).

[14]In his fifth report the Special Rapporteur, when addressing the scope of the duty to cooperate, considered that: "*the nature of cooperation has to be shaped by its purpose, which in the present*

usefulness of such a provision, which was doubted by some State delegations,[15] is compensated by the addition of a second paragraph, which reads:

> When external assistance is sought by an affected State by means of a request addressed to another State, the United Nations, or other potential assisting actor, the addressee shall expeditiously give due consideration to the request and inform the affected State of its reply

The discretionary nature of the offers is thus limited by a procedural obligation, which imposes on those States that are the addressees of a *specific* request—and not in place of a general appeal[16]—to respond to such a request in due time. With this provision, the ILC timidly sought to re-balance the position, as well as the respective rights and obligations of the affected State and of the international community.[17] However, the end-result is still very unbalanced to the detriment of the affected State.[18]

Another difficulty pertains to the terminological and classificatory ambiguities that surround the whole project.[19] The former are epitomised by the constant recourse to the term "duty" to identify conduct that is more correctly qualified as "obligation" in the commentaries, in line with the Project's main purpose, which is to

---

context is to provide disaster relief assistance. Seen from the larger perspective of public international law, to be legally and practically effective the States' duty to cooperate in the provision of disaster relief must strike a fine balance between three important aspects. First, such a duty cannot intrude into the sovereignty of the affected State. Second, *the duty has to be imposed on assisting States as a legal obligation of conduct*. Third, the duty has to be relevant and limited to disaster relief assistance, by encompassing the various specific elements that normally make up cooperation on this matter" (Fifth report, para. 81, emphasis added). Despite these promising reflections, he deemed that "the duty to cooperate in relief matters does not currently include a legal duty for States to provide assistance when requested by an affected State. This conclusion is confirmed by *the overwhelming majority* of States that submitted comments in the Sixth Committee" (ibid. para. 68, emphasis added). To be true, though, this reading of States opinions appears excessively conservative. Indeed, although fifteen States denied the existence of a *general duty to provide*, four other delegations (Poland, Thailand, Pakistan, and Sri Lanka) were favorable to admit in the Project a duty *to offer* (ibid. and references thereof). Moreover, the French delegation clearly affirmed that "[t]he duty to cooperate [i]s a fundamental principle of international affairs that [i]s embodied not only in international humanitarian law instruments, but in general international law" (UNGA Sixth Committee, *Summary record of the 21st meeting*, A/C.6/64/SR.21, 30 October 2009, para. 24).

[15]United Kingdom (A/C.6/66/SR.23, para. 45), Russian Federation (A/C.6/66/SR.24, para. 37).

[16]Cf. commentary DA 12, para. 8.

[17]"The paragraph aims at introducing a greater balance within the text of the draft articles as a whole, by providing a countervailing obligation on the part of States, or other potential assisting actors, when confronted with a request by an affected State for external assistance" (ibid., para. 7).

[18]The opinion that the ILC has not found a good balance between the rights and obligations assigned to the affected States and those pertaining to the international community appears to be shared by G. Bartolini (cf. Bartolini 2017, p. 702).

[19]The use of ambiguous language, if it is understandable when used by treaty bodies, is much less the case for the ILC, which should help provide clarity on the actual scope of international norms and notably of States' obligations. Nonetheless, this trend goes hand in hand with the practice of recent ILC projects of not elucidating in the commentaries which provisions pertain to the lex lata and which instead constitute lex ferenda.

define and clarify "the rights and *obligations* of States affected by a disaster in respect of persons present in their territory [...] or in territory under their jurisdiction or control, and the rights and *obligations* of third States and intergovernmental organizations and non-governmental organizations and other entities in a position to cooperate".[20] Indeed, the term "duty" evokes a *moral* rather than a legal obligation, with the risk of perpetuating confusion concerning the actual scope of general international law obligations in a disaster context.[21] The second type of ambiguities instead concerns solidarity, which is regarded as a "fundamental" *value* in the preamble, but is upgraded to an indefinite *principle* in its references in the commentaries.[22]

In conclusion, the Project, in sketching the role of the international community, has not maintained the progressive stance shown vis-à-vis the position of the affected State. With respect to international assistance, its stance is instead quite regressive. The decision to avoid difficult issues—in primis the allocation of responsibilities in the provision of aid—accompanied by the spectre of the *interventionist* implications of R2P, has resulted in a weak and ambiguous framework that seems to contradict the crucial importance that should have been assigned to international cooperation and solidarity.

9.2 Taking Stock of Solidarity and Cooperation in Disasters: Concluding Remarks and Suggestions

Since the Lisbon earthquake of 1755, disasters have been treated as a privileged field of action of international solidarity. The immense tragedy caused by such a mega-disaster was the paradigmatic example upon which Vattel could set out his well-known imperative.

As has been demonstrated, international solidarity has certain features that distinguish it from mere cooperation, specifically the existence of a community of formal equals—sovereign States—which are tied together by some common

---

[20]Cf. ILC, DAs commentaries, DA 1 (Scope), para. 2, emphasis added.

[21]"[T]he term 'duty' ('devoir' in the French version), was not devoid of ambiguity and was capable of bearing either the meaning of an all-encompassing legally binding obligation or one of a mere political or moral engagement" (Report of the Debate on Draft Article 12 [9] (Role of the affected State), in Bartolini, G., Natoli, T. & Riccardi, A. (2015). Report of the Expert Meeting on the ILC's Draft Articles on the Protection of Persons in the Event of Disasters. *International Law and Disasters Working Papers Series*, *3*, 48). See also the statement by ILC member Shinya Murase, who so affirmed: "[...] the Special Rapporteur was right to use the term 'duty' rather than 'obligation': in his own view, the notion of 'duty' fell somewhere between a moral dictate and a legal obligation" (cf. Provisional summary record of the 3102nd meeting, A/CN.4/SR/3102, 25 January 2012), p. 14.

[22]Cf. in particular the commentaries to DA 11 (para. 9) and DA 12 (para. 1). The "*spirit* of solidarity and cooperation" is instead mentioned in the commentary to DA 17 (Termination of external assistance (cf. para. 8, emphasis added).

interests (and concerns) whose achievement can require the postponement of individual interests and objectives. International solidarity, if and to the extent that it is realised in a given domain, should thus result in the (re)-establishment of *substantial* equality among States.

The research carried out in this part highlights that the Vattelian imperative remains a partially unfulfilled promise in international relations, where solidarity is more often evoked than put into practice. It follows that, within the international legal order, at present solidarity is still essentially a (moral) value. Nonetheless, the steady and continuous progress made by international cooperation in disaster response is ultimately based on solidarity, which increasingly shapes disaster response as a veritable structural principle of the subject area.

In times of profound change, as was certainly true of the period following the end of the Cold War and the political instability that ensued at the regional level, as well as with the climate change challenge that has broken out at an ever faster pace in the last decade, it was felt that a sense of solidarity would be more easily develop within the international community. The occurrence of bloody conflicts like those in ex Yugoslavia and Rwanda that followed (and in a way resulted from) the first of the above led to the conceptualisation of the R2P doctrine. When it was launched, this doctrine seemed to have revolutionary potential, but in the end it was significantly downsized by the General Assembly. Remarkably, however, even in its limited endorsement by the GA it can be considered as an institutionalised form of solidarity that—at least in principle—could be applicable *also* in disaster scenarios. However, due to the reticence of UN MS to assume new legally binding obligations, the doctrine as enshrined in the WSO document merely sets out a *moral* standard of action whose application to disasters is contested by a number of States.

As to the second epochal change, i.e. the global changing climatic conditions, its strong connection with the occurrence of disasters has become undeniable.[23] As a result, disaster response in a broad sense (i.e. disaster management) is now amenable to the climate change challenge and thus—considering the latter's repercussions for the protection of *humanity* as a whole—to *the* ultimate common interest or concern of the international community.[24] While the latter still needs to agree on a common action plan capable of effectively tackling such overwhelming challenge, solidarity in disaster response has found realisation at the regional level, notably within the EU legal order.

As has been remarked, solidarity has connoted the EU order since its inception and can be considered as an immanent or structural principle of the system. Disaster response is moreover the field in which it has found most expression. Among the multiple forms that European solidarity can assume in disaster management, the

---

[23]See e.g. International Strategy for Disaster Reduction (2008). Climate Change and Disaster Risk Reduction. *Briefing Note 01*. Geneva (2008).

[24]Not coincidentally, one of the most recent doctrinal contributions on the issue (Benvenisti and Nolte 2018) devotes a chapter to disasters, whose title is also very evocative for our purposes (Law on Natural Disasters: From Cooperation to Solidarity?).

most relevant is the Union Civil Protection Mechanism (UCPM). This mechanism realises solidarity internally (among EU MS) but also externally, and in this latter respect it is part of the broader framework of EU development cooperation. UCPM's recent reform seems to confirm that a system centred—at least theoretically—on voluntariness instead of strict obligations, if accompanied by various incentives to contribute, alongside a strong institutional framework, is capable of strengthening effectiveness and thus ultimately solidarity, too. Furthermore, the enhancement of the prevention and preparedness phases, with corresponding obligations attributed to MS, has reinforced the crucial link between national sovereignty and responsibility on the one hand and international rectius European solidarity on the other.

The success of European solidarity in disasters certainly rests upon the solid foundations of European integration; however, it also demonstrates that solidarity and the ensuing substantial equality that should derive from it are easier to realise in a regional context. Considering States' myopia towards the climate change challenge, geographical (but also cultural) proximity can facilitate group identification and afford even to the most sceptical countries a certain degree of mutuality in the short term. This is exactly what happened in the EU in 2017–2018, when massive fires, disavowing the cliché that southern MS are the major beneficiaries of the European disaster response tools, ravaged with the same intensity Greece, Portugal and the Scandinavian countries.

The EU model is already serving as a blueprint for disaster management in other regions of the globe.[25] In fact, disaster management is a policy area in which cooperation is rapidly progressing at the regional level, additionally because it is predominantly viewed as a technical rather than a political issue. Further, for the reasons already mentioned, even with respect to universal common interests/concerns, solidarity can be realised more easily and at a faster pace in a regional or sub-regional context. ASEAN is a case in point in this respect, as it sets out the most

[25]Cf. Ferris and Petz (2013).

developed disaster management framework after the EU[26] and has regarded the latter as a model in the field.[27]

As to the distinct and broader concept of international cooperation, we have seen that some UN human rights treaty bodies, starting from the CESCR, have increasingly assigned to it an ever greater role, of particular importance in disaster contexts. As clarified by the treaty bodies, cooperation obligations under the respective treaties have a multifaceted nature.

In fact, international cooperation and assistance may be carried out in various forms, engendering different obligations. Among the latter, the most relevant and at the same time the most controversial one is the so-called obligation to provide-fulfil, or more correctly to "support fulfilment".[28] This obligation has special relevance in the case of disasters, like more generally in emergency situations. However, for the time being, the extent of the obligation has not been clearly determined. As a consequence, the obligation to provide is still "imperfect".[29] The main problem is defining what it means in terms of *individual* contributions of States. In this respect, Alston's and Quinn's remarks have not lost their relevance: the existing international cooperation framework resulting from international human rights law cannot be interpreted as imposing "a legally binding obligation upon any particular state to provide any particular form of assistance".[30]

[26]Just 6 months after the Hyogo Framework for Action (HFA), ASEAN MS signed the ASEAN Agreement on Disaster Management and Disaster Response (AADMER), which is the most comprehensive regional treaty on disaster management. It has been in force since December 2009. A key role in implementing the AADMER is entrusted to the ASEAN Committee on Disaster Management (ACDM), which comprises MS' respective national agencies and acts as the executive body of the Agreement, as well as to the ASEAN Coordinating Centre for Humanitarian Assistance on Disaster Management (AHA Centre). The latter was established in 2011 through a separate agreement implementing Art. 20 AADMER (Agreement on the Establishment of the ASEAN Coordinating Centre for Humanitarian Assistance on Disaster Management, 17 November 2011) and aims to facilitate "co-operation and coordination among the Parties, and with relevant United Nations and international organisations, in promoting regional collaboration". Its functions include the management of standby arrangements, risk assessments, information and knowledge management and the facilitation of joint emergency responses. Concerning emergency response, the Centre channels the assistance made available, on a voluntary basis, by States parties following an explicit request by a disaster-stricken MS. More recently, in September 2016, ASEAN's MS signed a declaration whose objective is "to achieve faster response, mobilise greater resources and establish stronger coordination to ensure ASEAN's collective response to disasters (cf. ASEAN, ASEAN Declaration on One ASEAN, One Response: ASEAN Responding to Disasters as One in the Region and Outside the Region, 16 September 2016, para. 1).

[27]Cf. Pennisi di Floristella (2015). Remarkably, ASEAN has solidarity among its foundational principles.

[28]The concept of '[to] support fulfilment' of rights in other States was introduced by the Special Rapporteur on the Right to Food, Mr. Jean Ziegler (cf. ECOSOC, Report of the Special Rapporteur on the Right to Food, Jean Ziegler, E/CN.4/2005/47 of 24 January 2005, para. 56).

[29]De Schutter (2014), p. 222.

[30]Cf. Alston and Quinn (1987), p. 191.

UN treaty bodies, particularly the CESCR, have attempted to clarify the content of the obligation to fulfil with specific reference to development cooperation. Based on States' commitments in multiple fora, the Committee has affirmed that "developed" States parties should devote "at a minimum" 0.7% of their gross national income to international cooperation and assistance.[31] In other words, according to the CESCR, cooperation duties are not the same for every State party and the "responsibility" to provide weighs on those States that are "in a position to assist". Most authors agree that States' contributions to development cooperation in general and to official development assistance (ODA) in particular are still essentially voluntary. At the same time, however, there are some obligations attached to ODA that can be considered as a practical application of the good faith principle. First, developed States are obligated not to reduce the level of ODA and, to the extent possible, to take concrete steps to achieve the 0.7 target.[32] Secondly, the projects financed have to be submitted to a human rights impact assessment in order to verify their compatibility with internationally recognised human rights.

The *soft* character of the obligation to provide seems to be confirmed by the travaux preparatoires of the Optional Protocol to the ICESCR. Indeed, the trust fund established by this instrument has stimulated considerable debate among States and was finally accepted on the condition that contributions to it be purely voluntary.

Up to now, the thorny issue of defining the concrete extent of the obligation to provide and the ensuing distribution of responsibilities among States has not been resolved. As has been seen, the CESCR has utilised a sort of capacity criterion, whose concrete extent is circumscribed by the 0.7 target. However, even adhering to the opinion of whom, like Salomon, deems that the recurrent States' pledges concerning such a target have been translated into a corresponding opinio juris,[33] the absence of clear and binding criteria on the distribution of responsibilities among States prevents the operationalisation of the obligation to fulfil-provide.

Disaster response can certainly be re-comprised among those subjects with respect to which, collective action being frequently required, responsibility should

---

[31]Cf. supra, para. III.1.2.

[32]According to Gómez Isa, although there is no a general legally binding obligation to provide the 0,7 per cent of GNP, developed States are obliged not to reduce the level of ODA and to take concrete steps towards the goal recommended some decades ago by the United Nations, including the obligation of developed States to establish a time frame within which it will be achieved (Gómez Isa 2009, p. 30). More cautious is Vandenhole, who with respect to the EU and its Member States deems that this political commitment is "gradually evolving into a legal obligation at least not to reduce the level of spending on development cooperation, and to take all possible steps with the maximal use of available resources to reach and maintain the 0,7 per cent target as soon as possible, and at the latest at the date envisaged (2015)" (cf. Vandenhole 2007, p. 101). See also Ssenyonjo, according to whom instead "international assistance and co-operation entails procedural fairness. Thus, donor states and NSAs have a responsibility not to withdraw critical aid without first giving the recipient state reasonable notice and an opportunity to make alternative arrangements" Ssenyonjo (2009), p. 81.

[33]Cf. Salomon (2007).

be *shared*.[34] As a consequence, some authors have proposed the application of the principle of joint and several (or "solidary") responsibility.[35] Coming from the domestic private law domain, the principle enables the victim to recover the full amount of reparations from just one of the responsible actors, who can then in turn require compensation from the other actors that may have contributed to the damage.[36] It is clear that from the victim's perspective, this principle is the most protective one. Nonetheless, despite its increasingly frequent invocation by international law scholars,[37] its application to *public* international law is problematic.[38] In particular, joint and several responsibility is difficult to reconcile with State sovereignty[39] and could well "impact [...] upon the propensity of States to cooperate".[40] Moreover, it does not recognise that some States may or should be considered *more responsible* than others.

The difficulties mentioned above have been emphasised by "a paucity of judicial elucidation as to what directives would indicate that a given state was required to act in a particular situation, and how, in order to contribute to fulfilling socio-economic rights in the world".[41] Some inspiration can nonetheless be found in the judgement of the International Court of Justice in *Bosnian Genocide*.[42] In this case, the ICJ identified several parameters to take into account in order to assess whether "a State has duly discharged the obligation [to prevent genocide]",[43] such as "means reasonably available", "the capacity to influence effectively [the action of persons likely to commit, or already committing, genocide]" and "the geographical distance of the State concerned from the scene of the events".[44]

---

[34]On the subject, see generally Nollkamper and Jacobs (2013), p. 359 ff.

[35]On the issue, see generally Besson (2016), pp. 245–259.

[36]Cf. European Group on Tort Law, Principles of European Tort Law: Text and Commentary, art. 9:101(3) (2005).

[37]V. supra, at para. 2 of this Chapter.

[38]It must be noted that the ILC in the commentary to the Project on Responsibility of States for Internationally Wrongful Acts so affirms:

> Terms such as 'joint', 'joint and several' and 'solidary' responsibility derive from different legal traditions and analogies must be applied with care. In international law, the general principle in the case of a plurality of responsible States is that each State is separately responsible for conduct attributable to it in the sense of article 2 [Elements of an internationally wrongful act of a State] (cf. ILC, Commentary to art. 46. Plurality of injured States, in Draft articles on Responsibility of States for Internationally Wrongful Acts, with commentaries, 2001, p. 124).

[39]Cf. Nollkamper and Jacobs (2013), p. 422.

[40]Cf. Van Aaken (2015), p. 157.

[41]Salomon (2014), p. 7.

[42]ICJ, Application of Convention on Prevention and Punishment of Crime of Genocide (Bosnia & Herzegovina v. Serbia & Montenegro), Judgment, 2007 I.C.J. 43, [379 (Feb. 26).

[43]Ibid., para. 430.

[44]Ibid.

If applied collectively to international cooperation's obligations, these criteria could mitigate the criticalities of the recourse to resource capacity alone.[45] Indeed, rather than constituting the sole parameter, capacity should be conceived as a pre-condition. Otherwise, it risks not being accepted by (mostly affluent) States and being perceived as a masked form of assistentialism towards developing countries, de facto encouraging the latter to fail to meet their primary responsibilities. Furthermore, geographical proximity is an important factor in cooperative behaviour and responsibility sharing in disaster response. In fact, in disaster contexts, given that many of the benefits of cooperation in the short term are localised, it is not a coincidence that the most integrated and cohesive cooperation mechanisms have been created at the regional level.

Aside from the distribution of responsibility, another critical issue of international cooperation in disaster response concerns its funding mechanisms, in particular the inequitable distribution of financial aid among disaster-affected countries and related emergencies. Today as never before, humanitarian emergencies are funded through international assistance. Nonetheless, humanitarian needs have also grown at a faster pace than in the past, as a consequence of the outburst of conflicts and natural disasters.[46] The result has been a dire humanitarian financing gap and, as far as disasters are concerned, a still insufficient degree of engagement in their prevention with the funding of DRR activities.

Despite the recognition, including recently by the ILC, that humanitarian principles apply to disasters in all their different phases (prevention, response and recovery/reconstruction) and that a human-rights based approach, as reminded by the CESCR, must also inform development projects, there are still huge inequities concerning the distribution of funding *among* crises and the respective affected States on a global scale. In other terms, although it is now undisputed that humanitarian aid in a broad sense must be provided or distributed without discrimination, there is not yet a corresponding degree of engagement by States to guarantee equality and non-discrimination in the funding of different crises—a sort of *external* non-discrimination—at the international level.[47]

External discrimination manifests itself in the earmarking[48] that characterises much of the humanitarian financing system today. Notwithstanding the various attempts that have been made to reform the system in order to render it more

[45]As effectively stated by Fukuda-Parr and McNeill, 'response-ability' is necessary for those who are assigned obligations Fukuda-Parr and McNeill (2015), p. 11.

[46]"Never before has the world been so generous towards the needs of people affected by conflicts and disasters, and never before has generosity been so insufficient" (High-Level Panel on Humanitarian Financing, Too important to fail—addressing the humanitarian financing gap. Report to the Secretary-General, January 2016, p. 11).

[47]Unfortunately, this aspect is still hardly investigated by the legal doctrine.

[48]Earmarking consists of "any condition applied by a donor to restrict a contribution or part of a contribution to a specific project activity/purpose and/or geographic area" (Inter-Agency Standing Committee (IASC) Humanitarian Financing Task Team, Donor conditions and their implications for humanitarian response, April 2016, p. 10).

equitable as well as more efficient and predictable,[49] States' promises in this respect are still largely unfulfilled. The Central Emergency Response Fund (CERF), established by the General Assembly in 2005 as the UN global emergency response fund,[50] provides only a minimum amount of initial funding for rapid response in sudden-onset disasters and more generally for the most urgent life-saving programmes that are critically under-funded. The biggest share of funding is instead provided by Member States on a purely voluntary basis following specific appeals concerning a given country or region (the so-called Consolidated Appeals Process—CAP).

As a result, at present veritable equitable, solidarity-based funding mechanisms for disaster response exist only regionally (notably at EU level) or within the Red Cross Movement. Indeed, the latter has a Disaster Relief Emergency Fund (DREF) that allows National Societies to immediately respond to needs in large, sudden-onset disasters, as well as in small-to medium-scale emergencies that would not otherwise benefit from international disaster assistance through the provision of start-up loans, small/medium scale grants and allocations.[51]

List of Documents

European Commission, Implementing Decision (EU) 2018/142 of 15 January 2018 amending Implementing Decision 2014/762/EU laying down rules for the implementation of Decision No 1313/2013/EU of the European Parliament and of the Council on a Union Civil Protection Mechanism

European Commission, Communication from the Commission to the European Parliament and the Council. Towards a stronger European disaster response: the role of civil protection and humanitarian assistance, COM(2010) 600 final, 26 October 2010

European Commission, Interim Evaluation of the Union Civil Protection Mechanism. 2014-2016. Final Report, August 2017, available at https://publications.

[49]We refer notably to the Good Humanitarian Donorship initiative (cf. http://ghdinitiative.org/), the Grand Bargain agreed upon at the World Humanitarian Summit in May 2016 by more than thirty of the biggest donors and aid organisations (https://www.agendaforhumanity.org/initiatives/3861), as well as the Global Partnership for Preparedness, also launched at the World Humanitarian Summit to support risk-prone countries in becoming better prepared to responding to and recover from natural disasters (https://www.agendaforhumanity.org/initiatives/3840).

[50]Cf. UN General Assembly Resolution 60/124, Strengthening of the coordination of emergency humanitarian assistance of the United Nations, 15 December 2005.

[51]The DREF was established by the IFRC in 1985. None of the contributions to the DREF is earmarked, allowing the IFRC the freedom to allocate funds exclusively on the basis of needs. Unfortunately, though, the DREF cannot be used to fund DRR activities (cf. IFRC, The Disaster Relief Emergency Fund. What is DREF?, 2012, available at www.ifrc.org/PageFiles/40861/DREFBackgroundpaper.pdf).

europa.eu/en/publication-detail/-/publication/eb41bfee-78c3-11e7-b2f2-01aa75ed71a1/language-en/format-PDF (last accessed on 24 August 2020)
EU, Decision 1313/2013/EU on a Union Civil Protection Mechanism of the European Parliament and of the Council of 17 December 2013 on a Union Civil Protection Mechanism
EU, Decision 2019/420 of The European Parliament and of the Council of 13 March 2019 amending Decision No 1313/2013/EU on a Union Civil Protection Mechanism
Council of the EU, Regulation (EC) No 2012/2002 of 11 November 2002 establishing the European Union Solidarity Fund
Council of the EU, Decision 2014/415/EU of 24 June 2014 on the arrangements for the implementation by the Union of the solidarity clause
ECJ, *Premiums for slaughtering cows*, Case 39/72 72, Judgement of 1 February 1973
ECJ, *N.S. and others*, Joined Cases C-411/10 and C-493/10, Judgement of 21 December 2011
ECJ, Thomas Pringle v. Government of Ireland, Ireland and the Attorney General, Case C-370/12, View of Advocate General Kokott delivered on 26 October 2012
EU, Decision 1313/2013/EU of the European Parliament and of the Council of 17 December 2013 on a Union Civil Protection Mechanism
EU, Regulation 661/2014 of the European Parliament and of the Council of 15 May 2014 amending Council Regulation (EC) No. 2012/2002 establishing the European Union Solidarity Fund
European Commission, Communication from the Commission to the European Parliament and the Council of 26 October 2010—Towards a stronger European disaster response: the role of civil protection and humanitarian assistance (Text with EEA relevance) [COM(2010) 600 final.
European Commission, Communication from the Commission to the European Parliament, the Council, the European Economic and Social Committee and the Committee of the Regions—Renewed social agenda: Opportunities, access and solidarity in 21st century Europe (COM(2008) 412 final, 2 July 2008
European Parliament, Resolution of 22 November 2012 on the EU's mutual defence and solidarity clauses: political and operational dimensions, 2012/2223(INI)
ILC, Sixth report on the protection of persons in the event of disasters, A/CN.4/662
International Commission on Intervention and State Sovereignty (2001), *The Responsibility to Protect. Report*. Ottawa: International Development Research Centre
UN GA, A more secure world: our shared responsibility. Report of the High-level Panel on Threats, Challenges and Change, 2 December 2004, A/59/565
UN GA, In larger freedom: towards development, security and human rights for all: report of the Secretary-General, 21 March 2005, A/59/2005
UN GA, Resolution 60/1 of 16 September 2005, A/RES/60/1
UN GA, Implementing the responsibility to protect. Report of the Secretary-General, A/63/677, 12 January 2009
UN GA-SC, Prevention of armed conflict. Report of the Secretary-General, A/55/985–S/2001/574, 7 June 2001

UN SG, Implementing the Responsibility to Protect: Accountability for Prevention. Report, A/71/1016–S/2017/556, 10 August 2017

References

Allan C, O'Donnell T (2013) An offer you cannot refuse? Natural disasters, the politics of aid refusal and potential legal implications. Amsterdam Law Forum 5(1)

Allan C, O'Donnell T (2016) A duty of solidarity? The international law commission's draft articles and the right to offer assistance in disasters. In: Breau SC, Samuel KLH (eds) Research handbook on disasters and international law. Edward Elgar, Cheltenham, pp 453–478

Alston P, Quinn G (1987) The nature and scope of states parties' obligations under the international covenant on economic, social and cultural rights. Human Rights Q 9(2):156–229

Bartolini G (2017) Il progetto di articoli della Commissione del diritto internazionale sulla "protection of persons in the event of disasters". Rivista di diritto internazionale 3:677–718

Bartolini G, Natoli T, Riccardi A (2015) Report of the expert meeting on the ILC's draft articles on the protection of persons in the event of disasters. Int Law Disasters Work Pap Ser 3:48

Benvenisti E, Nolte G (eds) (2018) Community interests across international law. Oxford University Press, Oxford

Besson S (2016) L'application extra-territoriale des droits de l'homme internationaux en pratique: juridictions concurrentes, obligations conjointes et responsabilités partagées. In: D'Argent (ed) Droit des frontières internationales. Actes des journées franco-allemandes de droit international. Pedone, Paris, pp 245–259

De Schutter O (2014) International human rights law: cases, materials, commentary. Cambridge University Press, Cambridge

Ferris E, Petz D (2013) In the neighborhood: the growing role of regional organizations in disaster risk management. The Brookings Institution, Washington DC

Fukuda-Parr S, McNeill D (2015) Post 2015: a new era of accountability? J Global Ethics 11 (1):10–17

Gómez Isa F (2009) Transnational obligations in the field of economic, social and cultural rights. Revista Electrónica De Estudios Internacionales 18:1–30

International Strategy for Disaster Reduction (2008) Climate Change and Disaster Risk Reduction. Briefing Note 01. Geneva (2008)

Nollkamper A, Jacobs D (2013) Shared responsibility in international law: a conceptual framework. Mich J Int Law 34:359 ff

Pennisi di Floristella A (2015) Building the ASEAN Center for Humanitarian Assistance and Emergency Response. KFG Working Paper, 62

Salomon ME (2007) Global responsibility for human rights: world poverty and the development of international law. Oxford University Press, Oxford

Salomon ME (2014) How to keep promises: making sense of the duty among multiple states to fulfil socio-economic rights in the world. SHARES research paper, 53. Amsterdam Center for International Law, Amsterdam. Available at http://www.sharesproject.nl/publication/how-to-keep-promises-making-sense-of-the-duty-among-multiple-states-to-fulfil-socio-economic-rights-in-the-world/ (last accessed on 24 August 2020)

Ssenyonjo M (2009) Economic, social and cultural rights in international law. Hart, Oxford

Van Aaken A (2015) Shared responsibility in international law: a political economy analysis. In: Nollkamper A, Jacobs D, Schechinger JNM (eds) Distribution of responsibilities in international law. Cambridge University Press, Cambridge, pp 153–191

Vandenhole W (2007) EU and development: extraterritorial obligations under the international covenant on economic, social and cultural rights. In: Salomon ME, Tostensen A, Vandenhole W

(eds) Casting the net wider: human rights, development and new duty-bearers. Intersentia, Cambridge, pp 85–106
Zorzi Giustiniani F (2012) The works of the international law commission on 'protection of persons in the event of disasters'. A critical appraisal. In: De Guttry A, Gestri M, Venturini G (eds) International disaster response law. Springer, pp 65–84

Part IV
Civil-Military Relations in Disaster Contexts

Chapter 10
Civil-Military Relations in Disaster Contexts

Contents

10.1 Preliminary Remarks

Even in cases in which a disaster breaks out in a country where there is no conflict, military personnel and assets play an increasingly common role in disaster response. At the national level, the military is generally the first to intervene in a disaster scene. Indeed, with obvious differences across countries, the national military is usually the best equipped, and for this reason can mobilise and reach a disaster-affected zone in a short time. More generally, in various sectors military personnel have unique capabilities that are crucial for disaster response, such as: technical assistance and facilities (especially logistics and communications), search and rescue capacities and transport.

Foreign military personnel are also increasingly often involved in disaster relief operations. The engagement of foreign and international military forces in the delivery of assistance after a disaster is not a new phenomenon, but it has reached a certain level since the response to Hurricane Mitch in 1998, which saw the involvement of military forces from twelve States out of thirty contributing countries, and its importance is destined to grow as a result of both the increase in the

F. Zorzi Giustiniani, *International Law in Disaster Scenarios*,
https://doi.org/10.1007/978-3-030-50597-4_10

incidence of natural disasters and the growing assignment of civil protection functions to national armies.[1]

This situation brings with it a number of problems and challenges.[2] First of all, the presence of foreign military forces may well be perceived as a threat to the affected State's sovereignty; a fortiori given that it frequently occurs in countries with fragile institutions, which is often true of States that are particularly prone to natural disasters. Regardless of this perception and its foundation, concrete challenges are then posed by the need to coordinate the work of foreign military actors and that of their international and national *civilian* counterparts. In order to cope with these problems, the international community has engaged in various forms of civil-military coordination for humanitarian operations,[3] notably concerning the use of foreign military assets and of military or armed escorts for humanitarian convoys.

10.2 The Use of Foreign Military Assets

While the majority of IDL treaties are concerned with various aspects of disaster response, and in particular with disaster relief, only a few of them expressly regulate military relief.[4] Among those that cover military relief, we find several regional agreements such as the ASEAN ADMER, CDERA[5] and BSEC Agreements.[6] Pertinent legal issues are also addressed by existing status of forces agreements (SOFAs) established at the bilateral and regional level.[7] However, a thorough

[1]On the issue, see generally: Metcalfe et al. (2012); Wiharta et al. (2008); Park (2008), p. 895.

[2]On the issue, see the research conducted by Haugevik and de Carvalho (2007).

[3]Humanitarian civil-military coordination is defined by IASC and OCHA as "the essential dialogue and interaction between civilian and military actors in humanitarian emergencies that is necessary to protect and promote humanitarian principles, avoid competition, minimize inconsistency, and when appropriate pursue common goals. Basic strategies range from coexistence to cooperation. Coordination is a shared responsibility facilitated by liaison and common training" (cf. UN-CMCoord, Field Handbook Version 2.0 (2018), p. 8).

[4]Cf. ILC, Memorandum of the Secretariat, Protection of Persons in the Event of Disasters, 31 March 2008 (11 December 2007), A/CN.4/590, paras. 190 ff. See also Fisher (2007a), p. 155.

[5]Agreement Establishing the Caribbean Disaster Emergency Response Agency, 26 February 1991.

[6]Agreement among the Governments of the Participating States of the Black Sea Economic Cooperation (BSEC) on Collaboration in Emergency Assistance and Emergency Response to Natural and Man-Made Disasters, 15 April 1998.

[7]Cf. e.g. NATO, Model Agreement Covering the Status of National Elements of the EADRU on Mission on the Territory of a Stricken Nation, in annex 4 of the *Standing Operating Procedures for the Euro-Atlantic Disaster Response Unit (EADRU)*, 16 April 2007.

regulation of various aspects of the use of foreign military assets at universal level is contained in a couple of non-binding instruments developed by the Inter-Agency Standing Committee (IASC): the Oslo Guidelines[8] and the MCDA Guidelines.[9] The first document regulates the use of foreign military and civil defence assets (MCDAs) following disasters—that is, "natural, technological and environmental emergencies"—occurring in times of peace, while the second one addresses the same topic in the context of complex emergencies. Both guidelines try to respond to the need to bring order in an area that has traditionally been, and in some cases still is, a source of tension between humanitarian and military actors.[10] They lay down principles and standards that aim to improve coordination and ensure the most appropriate use of MCDAs in emergency situations.

The two documents try to respond to the main concerns and problems that generally arise from recourse to MCDAs, such as the risks for the impartiality of the relief, the blurring of the distinction between civilian and military action, and the lack of the required sensitivity to carry out the humanitarian assistance. In order to do so, the documents reiterate the crucial roles of core humanitarian principles (and consequently the need for all actors—starting with the military ones—to respect them) and national emergency response mechanisms, thus treating foreign MCDAs as complementary to, and not as replacements, of such mechanisms.[11] Among the other key concepts that guide the use of MCDAs, the most relevant one is certainly the principle of last resort.[12]

---

[8]Guidelines on The Use of Military and Civil Defence Assets In Disaster Relief, Rev.1.1, November 2007 (Oslo Guidelines). These guidelines were developed by the United Nations and then accepted, at an international conference held in Oslo in 1994, by all the participating States (45) and organizations (25). Their most recent revision dates from 2007. They are based on the assumption that the affected State has a stable government and can provide the necessary security to international organisations utilising MCDAs. Non-binding in character, they can be used to establish an interim SOFA between a host country and another State's military, if no bilateral or multilateral agreements exist.

[9]Guidelines on the use of military and civil defence assets to support United Nations humanitarian activities in complex emergencies, March 2003, Revision I, January 2006 (MCDA Guidelines). This document aims to "provide guidelines for the use of international military and civil defence personnel, equipment, supplies and services *in support of the United Nations* (UN) in pursuit of humanitarian objectives in complex emergencies" (ibid., p. 5, para. 11, emphasis added). Nonetheless, it is also relevant for the humanitarian actors at large to enable them to understand the wider operational context in which they may find themselves.

[10]Cf. Calvi Parisetti (2012), p. 587.

[11]The "fundamentally civilian character of humanitarian assistance" and the fact that military assets must be used "in conformity with international humanitarian law and humanitarian principles" is routinely underlined by the UN General Assembly (cf. e.g. GA Res. 59/141, 25 February 2005, para. 11). "[T]he primary position of civilian organisations in implementing humanitarian action, particularly in areas affected by armed conflict" is also reaffirmed by the Good Humanitarian Donorship Principles (see Meeting Conclusions, International Meeting on Good Humanitarian Donorship, Stockholm 16–17 June 2003, para. 19).

[12]The term "last resort" was first introduced, by consensus, by the Drafting and Review Committees of the 2003 'MCDA Guidelines'. It then appeared in the 2007 revision of the Oslo Guidelines.

As enshrined in the said guidelines, the principle of last resort demands that MCDAs be used to support the humanitarian response only if they meet four criteria.[13] First, unique capability: there must be a *unique* specific capability or asset requirement that cannot be met appropriately with available civilian alternatives. Second, timeliness: the urgency of the task must require immediate action. Third, civilian control: the humanitarian operation as a whole must maintain a civilian character under the overall authority of the responsible humanitarian organisation.[14] Fourth, time-limited: the recourse to military assets must be limited in time and scale.

Despite the apparent clarity of this principle, there has been wide disagreement over its interpretation and practical application within the humanitarian community and, more broadly, among the different actors involved on the ground. Indeed, while it is generally uncontested that the military possesses certain unique capabilities in crucial sectors of disaster response, the opinions of governments and humanitarian actors opinions diverge "about how much weight to give these 'unique' characteristics when balancing them against issues such as cost burdens, the risk of militarizing the relief effort and how the presence of foreign troops affects civilian humanitarian actors' safety and freedom to operate".[15]

In this respect, the country-specific guidelines that are typically developed by the OCHA country office do not help much, as they reproduce the generic language of the global guidelines on key issues, including last resort.[16]

10.3 The Use of Military or Armed Escorts for Humanitarian Convoys

Another important aspect of civil-military relations concerns the use of armed protection for humanitarian convoys. While the issue is obviously crucial in armed conflict situations as well as in complex emergencies, at first sight it could appear to be not very relevant in 'pure' disasters. Nonetheless, even outside contexts of generalised violence, humanitarian operators are easy targets for common criminals. Moreover, armed escorts are generally supplied by the affected State's authorities, and this remains true in times of disaster. This is what happened, for instance, to humanitarian organisations arriving in Indonesia after the 2004 tsunami.

The attitude of the humanitarian community to this issue has always been extremely varied, but, over time, resort to armed protection has become more and more common. To invert this trend and reaffirm the fundamental civilian character of

[13]Cf. Oslo Guidelines, paras. 32 ii, 35, 38; MCDA Guidelines, paras. 26 ii and 33.

[14]Cf. Oslo Guidelines, para. 37; MCDA Guidelines, para. 6.

[15]Cf. Wilharta et al. (2008), p. xi.

[16]Cf. Metcalfe and Berg (2012), p. 9.

relief, a specific set of guidelines was devised in 2001 by the IASC.[17] These guidelines provide that "as a general rule" armed protection will not be used by humanitarians.[18] Only "in exceptional circumstances" may the use of armed escorts be considered necessary as a "last resort" to enable humanitarian action.[19] The criteria to be satisfied in order to deviate from the general rule are multiple: 1. humanitarian need and programme criticality (the transport of essential personnel and relief supplies to avoid "unacceptable human suffering" cannot be undertaken without the use of armed escorts); 2. responsible authorities (national or local authorities do not provide the necessary support without the use of armed escorts); 3. safety and security (the armed escorts can provide the safety of humanitarian personnel without compromising their security or that of the beneficiaries); 4. sustainability (the use of an armed escort will not irreversibly compromise the humanitarian operating environment not even in the future).[20]

However, the application of the Guidelines proved problematic in practice. As was shown, inter alia, by the response to the 2010 Haiti earthquake,[21] resort to armed protection is indeed still the rule, irrespective of the existence of real security risks on the ground.

10.4 The 2010 Pakistan Floods Response: A Case Study

The 2010 Pakistan flood response is a case in point since it perfectly epitomises certain problems and challenges concerning civil-military coordination and, notably, the use of foreign military assets in complex emergencies.

The monsoon floods that hit Pakistan in 2010 constituted one of the most devastating disasters of recent times, displacing as they did over 20 millions people, or a tenth of the country's population. This catastrophe can be counted among the real mega-disasters that have ever happened worldwide.[22] Moreover, the floods occurred in a context of continued armed violence and in the aftermath of a displacement crisis stemming from major military operations conducted by the government in the north-west of the country against Taliban militants.

[17]Cf. IASC Guidelines on the Use of Armed Escorts for Humanitarian Convoys, 27 February 2013. The latest version of the Guidelines takes into account the evolution of security risk management procedures within the UN and non-UN organisations, and the increasing complex nature of the scenarios in which a growing number of humanitarian and military actors operate on the ground.

[18]Ibid., 3.

[19]Ibid., 2, 4 ff.

[20]Ibid., 7.

[21]IASC, Challenges in Humanitarian Civil–Military Coordination, 79th IASC Working Group Meeting, WO/1106/3732/7, 2011.

[22]As was noted by A. Madiwale and K. Virk, the people affected by the Pakistani floods were "more than the total number of people affected by the 2004 Indian Ocean tsunami, the 2005 Pakistan earthquake, and the 2010 Haiti earthquake combined" (2011, p. 1091).

Against this background, the first problem that was posed to the actors carrying out interventions concerned the definition of the situation: was it *merely* a natural disaster or, rather, was it a complex emergency? While the latter choice would have appeared to be the more correct one, several humanitarian organisations, including some UN agencies and intergovernmental organisations as well as Pakistani authorities and organisations, thought differently; as a result they relied on the MCDA Guidelines rather than on the Oslo Guidelines, or, at least, they took a more lax approach to civil-military relations.[23]

As to country-specific guidelines, just a few months before the disaster the United Nations, through the Humanitarian Country Team (HCT) established in the country, had adopted the Pakistan Civil–military Guidelines.[24] This document was more detailed than comparable country-specific guidelines as to the relationships between the affected State's institutions and military and humanitarian actors. Nonetheless, the process whereby it was developed was not very inclusive, as only a core group of international NGOs participated, while local and national actors were completely excluded.[25] The lack of involvement of the national authorities was particularly serious in a country like Pakistan, where, since the 2005 earthquake, the army had played a leading role in disaster management.[26] This, combined with the fact that the resulting guidelines were endorsed neither by the government nor by the army, obviously affected the interaction among civil and military actors in the disaster response.[27]

In the case at hand the picture was further complicated by two elements. The first was the dual role played by the affected State, which, through its military, was the first responder to the disaster and also a belligerent in the ongoing conflict in the country. The second was the deployment of foreign military assets, including assets from States that were fighting in the neighbouring Afghanistan and that had, in some cases, undertaken air operations in parts of Pakistan.[28] Specific challenges, in this

[23]Ibid., p. 1104.

[24]The Guidelines were formally adopted by the HCT on 5 March 2010.

[25]Cf. Greenwood and Balachandran (2014), p. 11.

[26]Not coincidentally, Pakistan's representative, in commenting at the first reading on the ILC draft articles before their adoption, "considered draft article 12 [now Article 10, Role of the affected State] to be the essential provision in the draft articles, and indicated that the primacy of the affected State in the provision of disaster relief assistance was based on the central principle of international law, i.e., State sovereignty" (ILC, Eighth Report on the Protection of Persons in the Event of Disasters, 17 March 2016, A/CN.4/697, para. 215).

[27]Cf. Greenwood and Balachandran (2014), p. 1 ff. And though, almost paradoxically, the Pakistan guidelines are the only country-specific guidelines which regulate in detail the relationship between national authorities and foreign actors.

[28]According to E. Ferris: "In these complex environments national military forces, as in Myanmar and Pakistan, can take the lead and limit the ability of other parties - civilian or military, national or international - to provide assistance. The role of international military forces in responding to disasters in conflict areas will carry with it the baggage of tension and suspicion that characterises the forces' involvement in humanitarian work in complex emergencies" (Ferris 2012, p. 7).

latter respect, concerned the interpretation and application of the principle of last resort.

On 20 August NATO announced its decision to deliver in-kind donations from its Member States using an air bridge to Pakistan. The organisation also offered this service to humanitarian agencies, and publicised it without prior consultation. After broad internal consultations, the HCT decided that the military capability offered by NATO could not be approved, particularly because of the security risks deriving from the obvious association of NATO assets with the conflict in Afghanistan; moreover Alliance convoys had been attacked several times in Afghanistan. Last but not least, and conclusively, the HCT determined that the air bridge was not a last resort option, since air and sea transport were also available commercially. Despite the decision of the HCT, some UN agencies and several small NGOs made use of the air bridge, although only occasionally.[29]

More broadly, differences on the last resort principle existed among humanitarian as well as governmental actors (Pakistan, the United States and the United Kingdom). As to humanitarians, while the HCT interpreted the principle as allowing recourse to military capabilities only when saving lives and alleviating suffering, even indirectly, was at issue, others considered that the cost of the operation had to be evaluated in the assessment of "last resort".[30] As was rightly remarked, "[t]he fact that 'last resort' and the guidelines themselves can be interpreted in such vastly different ways undermines the very value of guidance and points to an urgent need for greater clarity and agreement on the principle".[31]

Last but not least, it must be taken into account that the various existing guidelines on civil-military relations are non-binding documents and that as such, respect for them rests upon their persuasiveness as well as the participatory character of the drafting process. In this regard, the case at hand does not differ from most other disaster or complex emergency contexts in which country-specific guidelines were not accepted by national governments and military forces.[32] Nonetheless, the primary role of national authorities in disaster response makes their involvement in decisions directly affecting their sovereign competences unavoidable, because otherwise they would threaten the effectiveness of the whole relief operation. This is all the more true when foreign aid consists of military personnel or assets, since the latter inevitably raise "special sovereignty and security concerns".[33]

[29] Cf. Madiwale and Virk (2011), p. 1096.

[30] Organisations like Médecins sans Frontières (MSF) and the ICRC, instead, preferred not to recur at military assets in order to safeguard their perceived impartiality.

[31] Madiwale and Virk (2011), p. 1104.

[32] In the Pakistani case the scarce attitude to coordinate on the part of international organisations was so much more serious considering that "international actors had greater capacity to influence [Pakistan's] strategies and behaviour than local actors and affected populations" (Metcalfe and Berg 2012, p. 17). See also Shah (2011).

[33] Cf. Fisher (2007b), p. 307.

10.5 Foreign Military Relief in the ILC DAs

The resort to foreign military relief (material and personnel) is also envisaged by the Draft Articles, as part of the broad notion of external assistance. However, despite some refinements made in the second reading, the ILC's commentaries touch upon the topic only tangentially.

A first reference to foreign military relief is found in DA 3e) (Use of terms), which defines "relief personnel" as "civilian or *military* personnel sent by an assisting State or other assisting actor for the purpose of providing disaster relief assistance".[34] This definition is expressly inspired by two documents, the Oslo Guidelines and the 2010 Framework Convention on Civil Defence Assistance. The DAs as approved at the first reading specifically mentioned "civilian and military relief personnel" in DA 17 (now 15) (Facilitation of external assistance) too, while DA 18 (now 16) (Protection of relief personnel, equipment and goods) referred to relief personnel tout court. This inconsistency was reported by several States, and was subsequently eliminated in the second reading, where there is only a specific reference to civilian and military personnel in DA 3. More importantly, several States lamented the lack of reference to the Oslo Guidelines, and in particular to the principle of last resort.[35] However, despite the Special Rapporteur's proposal to take this suggestion into account,[36] the last resort concept is absent from the final text. It could certainly be argued that the limited and complementary role of military relief is recognised implicitly by the DAs, with, on the one hand, their emphasis on the sovereignty of the affected State and the corollaries of this sovereignty[37], and the recognition of the fundamental principles of humanitarian assistance, on the other hand. Nonetheless, the particular relevance of the last resort formula hardly renders its omission from a codification exercise justifiable.[38] A fortiori this is true, given that the final text

[34]Emphasis added. The term "relief personnel" is incorporated in the more general notion of "external assistance", that is "relief personnel, equipment and goods, and services provided to an affected State by an assisting State or other assisting actor for disaster relief assistance" (cf. DA 3 e)).

[35]For instance the Czech Republic, Germany, the European Union and OCHA had recommended to "take into account the Oslo Guidelines, which specify that international military assets are to be used only as a last resort when civilian alternatives are exhausted" (cf. ILC, A/CN.4/697, para. 85).

[36]The Special Rapporteur in particular proposed to specify in DA 4 e) (now DA 3 e)) that "military assets shall be used only where there is no comparable civilian alternative to meet a critical humanitarian need" (ibid., para. 91).

[37]We refer in particular to the consent rule and the possibility to pose conditions on external assistance (cf. Bartolini, G., Natoli, T., & Riccardi, A. (2015). Report of the expert meeting on the ILC's Draft Articles on the Protection of Persons in the Event of Disasters. Roma Tre University Department of Law - 8 and 9 June 2015. *International Law and Disasters Working Papers Series*, *3*, 27).

[38]More nuanced is the critique of Bartolini, who affirms that "a mention of this principle in the commentary would have reaffirmed a basic tenet of international relief operations" (Bartolini 2017, p. 1115).

contains several references to the Oslo Guidelines[39] and that the ILC claimed that the choice of mentioning military relief personnel was a "recognition of the *important role* played by [the latter] [. . .] in the provision of disaster relief assistance".[40]

The said omission also stands in stark contrast with the treatment of the use of armed protection, whose exceptional character as well as basic requirements are recalled in the commentary to DA 16 (Protection of relief personnel, equipment and goods). In this regard the Commission affirms that "the possibility of resorting to armed escorts in disaster relief operations to dispel safety concerns should be strictly assessed according to the best practices developed in this area by the main humanitarian actor",[41] and refers in particular to the 2013 Guidelines on the Use of Armed Escorts for Humanitarian Convoys. It then underlines that, before using such military assets, "[their] consequences [. . .] and [. . .] possible alternatives [. . .] should be considered by the relevant actors, especially taking into account that the security concerns that may prevail in disaster situations may be far less serious than those present in other scenarios".[42]

10.6 Concluding Observations

As been seen in this chapter, the growing involvement of foreign military personnel and assets in disaster response poses a number of problems and operational challenges, thus rendering an effective coordination between all the civilian and military actors present on the ground indispensable. Such coordination is particularly difficult because of the different mandates, capacities and cultures of the various actors, as well as the primary and unavoidable role of the State directly hit by the emergency.

Civil-military relations are regulated mainly through non-binding guidelines, which create distinct legal frameworks for complex emergencies and *mere* disasters. Consequently, the definition of a crisis has a crucial importance for the legal and practical implications. As was shown by the Pakistani case, however, this is often a first issue of contention among the intervening actors.

A particularly relevant question that is addressed by the existing guidelines concerns the limits of the resort to foreign military assets and personnel. On the basis of the principle of 'last resort', military assets, as well as armed protection, should be used in exceptional circumstances in order to fulfil a humanitarian gap, notably where there is no comparable civilian alternative and only if the use is necessary to meet a critical humanitarian need. The frequent divergences in the

[39] After the IFRC Guidelines, which before the DAs constituted the major reference document on IDRL at international level, the Oslo guidelines constitute the non-binding instrument that is referred to most often in the text.

[40] Cf. ILC, DAs commentaries, DA3, para. 27, emphasis added.

[41] Cf. Ibid., DA16, para. 9.

[42] Ibid.

interpretation and application of this principle, and more broadly of the guidelines, show, however, that "the diplomatic skills required to obtain buy-in are as important as, if not more important than, the technical skill required to develop solid guidelines".[43]

A military component of foreign assistance is also envisaged by the DAs. Nonetheless, despite the suggestions of various States, the final text contains only scant references to the topic and completely ignores the last resort principle with respect to the use of military assets. This absence, coupled with the recognition of the important role of the military which is acknowledged in the commentaries, creates a limited and ambiguous picture of the topic that is all the more disappointing for a codification work.

List of Documents

Agreement Establishing the Caribbean Disaster Emergency Response Agency, 26 February 1991

Agreement among the Governments of the Participating States of the Black Sea Economic Cooperation (BSEC) on Collaboration in Emergency Assistance and Emergency Response to Natural and Man-Made Disasters, 15 April 1998

Bartolini, G., Natoli, T., & Riccardi, A. (2015). Report of the expert meeting on the ILC's Draft Articles on the Protection of Persons in the Event of Disasters. Roma Tre University Department of Law - 8 and 9 June 2015. *International Law and Disasters Working Papers Series, 3*

Guidelines on the Use of Foreign Military and Civil Defence Assets in Disaster Relief - (1994/Updated Nov. 2006/Rev.1.1 Nov. 2007) (Oslo Guidelines)

Guidelines on the Use of Military and Civil Defence Assets to Support United Nations Humanitarian Activities in Complex Emergencies (March 2003/Rev. I Jan. 2006)

Guidelines on the use of military and civil defence assets to support United Nations humanitarian activities in complex emergencies, March 2003, Revision I, January 2006 (MCDA Guidelines)

HCT, Pakistan Civil–military Guidelines, 5 March 2010

IASC, Non-Binding Guidelines on the Use of Armed Escorts for Humanitarian Convoys, 27 February 2012

IASC, Guidelines on the Use of Armed Escorts for Humanitarian Convoys, 27 February 2013

IASC, Challenges in Humanitarian Civil–Military Coordination, 79th IASC Working Group Meeting, WO/1106/3732/7, 2011

ILC, Eighth Report on the Protection of Persons in the Event of Disasters, 17 March 2016, A/CN.4/697

[43] Madiwale and Virk (2011), p. 19.

ILC, Memorandum of the Secretariat, Protection of Persons in the Event of Disasters, 31 March 2008 (11 December 2007), A/CN.4/590

NATO, Model Agreement Covering the Status of National Elements of the EADRU on Mission on the Territory of a Stricken Nation, *in annex 4 of the* Standing Operating Procedures for the Euro-Atlantic Disaster Response Unit (EADRU), 16 April 2007

UN-CMCoord, Field Handbook Version 2.0 (2018)

UN GA, Resolution 59/141, 25 February 2005

References

Bartolini G (2017) A universal treaty for disasters? Remarks on the International Law Commission's Draft Articles on the protection of persons in the event of disasters. Int Rev Red Cross 99 (3):1103–1137

Calvi Parisetti P (2012) The use of civil and military defense assets in emergency situations. In: De Guttry A, Gestri M, Venturini G (eds) International disaster response law. Springer, New York, p 587

Ferris E (2012) Future directions in civil-military responses to natural disasters. Australian Civil-military Centre, Paper 05

Fisher D (2007a) Law and legal issues in international disaster response: a desk study. International Federation of Red Cross and Red Crescent Societies, Geneva

Fisher D (2007b) The law of international disaster response: overview and ramifications for military actors. Int Law Stud 83(1)

Greenwood L, Balachandran G (2014) The search for common ground. Civil-military relations in Pakistan. HPG Working Paper, March

Haugevik K, de Carvalho B (2007) Civil-military cooperation in multinational and interagency operations discussion paper on operational terminologies and assessment for security in practice, no. 2. Norwegian Institute of International Affairs

Madiwale A, Virk K (2011) Civil-military relations in natural disasters: a case study of the 2010 Pakistan floods. Int Rev Red Cross 93(884)

Metcalfe V, Berg M (2012) Country-specific civil-military coordination guidelines. HPG Working Paper

Metcalfe V, Haysom S, Gordon S (2012) Trends and challenges in humanitarian civil–military coordination. A review of the literature, HPG Working Paper

Park W (2008) Civil-military co-ordination in complex humanitarian situations, Report on Wilton Park Conference, 895

Shah Z (2011) Military–humanitarian relations in Pakistan. Humanitarian Exchange 49

Wiharta S et al (2008) The effectiveness of foreign military assets in natural disaster response. Stockholm International Peace Research Institute

Wilharta S, Ahmad H, Haine J-Y, Löfgre J, Randall T (2008) The effectiveness of foreign military assets in disaster response. Stockholm International Peace Research Institute

Part V
General Conclusions

Chapter 11
General Conclusions

The increasing quantity and severity of disasters in the last decades has led to an exponential growth in the number of instruments, of both a binding and a non-binding character, that regulate the response to such events. Nonetheless, the failure of initiatives that aimed to provide a binding (institutional as well as legal) framework of comprehensive scope at the universal level explains why such a framework has been developed in a piecemeal and fragmented manner. Over time, the various instruments and frameworks that address disaster response have progressively been identified as being part of a separate regime, originally named IDRL and more recently, as a result of its broadening scope, IDL tout court. Regimes, or distinct sets of rules governing specified subject areas ratione materiae, are a doctrinal construct that is intended to describe the increasing specialisation and perceived fragmentation of international law. However, any doctrinal construct can give only a partial description of reality. This is all the more true for the field of disaster response, as disasters and their management are a cross-cutting issue. Consequently, the rules applicable to disaster contexts cannot be contained within the boundaries of any given regime. The situation is even more complicated in complex emergencies, when the rules governing armed conflicts (IHL), as well as those protecting internationally recognised human rights (IHRL), if there is no derogation from them, continue to apply. The scrutiny of the two major models for selecting a regime has shown that both the models and, more generally, the reasoning in terms of regimes, are insufficient. Indeed, the choice of the applicable legal framework should instead be made at the level of single norms and on a case-by-case basis, taking into account the following factors: the level of detail of the norms and the more or less precise scope of their application; the nexus of the situation with the armed conflict or the disaster; the geographical proximity of the disaster to areas of active hostilities; and, ultimately, the exigencies of military necessity. As a result of the multiplicity of subjects acting in such mixed scenarios—mainly states, armed groups and humanitarian organisations of both an inter-governmental and a non-governmental character—and the scarcity of customary

F. Zorzi Giustiniani, *International Law in Disaster Scenarios*,
https://doi.org/10.1007/978-3-030-50597-4_11

norms specifically addressing disasters, the applicable framework is *necessarily* varied and case-specific. Scholars as well as states and the broader international community should thus devote greater attention to the identification of criteria and standard situations that could facilitate the selection of norms in the field.

Disasters, like other national emergencies, fall within the sovereign competences of a state, which is entitled to address them as it deems appropriate while respecting the constraints imposed by international law. The affected state's primacy in disaster response has two facets, which are amenable, respectively, to a more traditional vision of sovereignty and to a people-centred vision. The first understanding of sovereignty is expressed by the control of relief activities in all its phases. The primary role of the affected state in disaster response has long been dismissed by humanitarians as well as by donors but, even today, it cannot be ignored. Moreover, as a result of the DRR agenda, the centrality of territorial states in addressing disaster (risk) management is increasingly recognised.

The second facet is, by contrast, expressed internally by the sovereign state's primary duty to protect and assist its population and externally by the stronger limits set by international law on an outright refusal of any offer of external help. Implicit limits on the absolute character of the requirement for consent are imposed by international human rights law and, notably, by the obligations of international cooperation in that domain as epitomised by Art. 2.1 of the ICESCR.

Overall, the role of external action needs to be *complementary* to that of the affected state, so as not to undermine national capacities and responsibilities or disempower the affected population. Indeed, sovereignty on the one hand and international cooperation and solidarity on the other are the two main pillars of the international legal framework on disaster response.

International cooperation and solidarity are increasingly evoked in international fora as well as in the legal literature to address common interests and concerns, with disaster response featuring prominently among the latter. Cooperation and solidarity were also referred to by the ILC Special Rapporteur Valencia-Ospina as some of the "underlying principles" of the Project "Protection of persons in the event of disasters". In its most specific sense, cooperation marks the new historical era of international relations inaugurated by the UN Charter, and is conceived by the latter as the main instrument for promoting truly peaceful relations among states. It features the law of cooperation, as opposed to the law of coexistence that prevailed in classic international law and was mainly based on obligations to abstain and the predominance of the egoistic interests of states. Progressively, cooperation has built some new layers of law whose aim is to improve inter-state relations through the realisation of community values such as equality, justice, order and peace.

The idea of solidarity began to be used quite recently in international legal thinking and practice. Despite the increasingly common evocation of the crucial relevance of solidarity in today's globalised world and also in international fora, solidarity remains an elusive concept whose meaning and status in international law is still contested. In our analysis we found that the main features of solidarity can be identified in the following: the existence of a group whose members, tied together by certain common interests and objectives, agree to realise those interests and objectives even if this implies the postponement of *individual* interests and objectives. Unlike altruism, it necessarily requires a degree of group identification. Moreover, and unlike charity, it is a relationship among formal equals that is based on interdependence and a certain element of mutuality, even if not strict reciprocity. It was affirmed only recently in the international legal order, since this order is premised on the autonomy of its members, as expressed in the concept of sovereignty. However, solidarity should not be considered to be opposed to sovereignty. The relationship between the two concepts is, rather, a mutually reinforcing one. In particular, international solidarity is functional to the effective realisation of *substantive* equality among states. As has been seen, Vattel was a precursor in this regard, as he conceived the society of nations as necessarily united, on the basis of the concept of common humanity.

Unlike cooperation, solidarity at present shapes only a limited number of branches, or, to put it better, subject matters of international law. Disaster response is certainly one of these. As shown by our analysis of international cooperation obligations in Part III, international solidarity can be considered as a *value* that lies at the foundation of these obligations, as interpreted and applied in the practice of UN treaty bodies. More generally, though, the steady and continuous progress made by international cooperation in disaster response allows us to affirm that disaster response is increasingly informed by solidarity as a structural principle in this subject area.

At present, it is within the EU order that solidarity in disasters has found its most complete expression, and in its internal dimension it is not only a value but already a definite principle of EU law. European solidarity in disasters has been realised in different forms, the most relevant being the UCPM. The functioning of the UCPM proves, in particular, the efficacy of a system in which, through various incentives, states are *induced*, but not obliged, to contribute and which is governed by a strong institutional framework. Apart from the peculiarities of the European integration process, this success proves that solidarity, and the ensuing substantive equality that should derive from it, is easier to realise in a regional context. Indeed, the regional level renders group identification smoother, through geographical and cultural proximity as well as a certain mutuality in the short term. Moreover, disaster management, being perceived as a technical rather than a political issue, has been the object of multiple regional and sub-regional cooperation frameworks. For its part, the EU has already served as a model in this respect, being the source of inspiration for the development by ASEAN of a more integrated and solidary system for disaster response.

As to the broader notion of international cooperation, some UN human rights treaty bodies, starting from the CESCR, have interpreted and applied it as engendering various obligations. Among these obligations, the most relevant and at the time the most controversial is the so-called obligation to provide–fulfil, which is particularly relevant in emergency situations and, even more specifically, in disaster contexts. However, for the time being this obligation still has *imperfect* results, mainly because it is not clear what it means in terms of individual contributions by states. The CESCR has utilised a sort of capacity criterion, whose concrete extent is circumscribed by the 0.7 target. Nonetheless, the absence of clear and binding criteria on the distribution of responsibilities among states prevents the obligation to fulfil–provide being operationalised. Another critical problem, which affects international cooperation in disaster responses at large, concerns its funding mechanisms, notably the inequitable distribution of financial aid among disaster-affected countries and related emergencies. Humanitarian emergencies are funded through international assistance as never before. Nevertheless, despite the recognition that humanitarian principles apply to disasters in all their phases and that an approach based on human rights must also inform development projects, the distribution of funding among crises and the respective affected states is still characterised by huge inequities. Non-discrimination informs humanitarian action only at the level of a single operation or within a given recipient country, while, externally, humanitarian funding is still largely characterised by earmarking. Genuine solidarity-based—and thus non-discriminatory—funding mechanisms can be found only regionally (notably at the EU level) or within the Red Cross Movement.

Against this background, the ILC's work provides an important, albeit limited, contribution to the clarification and development of the international legal framework. As a whole, the DAs are marked by an asymmetry in the roles assigned to, respectively, the affected state and the international community. With respect to the affected state, it is notable that the ILC has devised a qualified consent regime that, despite the shortcomings and ambiguities described, provides a welcome and progressive reading of international law. The same cannot be said of the position assigned to the international community. Indeed, the concern expressed by several states about the respect for sovereignty and the principle of non-intervention is reflected in the DAs by a reticence about assigning a fully complementary role to the international community that is in line with the solidarity evoked.

Index

F. Zorzi Giustiniani, *International Law in Disaster Scenarios*,
https://doi.org/10.1007/978-3-030-50597-4

The manufacturer's authorised representative in the EU is Springer Nature Customer Service Centre GmbH, Europaplatz 3, 69115 Heidelberg, Germany. If you have any concerns regarding our products, please contact ProductSafety@springernature.com

Printed and bound by CPI Group (UK) Ltd, Croydon, CR0 4YY
30/09/2026
02225497-0003